Miracles

of

the

Cross

Foreword by Mother Angelica

Journeys of Faith®
1-800-633-2484

Bob and Penny Lord

Other Books by Bob and Penny Lord

THIS IS MY BODY, THIS IS MY BLOOD
Miracles of the Eucharist - Book I & BOOK II
THE MANY FACES OF MARY - a Love Story
SAINTS AND OTHER POWERFUL WOMEN
IN THE CHURCH
SAINTS AND OTHER POWERFUL MEN
IN THE CHURCH
HEAVENLY ARMY OF ANGELS
SCANDAL OF THE CROSS AND ITS TRIUMPH
MARTYRS - THEY DIED FOR CHRIST
THE ROSARY - THE LIFE OF JESUS AND MARY
VISIONARIES, MYSTICS AND STIGMATISTS
VISIONS OF HEAVEN, HELL & PURGATORY
TRILOGY BOOK I - TREASURES OF THE CHURCH
TRILOGY BOOK II - TRAGEDY OF THE REFORMATION
TRILOGY BOOK III - CULTS - BATTLE OF THE ANGELS
SUPER SAINTS BOOK I - JOURNEY TO SAINTHOOD
SUPER SAINTS BOOK II - HOLY INNOCENCE
SUPER SAINTS BOOK III - DEFENDERS OF THE FAITH
BEYOND SODOM AND GOMORRAH
THE JOURNEY AND THE DREAM
ESTE ES MI CUERPO, ESTA ES MI SANGRE
Milagros de la Eucaristía
LOS MUCHOS ROSTROS DE MARIA - una historia de amor

Table of Contents

Foreword

If there is any subject that needs to be addressed in this day and age, it's suffering! That is precisely why this particular book is so necessary. Many of us shirk from suffering and run from the Cross. In the face of suffering, how many of us can muster up the courage and faith to proclaim with Saint Andrew, the Apostle, *"O Good Cross, made beautiful by the Body of the Lord:* **long have I desired you, ardently have I loved you, unceasingly have I sought you out;** *and now you are ready for my eager soul. Receive me from among men and restore me to my Master - so that by means of you He may receive me, who by means of you, dying redeemed me?"*

Mother Mary Angelica, PCPA

To the obstinate and irreligious, suffering is a cruel mystery. But to those sincerely striving for union with God, suffering is a coveted treasure. To prove this point, we can look to the Prophets, the Apostles, and the Saints. The Prophets considered suffering to be a call from God to repentance, while Apostles saw it as "a happy privilege" to imitate their Master. The Saints ardently desired a share in the Passion of Christ and thought of His Cross as a rare and beautiful diamond. But above all, to discover the true value of suffering, we look to Mary, the Queen of All Saints. It was her silent "fiat" at the Foot of the Cross that revealed the hidden grandeur of every cross.

If we desire holiness, we-like all the holy ones who have gone before us-must follow in the blood-stained Footprints of Our Savior. To do this, we must accept our crosses with love. Let us not be afraid to boldly proclaim: *"Jesus, I accept all of the sufferings in my life with the same love that You accepted the pain in Your Life. I do not understand Your Plan, but I trust Your Love and my love reaches out to You with the hope of being lost in Your embrace!"*

Stretched out upon the Cross, Jesus' arms are opened wide to receive us- *"And when I am lifted up from the earth, I shall draw all men to Myself"* (John 12:32). At that moment, a moment of "great weakness", the act of Redemption was wrought. At that moment of humiliation and infamy, all men of faith obtained the strength to endure the sufferings that the Father permitted in their lives.

Jesus continually tells us that the cross is a vital part of our lives: *"If anyone wants to be a follower of Mine, let him renounce himself and take up his cross every day and follow Me"* (Luke 9:23). But along with this admonition, Our Lord assures us that we will never be abandoned under the weight of the cross: *"Come to Me, all you who labour and are overburdened and I will give you rest"* (Matthew 11:28). Finally, Jesus exhorts us to recognize that our cross is truly a share in His Cross: *"Shoulder My yoke and learn of Me, for I am gentle and humble of heart"* (Matthew 11:29).

As we carry our cross, like Jesus, we sometimes tire and are in need of a "Simon of Cyrene" to help us along the way. Bob and Penny Lord have been just that to so many. Their praiseworthy ministry and inspiring books have steadied and strengthened many who were stammering under the weight of the cross. We are all indebted to Bob and Penny, for their tireless work to reestablish devotion and zeal in the hearts of the faithful. They work in the midst of the darkness of the world, in order to bring to this darkness the Light of the Timeless Truth, Who is Jesus Christ. For this - and on behalf of all who have been touched by their example, their writings, their zeal, and their love-I want to thank them.

Mother Mary Angelica, PCPA

Why Miracles of the Cross?
Why now?

"We kill you when you make the sign of the Cross!"

These words spoken by an Indian Chief to St. Isaac Jogues, expressed the sentiment some tribes, in North America, had toward the Cross and the Black Robes who venerated It, and preached on It, and showed It. St. René Goupil was the first North American Jesuit[1] evangelist to be martyred, while a captive of the Iroquois Indians in Albany, New York. One day, as he was walking back to the camp from a work detail, he passed a young Indian boy and made the Sign of the Cross on his head. The boy's grandfather, an Iroquois chief, became furious, and had René Goupil ambushed and tomahawked. He was killed instantly. He was a Martyr of the Cross.

✞✞✞

In a major renovation of a Catholic Church in an upscale community in Minnesota, the Crucifix was taken down from the main Altar, to be replaced by decorative silver and gold bars. And yet over a million dollars was spent on an organ around which the choir stood in all their regalia,[2] the focus of attention, while the Cross was relegated to those silver and gold bars in an inconspicuous position. The reason given for this was that the Crucified Christ had no place in our modern church. People didn't want to remember Him as the Crucified Christ, but the Risen Christ, not the bruised, bloody Christ on the Cross, but the spanky-clean, risen Christ. They were an Alleluia people, not a Crucifixion people. And yet, someone forgot to tell them that you cannot have an Easter Sunday without a Good Friday; you cannot have the Resurrection without the Crucifixion.

✞✞✞

On November 23, 1927, on the grounds of what is today the

---

[1] He was not an ordained priest, but a volunteer, called a Doneé
[2] choir gowns

National Lottery building in downtown Mexico City, Blessed Miguel Pro stood in front of a firing squad. He held both arms out in the form of a Cross, with the Crucifix he was given on the day of his ordination in his right hand, and a rosary he received at the Shrine of Our Lady of Lourdes in his left, and as the soldiers prepared to fire upon him, he cried out, *"Viva Cristo Rey,"* which translates to *"Long live Christ the King."* With that, the soldiers fired an overabundance of bullets into his body, but he didn't fall. He stood, in the form of a Crucified Christ, for a few minutes, while flashbulbs popped like firecrackers as he was photographed by all the newsmen in Mexico, photographs which created a Martyr for Christ.

Last year, at a major Marian Shrine in Europe, a Sister, dressed in a business suit with earrings and all the secular trappings, explained to us why they had to take the Crucifix down in the Church, because it offended the sensibilities of many of the non-Catholics who visited the Shrine. They replaced the Crucifix with flowers.

What have we done to the Cross?

What have we done with that symbol of the price Our Savior was willing to pay for our Redemption? How have we dishonored the symbol of our Faith for which many of our Martyrs gave their lives? The disrespect, dishonor and disdain for the Cross and Jesus on the Cross is no new thing. It has been going on for centuries, actually from the time Our dear Lord Jesus died for us. The battle has raged on constantly, between those who would denigrate the Sacrifice Jesus made for us on the Cross, and those who would honor and glorify His action on the Cross.

In a letter to the Dominicans in July 2001, on the occasion of their choosing a new master general, Pope John Paul II begged them to evangelize the importance of keeping Jesus and His role in our Church key in their preaching. He said in his letter:

"One of the first tasks of the Dominicans at their founding was to respond to the Albigensian heresy, which was a new form of the recurrent Manichaean heresy...at whose core was the denial of the Incarnation. It is clear," His Holiness continued: "that the ancient afflictions of the human soul and the great untruths never die but lie hidden for a time, to reappear later in other forms. We live in a time marked in its own way by a denial of the Incarnation. For the first time since Christ's birth, 2000 years ago, it is as if He no longer had a place in an ever more secularized world. Not that He is always denied explicitly; indeed many claim to admire Jesus and to value elements of His teaching. Yet He remains distant; He is not truly known, loved and obeyed."

Our dear Pope, in effect, was telling the Dominicans, and us, that in the eyes of many, Our Dear Lord Jesus and all that He stands for, is no longer relevant. Can you picture that? ***Our Lord Jesus is not relevant!*** That's the goal of the enemy of God, to have us neither love nor hate Jesus, but just become completely apathetic to Him and all that He stands for. This is the conflict that the Lord and the Church have been battling since the day He was put on the Cross. Take away the importance of the Cross! Take away the value of the Cross! As Archbishop Sheen said, and he was quoting Scripture,[3] Satan was in the crowd that day. He wanted to counteract the significance of what was taking place. And he has continued to work for that objective from that day unto this.

But the Lord fights back. We made a statement with regard to Miracles of the Eucharist, which just as easily will refer to the Miracles of the Cross:

"In times of crisis, the Lord sends us special grace. This grace may come from Miracles of the Eucharist, Apparitions by Our Lady, and Saints and other Powerful

---

[3]Mt 27:40

*Men and Women in the Church. It may come in the form of
Angelic intercession. It will come from anywhere the Lord
deems necessary. There is only one think of which we can
be assured; **it will come.** "*

And it has come. The grace we want to share with you in
this book, that Signal grace[4] which had to come, is the grace of
Miracles of the Cross. In addition to doing intensive research,
we felt the need to actually go to Europe to the Shrines where
these Miracles of the Cross have taken place, to gather more
information than was readily available from the material we
originally used. (You can just bet we're going to make a
television series out of these Miracles.) They are not only
fascinating and breathtaking, but they are another way of God
showing us how much He loves us.

In times of crisis, He is willing to have Jesus actually come
down from the Cross and bring about Miracles. Oftentimes they
are to fortify our beliefs in His great sacrifice for us; at other
times He has come down in response to our prayers, to give us
physical or spiritual healing; He has also come down off the
Cross to convert men's hearts. We have seen Crucifixes in
churches in Europe with little plaques, simply stating,
"Miraculous Crucifix." We have tracked these instances of
Divine intervention. There is so much we want to share with
you, but bottom line, and most importantly, we want you to know
just how much your God loves you, how He's been willing to do
whatever it takes to prove it to you.

However, there is a greater question for you to consider.
Why now? This is always a key phrase for us. When we are
asked this question, we know the Lord is trying to break through
to us, to speak to us. We were asked that question when we
wrote our first book, *"This Is My Body, This Is My Blood,*

---

[4]Mother Angelica tells us: "Signal Grace is a special grace given to those
who have to perform special tasks for God, or undergo severe anguish for
God." We recall that she was very serious that evening on the Live Show
when she told us that. Her eyes were sad; her jaw was set.

Miracles of the Eucharist." In that instance, we actually thought we were writing about the riches of our Church, just recording an account of how the Lord has shown His power and renewed the belief of His people, (mostly His Priests) in His Real Presence in the Eucharist through these Miracles of the Eucharist at crucial times in the history of our Church. We were greatly shocked when we realized that instead, we were writing a defense on Our Lord's presence in the Eucharist. We never considered that the Real Presence of Jesus in the Eucharist *had to be defended.*

Why now? We have learned not to take that question lightly. We knew we had to ask ourselves: What is the Lord trying to tell us with Miracles of the Cross? What is happening in our Church and our world with regard to our belief in, and our reverence to the Person of Jesus on the Cross, as well as the Holy Trinity in the Sign of the Cross. When St. Bernadette of Lourdes was a young girl, being questioned by bishops and priests, as well as by civilian authorities, they marveled at how reverently she made the Sign of the Cross. They commented that the feeling they got from watching her make the Sign of the Cross was that she was truly calling the Trinity down into the room. Yet today, there are so many in our churches who make the Sign of the Cross as if they were shooing flies from around their faces. What is Jesus trying to tell us and more importantly, ***why now?***

Come with us on our Journey of Faith. See the marvels the Lord has prepared for us, to prove how much He loves us, how He is willing to overturn the laws of nature, how He's willing to come down off the Cross for us and give us Miracle. We pray that the words we write in this book are His words, and not ours. We pray that if we get in the way, the Lord just deletes our words and only puts into this book and your hearts, that which He wants you to hear and feel, and that is He is always here for you, to touch you, to hear you, to protect you and bring you *Home* to Him in Heaven. Come now, let's experience ***Miracles of the Cross.***

The Volto Santo of Lucca

The Lord has blessed us with what we have become accustomed to calling Holy Clusters. The area around Lanciano, where there is the oldest reported Miracle of the Eucharist, is in a cluster with San Giovanni Rotondo, home of Blessed Padre Pio, and the Cave of St. Michael in the Gargano. In the area between Florence and Pisa, there are many blessed clusters. As an example, in Pistoia, there is the body of an incorrupt Blessed. In Prato, there is the Shrine of St. Catherine de' Ricci, as well as the Miraculous cincture of Our Lady, which she dropped from Heaven to doubting St. Thomas the Apostle, when he could not believe that she was assumed into Heaven. Although Pisa is most known for the leaning tower, that is not the blessed cluster for which the city is famous. Pisa is where St. Catherine of Siena was gifted with the Stigmata of our Lord Jesus.

Lucca is also a very special city, sandwiched in between Florence and Pisa. It is protected by well-preserved walls which have graced the city since the time of the Romans, but then again in the Sixteenth century, a new set of walls, stronger, was placed around the city as a protective measure. However, even more than the protection that man has given to this city, God has blessed and graced Lucca with many Saints, the most famous of which are St. Gemma Galgani, a 20th century Visionary, Mystic and Stigmatist[1], who has two Shrines in Lucca, and St. Zita, an incorrupt Saint of the Thirteenth century, who is venerated in the Church of San Frediano in Lucca. These Saints are both important reasons to visit Lucca, and we bring our pilgrims to venerate them each year.

And while Sts. Gemma Galgani and Zita are both products of the town of Lucca, there is another important reason for us to come to this place. This other most important Shrine to visit came to Lucca by way of Jerusalem. It is called the Volto Santo, or Holy Visage. It is a priceless treasure, which, tradition

---

[1]Visionaries, Mystics and Stigmatist - Bob and Penny Lord

Above:
The Cathedral of Lucca, Italy which contains the Volto Santo

Right:
The Volto Santo, or Holy Visage of Lucca, Italy Tradition tells us, this Cross was sculpted by Nicodemus. He etched the image of Our Lord Jesus from his first-hand knowledge of the Savior on a large piece of Lebanese cedar.
It became a major Shrine of pilgrimage throughout all of Europe. Miracles attributed to Our Lord Jesus through the Volto Santo occurred almost immediately after the Miraculous Cross was placed in the Cathedral at Lucca.

tells us, was sculpted by Nicodemus. He etched the image of Our Lord Jesus from his first-hand knowledge of the Savior on a large piece of Lebanese cedar . It is pointed out more strongly in the tradition of the Crucifix, that the image of Jesus was actually sculpted by the Angels. It is also recorded that the Angels protected the Crucifix through the centuries of persecution by the Turks and Moslems until the Middle Ages, when an Italian bishop, named Gualfredo, came to the Holy Land on Pilgrimage. The Lord instructed the Angels to have him discover the revered Image in an equally miraculous way. He was so impressed with this superb treasure, that he virtually smuggled it out of the Holy Land. He brought it back to Italy on a boat with neither crew nor sails, in an effort to be inconspicuous. He actually floated to Italy, leaving the navigation of the boat to the Lord.

There had to be a tremendous amount of faith on the part of the bishop to be willing to make this treacherous journey, depending completely on the Lord for his safe passage. Also, the treasure he was carrying to Europe was of such immense value pirates would kill to steal it from him. Even the routing the boat took showed a complete abandonment on the part of the Bishop. He had no way to know what path the boat would take. It had to be guided by Angels, very similar to the voyage the Holy House of Nazareth took on its way to Europe and finally, Italy. Whereas in the case of the Holy House, it was transported by the Angels by air, in this instance, the Volto Santo went by sea. It had to go all the way out into the Mediterranean sea, around the tip of Greece, around Sicily, up the Tirrenian Sea, past Sardinia and Corsica, until the Angels finally floated It to land near the coast of La Spezia, to a little town called Luni.

We're not sure where the bishop would have prayed would be the final destination of the Miraculous Cross. Perhaps he desired to have as its home, the town of Luni, where it landed. At any rate, a battle ensued between the diocese where Luni was, and the diocese of Lucca. Each felt that the Volto Santo should be venerated in their diocese. But again, Divine Providence was given the lead. Another bishop took over; he would determine how the voyage of the Sacred Cross would progress, to wherever it was the Lord wanted it to stop. Bishop Giovanni I, of Lucca, was inspired by the Holy Spirit to let Divine Providence determine where the Cross would go.

The Cross was placed on a cart, driven by untamed oxen. They were not guided in any direction, but allowed to wander as the Lord would dictate. The oxen with the Miraculous Crucifix were followed by the Bishop of Lucca, and various dignitaries from the towns of Luni and Lucca. There have been reports of the sounds of Angels singing heavenly chants, in honor of the Son of God, whose miraculous Image they were guarding, as they followed the cart. Obviously, there had to be a Heavenly cortege surrounding and protecting the Image of Our Lord Jesus. The convoy traveled down the coast of Italy from La Spezia, almost to Pisa, whereupon the oxen moved inland. At last, the cart brought the miraculous Crucifix to the town of Lucca, where it stopped in front of three churches before it finally halted at the doors of the Cathedral. It was reverently placed in the Cathedral where it has stayed to this day.

It became a major Shrine of pilgrimage throughout all of Europe. It was almost obligatory for a pilgrim to stop at Lucca at the Shrine of the Volto Santo before continuing to Rome. There was even a certain road they were to travel in the Middle Ages, called the *Ria Romea* or *Francigena*.

Miracles attributed to Our Lord Jesus through the Volto Santo occurred almost immediately after the Miraculous Cross was placed in the Cathedral. Word of the miracles spread throughout Italy and, consequently, all over Europe. Lucca is a corridor city bringing wagons and carts from the Mediterranean Sea to Florence. The first miracle attributed to the Volto Santo was given to a man to save his life. A minstrel from France had sailed to La Spezia and wandered through the Italian countryside, playing for his room and board, to anyone who was willing to listen to him. When he arrived at Lucca, and beheld the beautiful

Volto Santo, he was completely taken back by the elegance and spirituality emanating from the Miraculous Cross. He had no gift to give to Our Lord Jesus, so he played his lute[2] in front of the Cross. Our Lord, who will not be outdone in generosity, rewarded the man by dropping one of His silver slippers from the Cross. It fell in front of the man, who was elated at this obvious gift from the Lord.

He took the gift and continued on his way, joyfully sharing with everyone with whom he came in contact, how the Lord graced him with the silver slipper from the Cross. However, not everyone accepted his explanation of how he came to be in possession of one of the most famous relics in the town. Word got out to the local authorities that a foreign wanderer stole the slipper from the Miraculous Cross in the Cathedral. The man was arrested in short order and placed in prison. He was accused of the theft of a blessed object from the Cathedral, which was as close to being a sacrilege as you could get. The sentence which was going to be imposed on him was death.

This was not at all what the innocent man had reckoned on when he was given the gift by the Lord. But how would he prove his innocence to the authorities? The only one who could help him would be Our Lord Jesus Himself in the form of the Volto Santo. The man prayed for all he was worth. When it seemed as if he were at the final hour of his life, Our Lord interceded for him and convinced the authorities of the truth of his story, by producing a beautiful young man who testified that he had been present when the slipper fell from the feet of the Crucifix in front of the minstrel. The vagabond was released from custody. As soon as this happened, the beautiful young man who was the witness for the minstrel disappeared, never to be seen again. Tradition has it that this young man was an Angel, sent from Heaven to defend and rescue the minstrel. So many miracles have been attributed to the Volto Santo that they have stopped recording them. But every now and then, a testimony is given of

---

[2]an old stringed instrument related to the guitar

a miraculous cure, or a conversion of heart as the result of praying for the intercession of Our Lord Jesus in the Volto Santo.

Royalty of Europe took to venerating the Volto Santo as their own private Shrine. Kings would wear medals struck in the image of the Volto Santo. Others would swear by the Volto Santo. William II, King of England, took his oath of office as King of the realm in 1087 *"per Vultum de Luca."* Another member of nobility, Pasquale II, commemorated the *"Vultus Sacrarium"* in 1107. This practice of royalty gave way to local colloquialisms as well as slang corruptions of the Name. Legends of saints cropped up whose names were variations of the Name Volto Santo. In France, a fictitious saint named Vaudeluc was venerated. Vaudeluc is a slang corruption of the French **Vault de Lucques**, which means Volto Santo.

Many would come and pray at the Shrine, as well as institute special ceremonies in their own countries, usually on May 3 or September 14, to coincide with the Feast Day of when the oxen brought the Miraculous Crucifix to Lucca. But no ceremony can compare with the honor and respect given to this most important Miracle than that in Lucca itself. At sunset of September 14, the Crucifix is taken from its home in the Cathedral and decorated with a golden tunic, a crown and jeweled ornaments; It is then processed through the entire town of Lucca, and ends back at the Cathedral. The festivities are attended not only by the people from the city, but from the farms and outlying areas as well. Parents and grandparents line children up in front of the Image of Jesus and explain the story to them. For the people of Lucca, to this day, this is one of the most important events of the year.

Over the centuries, coins have been struck with the Image of the Volto Santo. At one time it became the official seal of the guild of merchants in Lucca. It has been immortalized by Dante Aligheri in *Dante's Inferno*, as well as in song by the minstrels traveling through from France, England and the Flanders. This Miraculous Cross was given a permanent home at the Cathedral of Lucca for all to see and venerate. An octagonal temple was built in the fifteenth century by a famous artist of the day. It is very ornate and majestic, a fitting place of worship for the Miraculous Crucifix.

Our Lord Jesus is waiting for you there in that Cathedral. Line up with the rest of the faithful to speak to your Lord in this Miraculous Image. People come from all over Europe to put their joys and sorrows, their hopes and prayers into His Hands. He will answer your prayers. Miracles have abounded at this Shrine of the Volto Santo. Conversions have come about, miraculous healings; prayers have been answered; He's there, waiting for you.

Jesus has given us this Shrine for a very important reason. We have to know we are not hopeless and helpless. We have to know that there is a light at the end of the tunnel, a way for us to be pulled out of the pit the world has put us in. There's got to be hope. We heard a very bitter priest give a homily in which he talked about how Easter had come and gone, the Resurrection had occurred, and still there was no peace and love in the world. He referred to the Miracle of Easter as the Easter *stories*. He referred to the Resurrection as the Miracle *stories*. He said in effect, *"What do we do now? Where to we go from here? Peter and John experienced a great deal of opposition after Jesus rose from the dead. Everything was supposed to be peace and love. Where is it?"*

It is for reasons such as these, my brothers and sisters, that Jesus has given us miracles down through the ages, not only Miracles of the Cross, which are extremely important and powerful, but Miracles of the Eucharist, of which we've written for many years, apparitions of Our Lady, Angelic intercession as well as the intercession of the Saints, some of the most popular being St. Joseph, St. Anthony, St. Thèrése and St. Peregrine. However, they are but a few. We all have special Saints to whom we should ask for help. Of course, they couldn't do anything for you if it weren't for Our Lord Jesus and God the Father giving them the power. All of these we've mentioned in this paragraph are to counteract the negation and hopelessness this dear priest left the people with. God, through Miracles and apparitions, gave us tangible proof that He is with us, watching out for us, involved in our lives. Ironically, this priest, this purveyor of doom was of a religious Order, whose founder would not allow long-faced friars into his community. We have also heard a priest from that same Order teach *"It can be Heaven, Heaven, Heaven all the way to Heaven."*

Perhaps we should have used this as an introduction to this book. However, the point we want to leave you with is how much Jesus loves us, and how He shows us that love through Miracles, all kinds of Miracles, to help us on our pilgrimage of life. In this book the focus is on Miracles of the Cross. But no matter what Miracle the Lord gives us, just remember, He's there with us; He's involved with us; He loves us.

The Origin of the True Cross

St. Anthony uses the *History of the Greeks* from the Apocryphal Gospel to recount the story of the origin of the Cross. In his Opus for the Feast of *The Discovery of the Cross* St. Anthony tells the story of the tree from which the Cross came. This sermon became so popular that two hundred years later, the story was still being passed on; and subsequently inspired the well-known artist Piero della Francesca in the year 1435 to paint the story in breathtaking scenes.

St. Anthony began his Opus with Joel (2:22):

"The tree that bears its fruit, the fig tree and the vine give their yield." This tree is further mentioned in the book of Wisdom:

"When because of him (the unjust man) the earth was flooded, it was Wisdom again who saved it, directing the course of the just by contemptible wood.[1] *This contemptible wood is the Cross of Christ; contemptible because `accursed is anyone who is hanged on a tree,*[2] *where Christ, the Wisdom of God the Father, was scorned and derided: `So you would destroy the temple and rebuild it in three days! Then save yourself! If you are God's Son, come down from the Cross !'"* (Mt. 27:40)[3]

On this contemptible tree, Christ saved the world.

The Origin of the Cross

The Origin of the Cross goes back to Adam. When Adam became ill, he sent his son Seth to find some medicine to heal him. Seth went to an area near the Garden of Eden. There he approached an Angel guarding the gate to Paradise. Seth told him his father was dying and pleaded with the Angel to help him. The Angel broke off a limb from the tree from which Adam had eaten of the forbidden fruit, even after God the Father had forbidden him and Eve to do so. The Angel handed the branch to

---

[1] Ws 10:4
[2] Gal 3:13
[3] Saint Anthony

Below:
*The Queen of Sheba venerates
the wood of the tree that grew
on Adam's grave*

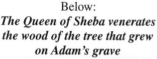

Above:
The burial of Adam
Saint Anthony tells us that when Adam became ill, he sent his son Seth to find some medicine to heal him. Seth went to an area near the Garden of Eden. There he approached an Angel guarding the gate to Paradise. Seth told him his father was dying and pleaded with the Angel to help him. The Angel broke off a limb from the tree from which Adam had eaten.
Seth rushed home, only to find that his father Adam had died and had already been buried. He planted the branch on Adam's grave. This branch later grew into a great tree!

Below:
Verification of the True Cross
It was placed on a dead man and he came back to life.

Above:
*A statue of
Saint Helena,
Mother of Emperor
Constantine holding
the True Cross.
Church of Holy
Cross of Jerusalem,
Rome*

Seth and with that he said, *Your father will be healed when this branch bears fruit.* Saint Anthony writes that the preface of the Mass of the Feast of the Discovery of the Cross, made a reference to this occurrence:

"The tree of man's defeat became his tree of victory. Where life was lost, there life has been restored."

Seth rushed home, only to find that his father Adam had died and had already been buried. He planted the branch on Adam's grave. This branch later grew into a great tree! It appears the Queen of Sheba saw the tree in *"the house made of wood,"*[4] as the Palace of King Solomon was called. She had a Vision, where the tree's origin and the circumstances involving the tree were revealed to her. Not daring to tell the king what she had learned, she instead wrote to him when she arrived home that she had seen a person hanging from the tree; and it was He who would bring about the downfall of the entire nation. Did he remember something from Scripture foretelling the One who was yet to come? Did he see in the queen's Vision a fulfillment of an ominous prophecy? All we know is that it is written, Solomon, fear overtaking him, buried the tree in the deepest bowels of the earth - the place that would later be called *the sheep pool.*

You may recall that we read in John's Gospel that the sick would come to the sheep pool in search of healing:

"...there were crowds of sick people - blind, lame, paralyzed - waiting for the water to move; for at intervals the Angel of the Lord came down into the pool, and the water was disturbed, and the first person to enter the water after this disturbance was cured of any ailment he suffered from.[5]

"When the time of the coming of Christ was approaching, the tree began to grow over the water, and it is then that `*the Angel would come to stir the water.*'[6] On Good Friday, when they looked for a tree on which to crucify Our Lord, they found this

---

[4]3 Kings 7:2
[5]Jn 5:3-10
[6]Saint Anthony

Above:

Reliquaries of the Inscription (INRI) on the Cross and a nail from the Crucifixion - Church of The Holy Cross of Jerusalem, Rome

Above:

Wood from True Cross that St. Helena brought back to Rome, now located in the Church of Santa Croce in Gerusalemme (The Holy Cross in Jerusalem)

Right:

The Wood of the True Cross, brought back by St. Helena

tree. They cut it down, and brought it to the place where Jesus stood ready to carry it to His crucifixion. And so it was on Calvary that the Angel's word to Seth was fulfilled. *"Thus, the tree bore its fruit, saving Adam and restoring him to health."*[7]

The Tree, *now the Cross of Salvation*, was once again buried deep in the bowels of the earth. Were they hoping it would rot and go away? But the tree and the message of the tree would not be stilled. Three centuries later, Saint Helena - Constantine's mother would discover the tree. This is why we have a Feast called The Discovery of the Cross.

Allow us to have Saint Anthony speak to your hearts:
"The Eyes of Our Beloved are now closed in death.
The Face, `upon Which the Angels desired to look'[8]
has turned pallid and pale.
The Lips, Which once uttered words of eternal life,
have now turned blue.
The Head, Whose sight made Angels tremble,
now hangs lifeless.
The Hands, Whose touch cured leprosy,
brought back life, restored sight,
put demons to flight and multiplied bread,
are now, alas, transfixed by nails
and stained with Blood."

Constantine and Miracle of the Cross at the Milvian Bridge

While preparing for battle at the Milvian Bridge, Christ appeared to Constantine in a dream. He told Constantine to paint an inverted X with what appears to be a P running through it[9] on his army's shields. At noon, the day of the battle, while praying to the pagan god of his father, Constantine saw a cross over the sun with the inscription, *"In this sign conquer."* That evening Jesus appeared to Constantine and told him to paint a cross on

---

[7]Saint Anthony
[8]1 Pet 1:12
[9]This formed the emblem used by the Christians.

Above:
The Vision of Constantine of the Cross
He saw a cross over the sun with the
inscription, "In this sign conquer."
Left:
The Dream of Constantine - Jesus
appeared to him and told him to paint a
cross on his soldiers' shields.

Above:
Battle of the Milvian Bridge, where Constantine was victorious because
he used the Cross as a banner for the battle.

his soldier's shields. Eusebius describes the sign as the Labarum.[10] Constantine did as the Lord dictated and was victorious over his enemies. He gave full credit to the Vision he had of the Cross at the Milvian Bridge.

When Constantine arrived in Rome, he accepted the honors bestowed upon him by the senate, but refused to participate in a pagan religious ceremony in the temple. In addition, to everyone's amazement, he gave the order that all persecution of Christians was to cease. He went further and gave a palace at the Lateran[11] to Pope Militades to be used as a papal residence. Then he erected a Christian church[12] at the Lateran. Imagine the reaction in the senate when he published a decree granting religious freedom to all Christians in his realm, and then when he ordered all property returned to the Christians in Africa.

Constantine had a statue of himself erected in the Forum, with him holding a vexilium, decorated with the Chi-Rho. Under the statue was an inscription which read: *"Through this salutary sign (referring to the Chi-Rho)...I have freed your city from the yoke of the tyrant."*[13] Silver coins were struck with his helmet inscribed with the Chi-Rho. Slowly but surely, pagan signs were replaced by Christian ones, until in 321, when they (pagan signs) disappeared all together. Although he did not enroll in the Catechumenate, believing himself divinely converted, he did read Holy Scripture. Pope Sylvester baptized Constantine in the baths of the Lateran, curing him of leprosy.

His mother Queen Helena, hearing of her son's fascination with the God of the Christians, came to Rome to dissuade him. Instead she converted! Constantine became a Defender of the Faith, fighting the heresies of his time that had cropped up, that

---

[10]staff capped with the Chi-Rho monogram

[11]This was located where the Holy Steps (Scala Santa) are now.

[12]It is now St. John Lateran *(or San Giovanni Laterano)* - the first Christian church, after the Church became legal

[13]This has all been testified by Eusebius

of Arianism.[14] He opened the Council of Nicea,[15] and on and on.

And how did this switch come about, him exchanging the comfortable life he had with fellow pagans to face controversy inside and outside the newly legitimized Church? In a letter to the Orient, Constantine wrote of his divine experience, giving full credit to God's Grace that he had converted.

Now Constantine had this deep desire to venerate the holy places, where Jesus had walked: He wanted to follow the Savior's steps: in Nazareth, where the Incarnation had taken place, in Bethlehem where Jesus was born, on Mount Tabor where He was transfigured, Calvary where He died on the Cross and on and on. He began by building an extraordinary church in Jerusalem, because he believed that it was the place most honored by Jesus' Presence and Passion. Some say Constantine sent his mother to the Holy Land to find the One True Cross upon which Jesus died.

The Discovery of the Cross by Saint Helena

Saint Ambrose (4th Century) was the first to write of the finding of the Cross by Saint Queen Helena.   Others would follow with additional information.

A newly baptized Christian, Queen Helena became fascinated by the stories circulating among the Christian world of the Christ Who gave His life for all on the Cross. In 326, she made a journey to Palestine and upon arriving there, began visiting all the holy places, in search of the Holy Cross. And she was close to eighty years old at that time! Now there was no visible sign left; heathens had destroyed or covered with stones anything pertaining to the life and death of Our Lord. It was as if they wanted to erase any memory of Our Savior and the price He paid. They even built a pagan temple to Venus on one of the

---

[14]More on this and other heresies that have attacked the Church, up till today, read Bob and Penny Lord's book: *Scandal of the Cross and Its Triumph, Heresies throughout the History of the Church.*

[15]You can find out about this and other Councils in Bob and Penny Lord's book: *Treasures of the Church.*

holy sites, so that when Christians came to adore Our Lord, where He lived and suffered for us, they appeared to be worshipping a marble idol of the pagan goddess. They went as far as erecting a statue to Jupiter, according to St. Jerome, on the site where Our Lord rose from the dead. It remained there through Adrian's reign, up to the time of Constantine.

She began intensive research and study on the Cross upon which Jesus died. She called in Jews and Christians alike, searching for clues as to the whereabouts of the Cross. They advised her to look for the Sepulcher where He had been buried. There she was most likely to find the instruments of torture. The custom of the Jews was to dig a hole near where the body was buried and place the means of punishment there, as they found them abhorrent and of need to be hidden. The queen ordered all pagan temples be torn down, statutes to the pagan gods smashed and then to remove it all as plain rubbish. Her eager pursuit of the Cross was rewarded. In the ruins, she found not one but three crosses, the nails which had pierced Our Savior's Body, and the plaque which had been nailed on His Cross - *Jesus of Nazareth, the King of the Jews.*

Imagine her dilemma when she found *three* crosses! Only one was that of Our Lord, the other two were of the thieves who hung on either side of Him. As the plaque was not attached to the Cross, it was impossible to ascertain which was the True Cross. One of the prominent ladies of Jerusalem lay critically ill. Bishop Macarius, suggested Queen Helena have all three crosses, one by one, placed on the ill woman. The Bishop believed they would discover the True Cross, by placing the crosses on the sick woman. The one which healed her would be the one upon which Jesus was crucified! After praying that God would show them which was the True Cross, he placed each of the crosses on the body of the ill woman. Only one of the crosses touching her, restored her; and the true Cross of Jesus was discovered.

Queen Helena immediately had a church built over the spot, as she later did over the other Holy Places where Our Lord lived, preached, healed and died. She made a magnificent case for it and brought a piece of the Cross to her son Constantine in Constantinople at the time. He reverently venerated the Cross, and thereafter cherished it. She left for Rome. Once there, she placed a piece of the Cross in the church, she had built, *Santa Croce in Gerusalemme* (The Holy Cross of Jerusalem), where it can be found till today. It is believed that the Cross was very possibly discovered in May or early Spring, because Queen Helena died in the arms of her son the eighteenth of August the same year the Cross was discovered. In the Lives of St. Cyril of Jerusalem, St. Porphyrius of Gaza, and St. Paulinus it is written that pieces of the True Cross were scattered to the four corners of the Catholic world, and yet the Cross remained the same size.

Other recounting of the finding of the True Cross

Now there is another tradition about the finding of the True Cross. It has been recorded that a Jew called Judas helped the Queen discover the whereabouts of the true Cross. Who had more authority than he, whose ancestors had been present when Jesus walked the earth and witnessed all that had come to pass! Judas was also instrumental in Helena's discovery of the nails which had pierced our Lord's Hands and Feet, and the exact location of Golgotha. After Judas was baptized, Queen Helena had him consecrated fifth Bishop of Jerusalem, by Eusebius, Pope and Bishop of Rome in 310. Judas[16] wrote, *"Behold more or less two hundred years the Cross has been hidden."*

Before Queen Helena found the true Cross, the Empress Protonica, wife of Emperor Claudius is credited with having discovered it in the years 41-54 A.D. The Empress had converted to Christianity from paganism, after seeing miracles performed by Saint Peter. Soon after, she departed from Rome and traveled with her two sons to Jerusalem. There Saint James showed her the Hill of Golgotha. She was responsible for the

---

[16]Not Judas Iscariot, but Judas the one who helped Helena discover the true Cross.

Jews turning Golgotha over to the Christians. Her daughter died soon after. Her eldest son called it a work of God, because when the true Cross was placed on the dead girl's body, she came to life, validating the Cross as the one upon which Jesus suffered and died. This account was written by Saint James himself.

It has been said that the Cross was then hidden and discovered by Saint Helena in a deep grotto that was 33 feet below the surface in one of the apses of the chapels of Saint Helena in the Church of the Holy Sepulcher.[17]

This first discovery was affirmed by Saint Cyril of Alexandria, who having knowledge of it, said, *"It has been said at different times that the Wood of the Cross has been discovered."*

The Feast of the Exaltation of the Cross has been celebrated from the year 326, when it was discovered, till today. It was originally observed in May; until the year 335, when Constantine had the *Church of the Resurrection* built in Jerusalem. As the church was dedicated on the thirteenth of September, and the following day the Cross was set up in the church, the tradition of celebrating the Feast Day passed from May to the fourteenth of September. This Feast Day is observed by both the Greek Church and the Roman Catholic Church.

The Cross is returned to Jerusalem

In the 7th Century, Heraclius, son of Heraclius, Exarch[18] of Africa, aided his father in overthrowing the unpopular Emperor Phocas. He traveled to Constantinople and conquered Phocas and executed him. Thereupon he was proclaimed Emperor. Heraclius spent his entire reign. battling forces within and without his palace. The East has always had strife, neighbor against neighbor. In 611 the Persians conquered Syria, Anatolia, Palestine and Egypt. Then in 614, they invaded and overran Jerusalem, taking to Persia their spoils, including the Holy Cross

---

[17]where one finds Golgotha and the Tomb where Jesus was buried.
[18]a governor of an outlying province in the ancient Byzantine Empire

of Jesus. Heraclius took singular delight vanquishing Phocas and his men from Anatolia and especially Armenia, as he was of Armenian descent. Whereupon he carried the war into Persia. There a battle ensued where Heraclius brought about the fall of Chrosroes, Persia's leader and caused the rise to power of Kawadh, who upon ascending the throne promised to restore all territory occupied by Persian forces and return the Cross to Jerusalem. When Heraclius arrived with the Cross in Jerusalem, he was greeted with cheering and great ceremony. But sadly, that was short-lived, as he was unable to block the Arabs from invading and occupying Palestine, Syria And Egypt in the name of Islam.

Why is the Cross so loved and so hated?

Why is the Cross so loved and so hated? It is loved by those who love Jesus, those who want to remember that it was on this Holy Cross that we were saved. We love the Cross because it was on this Cross that the Gates of Heaven were opened; that Death was conquered. With those who hate the Cross - Is it they do not want us to remember we were saved, and at what price? For if Our Lord would do this for us, that we might know eternal life with Him, if He would go through the Passion for us, then our souls are precious to Him.

The enemy of God tells us we are hopeless and helpless; we are too skinny, too fat, too tall, too short; we are evil and there is no hope for us. On the Cross, Jesus had pity on the repentant criminal next to him. If He would do that for him, what won't He do for us! When you think, He died for each of us; and He would have done it all if you or I were the only one on earth; and one of us would have had to have been the one who killed Him; when we think about that, we walk unafraid, knowing our Lord Who died for us will never give us a cross we cannot bear.

The Living Cross of Limpias

God is so powerful! He is involved with His children! The Lord works in mysterious ways, when He wants to make His presence known to His people. The fact that He is always working in our lives is affirmed by all the Miracles He gives us. He's also not beyond giving us a Miracle of the Cross to get our attention, to let us know beyond the shadow of a doubt that it was truly He who died on the Cross for us, and that it is He who continues to suffer for the sins of the world.

Following the unconditional love the Lord shows us through Miracles of the Cross is such a special and awesome gift. It bears witness to how strongly the Lord works with our welfare in Mind, in everything He does. Because of our conditional love, it's hard for us to believe that God unreservedly loves us. We know we don't deserve it. But as He proves to us in these Miracles, He loves us because He loves us. One time Penny asked the Lord how He could love her when she was ever going forward three steps and falling back two. The thought she was given was, *"I love you because I love you. Now just accept that and let's get on with it."*

The Lord proved His love for us, His children, through a Miracle of the Cross in a little town in northern Spain at the beginning of the Twentieth Century. It happened during Lent, the end of March, 1919. Two Capuchin priests were giving a Lenten retreat at their local church in the little village of Limpias, located in the area of Coruña. The Lord was blessing the congregation abundantly. You could feel the Power of His Presence in the church. You could tell that all was going well. The homilies were well accepted; the people were responding. The lines were long for the Sacrament of Reconciliation.

There was a large Crucifix on the back wall of the Church. Many in the parish had a great devotion to Our Crucified Lord and paid homage to Him on this Crucifix. But on this particular evening, they were coming to the close of the mission, and so the

Above:
Our Chapel at Holy Family Mission with a
replica of the Cross of Limpias

Right:
Mother Mary Angelica
with a replica of the Cross of Limpias
in the Nun's Chapter Room of Our Lady of
the Angels Monastery, Hanceville, AL
during the consecration of the Monastery
August 1999
This was brought from their convent in
Akron, Ohio when Mother first relocated to
Irondale, Alabama.

attention was not on the Crucifix, but on the priests, who were giving their last teachings.

Suddenly a child in the front of the church cried out, *"Father, the Holy Christ is moving. The Holy Christ is looking at me."* Everyone looked at the child incredulously, and then looked up at the Crucifix. Then, from another part of the Church, another child cried out; and then another. Pretty soon, all the adults in the Church were clamoring, some in awe, others in fear. Some were able to see the living Christ on the Cross. The murmuring spread throughout the church: *What could it be? Is it the end of the world? Is Jesus here to punish us for our sins?* The reported expressions on Jesus' face varied. Some said He looked at them with such love. Others said He was terribly angry with them. But they were all of one mind: Instead of a dead Jesus on the Cross, Jesus was alive, and He was sorrowfully suffering the Passion.

One of the priests, in an effort to try to determine if what was happening was truly coming to pass, ran over to the Crucifix and placed his hand on it. He pulled it away abruptly. The body was warm! He could feel perspiration on the body, the same as if he had touched the body of a *living,* suffering person! He shared, it also felt like he was touching flesh, rather than wood. He, too, began to perspire! He didn't know what to make of the entire situation, nor quite sure how to handle it.

Actually, the people came to the rescue. They began to sing hymns to the Lord, such as *"Hymn of the Pilgrimage," "Pardon, O my God,"* and other local hymns well-known by the people in the church. Soon the sounds of hymns rang throughout the church. During all this time, lights were out in the Church; the only light was the daylight streaming in from the stained-glass windows. *O my Lord,* they exclaimed! There seemed to be an aura coming from the image of Our Lord Jesus. Each person who witnessed the Miracle of the Cross had a different version of what happened, as truly each person had their own individual encounter with Our Lord Jesus, come to life on the Cross.

Needless to say, word spread like wildfire about the miraculous occurrence with the Cross of Limpias. Pilgrimages came from all over the country, and then even outside of Spain - from southern France, to view and venerate the Miracle of the Cross. They all shared their individual experiences. To some, the statue on the Cross remained dead and motionless the entire time they were at the Church. To others, Our Lord came to life for short periods of time. When the Image went from death to life, the Image appeared tortured, wracked with pain. The eyes, which depicted a suffering Christ, but a wooden representation, took on a completely different expression when the statue on the Cross seemed to come to life. The excruciating pain was immediately obvious. Our Lord's eyes projected His suffering. His Head turned from left to right, every move seemed like an eternity of pain.

His Hands and Feet appeared to move painfully in an effort to alleviate the torturous agony inflicted by the nails, which brutally pierced them. But with all of that, there were those who testified He had *smiled at them*. Can you picture Our Lord Jesus in so much agonizing pain, yet able and willing to smile at His beloved children, as if to reassure them?

We'd like to share some individual experiences which we believe shows the awesome power of God through this Miracle.

In the early days, when pilgrimages first came to the Shrine, a chauffeur brought his employer and wife to the church in Limpias, Spain. He chose not go in with his employer, as was his custom to wait outside. He never attended anything his employer did, but in this instance, he had a valid reason. It had to do with Church, and he wanted nothing to do with God or Church or anything of the kind. It was very obvious where his loyalties were, and if there was any doubt in your mind, he would have no problem telling you right off the bat.

So, on this day, he stayed outside the church, making fun, under his breath, of all the believers inside. He as much as called them simpletons, being taken in by the Catholic Church. But when his employer came out and gently ordered him to go in and view the Miracle of the Cross, he reluctantly obeyed. But to be sure that no one would think for a minute that he was taking any of this seriously, he put an insolent smirk on his face. He was not about to be manipulated, boss or no boss.

He was led inside the door of the church, right up to the Image of the Holy Crucified Christ. After a beat, his face turned gray. All the blood seemed to drain out of it. He collapsed to the floor. He was as limp as a rag. He screamed out one word, "***Pardon.***" He lay there for some time, sobbing. He could not get up! He had to be carried out of the church and placed in the back of the car. His employer had to drive him and his wife home! The people in the church were completely aghast at the behavior of the driver, as was his employer. Quite a bit later, after he regained his composure, he said the Lord looked at him with such a piercing glance it made his blood curl. He never quite explained it any more than that, but tradition has it that he changed his ways, and went back to the Church and the Sacraments. There's no mention whether he ever returned to the Shrine of the Miracle of the Cross of Limpias.

We may have mentioned that the Miracle of the Cross did not happen all the time, and not everyone saw the Miracle. In addition, when more than one person witnessed the Miracle at the same time, each one did not necessarily see the same thing. Although many people experienced the Lord's blessings in this way, it was by and large, an individual encounter. That's why the occurrence we're going to share with you now is so unusual.

On one of the pilgrimages to the Shrine, in a group of over two hundred and fifty people, over two thirds witnessed the *exact same thing!* They saw Our Lord Jesus, alive on the Cross, convulsing in the same way. He was experiencing the excruciating pain of the Passion right in front of them. In addition to His Head and Body writhing back and forth on the Cross, His horrifying facial expressions told the story of what was happening to Him *physically.*

One of the eyewitness, giving testimony, shared about his wife, who had not believed in the Miraculous Living Cross of Limpias when the group first arrived from Santiago de Compostela. However, knowing that she was outnumbered among so many believers, she said nothing. She prayed, if this was truly a Miracle, that the Lord would give her the gift of seeing it. Also, she prayed to Our Lord Jesus, if this Miracle were true, would He grant her special intentions for her husband and children, who were with her at the Church. At one point, she thought she saw something, but then chalked it up to her imagination. However, she asked her children if they saw anything, and what they shared corresponded exactly to what she thought she had seen - that Our Lord Jesus was alive and moving. She kept it to herself, until later that day when everyone was praying the Rosary at the foot of the Miraculous Cross, and the woman's daughter cried out that Jesus had raised His Head, opened and closed His lips, and then bowed His head again.

The mother, not wanting to appear ridiculous, and feeling uneasy about the child's testimony, told her it was her imagination. Then the Lord spoke to the mother through another pilgrim, praying next to them. She scolded the mother for not believing the Lord when He gave her proof positive of His Presence in this church, and in her life. The pilgrim added that she had not seen anything, but believed, because she knew that Jesus loved her and all the people in the church.

The disbelieving mother ceased her disbelief, opened her heart to Jesus in this Miracle, and towards the end of the day, she swore that He looked at her and smiled. A P.S. to this story is that all the petitions she had made to the Lord were fulfilled.

We would like to share with you an interesting fact about the Cross of Limpias. When we had made our commitment to build a Spanish style Mission in the United States, people from all over the country began to send us Sacred Art to put in the Mission. In particular, these dear friends from Louisiana, Curt and Mary Burns, gave us some pews, statues and a beautifully carved marble altar frontispiece, from a monastery in Louisiana, as well as a monstrance. Among them was a very broken-down crucifix. It had been at that monastery for forty or fifty years. Curt and Mary put it in the back of a truck and drove it from Madisonville, Louisiana, to Sacramento, California, where we lived at the time. We had it restored by this beautiful mother and daughter team who restored Hummel figurines. When they finished with the Crucifix, we brought it back to our offices in Rancho Cordova, California and placed it in our chapel. We noticed that Jesus' eyes were open. He appeared to be half alive, half dead. He was in that middle place before actually succumbing to Brother Death. But we could see that He was suffering. We were told that this was the Cross of Limpias. This particular Cross had suffered great abuse at the hands of some youth who had gone to the monastery. The arms were separated from the rest of the body. Parts of the body were broken. The head was smashed when a young person threw a full can of Sprite at it in a fit of anger. We felt very personal towards this Image of Our Lord Jesus.

We fell in love with this statue of Jesus. The Lord had preordained, it appeared, we move to Arkansas. We began to build the Holy Family Mission in Morrilton, Arkansas. The beautiful Cross would be hung in the little chapel of the Mission, until such time as we had enough money to build the Hall of Saints, a chapel/conference center. At that time, the Crucifix was to go into its new permanent home.

We felt very blessed to have this beautiful Cross in our Ministry. Then in August, 1999, we all went to Mother Angelica's new Monastery in Hanceville, Alabama. This was the day of the consecration of the Monastery. After this day, no one would be allowed behind the cloister area.

The consecration, at which the Bishop of Birmingham blessed each room, began and ended at the Nuns' Chapter Room. After a ceremony by the Bishop, their Crucifix was brought in to be placed ceremoniously, in the middle of the Chapter Room. As the Crucifix was brought into the room, the four of us, Bob, Penny, Luz Elena and Brother Joseph, gasped. The Crucifix was exactly the same as the one we had in our chapel in California, and which is now located in our little chapel at the Holy Family Mission in Morrilton, Arkansas! Mother Angelica shared she had brought it with her from Canton, Ohio to Birmingham, Alabama, and had it placed in the Cloister of her first monastery, which is still on the grounds of EWTN.

We always ask ourselves why? Why did the Lord feel it necessary to materialize in such a powerful way, in one of the most unusual Miracles of the Cross we have researched? What was going on in the world, and in Spain in particular in 1919 which would precipitate such a strong manifestation of the Presence of the Lord?

There had been a raging battle going on between the powers of God and the powers of evil from the time of the French Revolution and the rule of Napoleon. While he was defeated and thrown out of Spain, his philosophy and the anti church philosophy which ran rampant in France during the Revolution took hold in Spain. The next hundred years was like a seesaw, with the Church winning ground, only to lose it to liberal, revolutionary elements in the country. By the time we entered into the twentieth century, the last century of the second millennium, there was a strong undercurrent of bitterness towards the Church in Spain. This had been orchestrated by elements within the government in an effort to break the stronghold the Church had on the Faithful of the country. Many anticlericals had infiltrated into positions of importance within the Church, and so the battle was being fought on two fronts, those we knew were against us, and those we thought were on our side. It was a time of great violence.

Communism was gaining a stronghold in Spain, splitting the people in two. The militant elements of the Communist cult attacked the Church with a vengeance. It brewed like a massive flame bursting from the bowels of hell, until it would finally erupt into a volcano of hate. Most of this hate did not surface until after the Miracle of Limpias manifested itself. This was due in part to a benevolent dictator, who was able to subdue the attacks on the Church. But in 1931, when the communist Republic was installed into the government, it was open warfare against the Church. Within a few weeks of the Republic being created, convents were burned throughout the country, the Jesuits were dissolved and the Primate of Toledo was expelled. The people of Spain could not believe what was happening. Satan's horns were made evident, for all to see. He was raging! In spite of the masses' loyalty to the Church, his assault was very successful.

Could the Lord be revealing His Pain over this outrage against the Church and the people of God, in 1919 when He revealed this Miracle to the people of Spain? Was this Miracle of the Cross given to the people so that they would have strength and courage to bear what was to happen to the people and the country in the coming years? Was it to ask them to change their ways before holocaust was rained down on them? Was it to ask them to change the world before they destroy it?

It reminds us a great deal of the two apparitions of Our Lady in Belgium in 1932-1933, actually two weeks apart and 50 miles apart. There had always been a question left in the minds of all concerned. Why were there two apparitions so close together in time and proximity? In our book, "The Many Faces of Mary," we posed this possibility. We believe Our Lady was saying to them:

"Prepare yourselves for days of darkness. You will have much to endure. But know that I am always with you. Believe that you are beloved of God. If you can love yourself, I can love you. With the strength of that love, all things are possible. We can change the world.

"Our Lady was most definitely coming to the aid of her children of 1932/33, preparing them for the worst, which was to come.

"...Try to understand what she was saying. Do they (her

words) apply today as much, or even more so than in 1932? Why do women abort their children by the millions? Why do young people, people of all ages for that matter, abuse their bodies with drugs and alcohol to the point of death? Why do young people, and all people, commit suicide in staggering proportions today? Why are we as a world, determined to destroy ourselves?"[1]

The Miraculous Cross is still in the church in that little town of Limpias, nestled way up in the northwestern part of Spain, near the town of Santander, off the coast of the Atlantic Ocean. Pilgrimages go there from all over the world these days. We are sure that Our Lord Jesus manifests Himself to those who call on Him. And when they do, He goes beyond the limitations of human understanding to prove Himself to them, to let them know beyond the shadow of a doubt that He is here with them, in the Tabernacle, in the Miracle of the Cross, in any place where He is needed.

You don't have to go to Limpias, Spain, to venerate Jesus in this state, before He died. You can come to the Holy Family Mission in Morrilton, Arkansas. You can also go to your own Church and speak to Him, hanging, vulnerable, on the Cross. He is there for you. He waits for you. He listens to you. Listen to Him! He is talking to us, more than ever, pleading with us to convert before it's too late.

---

[1]From Bob and Penny Lord's book: *The Many Faces of Mary*

The History of the Cross

Our Faith belief is so rich, so strong. Even the symbol of the Cross, which symbolizes our Redemption through the Crucifixion of our Savior, is a perfect example of God taking a negative, and turning it into a positive. Like with St. Francis, who by his desire to be buried on the Hill of Hell,[1] turned it into the Hill of Paradise, so the Savior, by His choosing to die on a Cross would change its meaning forever. But it was to be a long and painful walk in man's desire to know the Truth. In order to truly understand the difficulty of the early Christians to accept the Cross, we must travel back thousands of years, to before Christ was born, to try to understand the struggles they had with the Cross.

Before the cross became the Cross of Salvation...

In studying the ancient beliefs of the cross, we discovered that before Christ, civilizations, in their search for signs explaining their existence, looked upon the cross with a more *human understanding*, one closely resembling the *astronomical*[2] or planetary, rather than the *Salvific* meaning of the cross that would follow through Christ's suffering. As the cross had two lines of equal length crossing one another, they took this to mean the cross symbolized the division of the world into four parts, or the four dimensions of the *Universe*.

There is so much that can theologically be drawn from this ancient symbolism of the cross, almost a foretelling of the whole Truth, which would come to pass. God the Father, *King of the Universe*, sent His only begotten Son Jesus Christ to make the final sacrifice which would free all men from the slavery of sin, *through the Cross!* With this earlier understanding of the Cross, was the Father not trying to send His children a tiny glimpse of the Light awaiting them at the end of their tunnel of darkness?

---

[1] somewhat like Potter's Field where criminals who had been executed for having committed the most heinous crimes were buried

[2] Scientific study of the Universe

With this earlier prefigurement of the Cross, was the Father not sending hope that through the Cross He would save the four corners of the world, the entire *universe?* You might ask why He did not open their eyes fully at that time. Because, as we hear Jesus saying to His Mother at Cana, "(His) *hour had not come.*"[3] God would save His children at the appointed time. Oh, He sent Prophets and Prophecies, to foretell the coming of their freedom. But it would only be through His Son's death on the Cross that all would be revealed.

A Light cuts through the darkness

Sin dimming their limited understanding of signs, the ancients were almost touching on what God had in store for them. The Gospel tells us, "...*the people who sit in darkness have seen a great light, on those dwelling in a land overshadowed by death light has arisen.*"[4] As *King of the Universe,*[5] God the Father sent His Son to uncover and destroy all that had kept them in darkness. The night, the Baby Jesus was born, a light shone in the darkness, which lighted the way for the shepherds and then the three Wise Men to find the Light of the world, the Light Who would save the world through the Cross.

The Swastika cross- an undetected symbol of Eternity

One of the most commonly used crosses of ancient times was the *swastika cross.* Consisting of four gammas joined at right angles - to some cultures of that time, it symbolized the spinning Sun - the source of light and power; or in other cultures - the glaring power of the elements, especially that of lightning. Originally known as the *gamma-cross,* the *swastika cross* derived its title from the Sanskrit. Meaning well-being, or long life, it consequently earned a reputation as a good omen symbol. The symbol they had perceived as *long life,* would later be understood, after the coming of Christ, as the promise of *eternity,*

---

[3]*cf*Jn 2:4
[4]Mt. 4:16
[5]You recall the ancients considered the cross, the two lines crossing each other as dividing the Universe in four parts.

the eternity gained from the Father in Heaven, through His Son's death on the Cross.

A symbol of love becomes a symbol of hate

Prior to Christ's coming, we not only find the *swastika cross* prevalent among the Hindus, Buddhists and Jainisists,[6] but as well with Germanic tribes. Because of this, many centuries later, remembering the powerful symbolism it had held in the ancient pagan Germanic tribes,[7] the German National Socialism Party, or NAZI party, seeking to instill pride and heritage in a beaten, starving people, adopted the *swastika cross* as its banner. By using this symbol of glorious days long gone by, this ancient symbol of long life did what the newly formed government had hoped, it united the German people, but at what cost! Under the *infamous* Adolph Hitler, it became Nazism's banner of fear and hate. And so, as the enemy of God loves to do, the devil took a symbol, meant to prophecy the coming of good - that of man's Salvation, and distorted it, turning good into evil.

The Scandal of the Cross

Prior to Christ's Sacrifice, the cross had always been looked upon as a scandalous symbol of punishment, a means used to crucify the most evil criminals. We believe that the weight of the Cross that threatened to crush Christ the third time He fell, was the sins of the world - past, present and future - the same sins He saw in the Garden of Gethsemane.

As He staggered, stumbling, along the Via Dolorosa, falling and getting up again, blood mixed with perspiration, burning His eyes, Jesus Christ could have ended His agonizing Passion anywhere along the way. *No! Instead,* He chose the Cross, heavily laden by our sins, as the instrument of our Salvation, transforming the *Cross of Death* into the *Cross of Life,* Life Eternal! Could it be that was why Christ held on, through inhuman torture, struggling more dead than alive, to die on the

---

[6]meaning tribe of conquerors
[7]although it did not originate with the Germanic tribes

Cross, so that our sins would die and we would enter into Heaven and dwell with Him and His Father?

Right from the Fall of Adam and Eve....

Through the fall of our first parents, Adam and Eve, man's vision has been blinded to the truth, from the very beginning. Yet man struggled to reach and understand a God he didn't know, a God Who filled the deep recesses of his heart with longing. We see many instances of how this longing manifested itself, like a whisper from the past, gnawing, persistently searching for that which it did not know but desired. We find it among natives who, never having had knowledge of God, when the Word of God came in their midst, freely accepted it, as if remembering, from some long-ago yesterdays, the seed of Faith, which had been planted; then lay dormant, only to flower in God's timetable.

An instance where this most dramatically happened was in Mexico, where it is believed a blonde missionary landed,[8] taught the natives Christianity and left them a glimpse of the Kingdom. But for centuries, having no one to continue guiding them along the path to Jesus and salvation, the truth became distorted. In their desire for the God Who shed His Blood for His children, they mistakenly ended worshipping a blood-thirsty god whose anger could only be satisfied by the shedding of his *children's* blood. As this gluttonous, ravenous pagan god's craving for blood could not be quenched, all they had left was a hole in their hearts.

This is what Our Lady of Guadalupe[9] came to in the 16th Century - Indians worshipping a series of gods, who demanded the Sacrifice of the Innocents by the tens of thousands. When the Mother of God appeared, their eyes were opened, they understood that *the Sacrifice* of the God-Man Jesus Christ *on the Cross* was all that was necessary to appease the One, and Only True God, the scales covering their eyes were lifted, and all

---

[8]possibly St. Brendan of Ireland

[9]For more on this apparition and other apparitions of Mother Mary, read Bob and Penny Lord's book: *The Many Faces of Mary, a Love Story.*

human sacrifice was ended.

The Cross, the price paid for our atonement, avoided...

But back to the Infant Church following Christ's death! Sadly, rather than acknowledge it as the means of salvation, the Sign of the Cross was shunned and avoided, for the most part, until the 5th Century. It posed an embarrassment, for the early Christians; because of its connotation in non-Christian cultures.[10] In the early centuries, following Christ's death, Christians wearing or displaying the Cross would be very much like venerating a man seated on an electric chair, today.

Take Christ off the Cross

Until the 4th Century, the Cross was not displayed in public; if at all, it was reserved for private devotion in the home. At that, it would be a plain wooden cross, deprived of the Wounded Corpus of Jesus Christ. A strong argument for this was that prior to the 4th Century, it was a death sentence to be found Christian; and so Christians identified themselves to each other with the sign of a fish.

Probably more important than all *human* reasoning, they were afraid if the Cross were found, it might be desecrated. So, although hidden from the world, in the deepest recesses of their hearts, the early Christians adored the Cross as a remembrance of the God-Man Who died that they might live. What gave the early Christians of the first four centuries, the strength to face lions and the most inhumane deaths, rather than deny Christ? It was the Cross and the price paid on that Cross!

Heresies rise up and the Church fights back

Something that both Pagans and Jews agreed to disagree upon was the incomprehensible belief that Christians held, that the Man Jesus crucified had also been God. Moslems insist, till today, they cannot believe that Jesus was God, because God

---

[10]Crucifixion was a method of capital punishment used in the Mediterranean countries from 6th Century B.C. to 4th Century A.D. reserved for the worst criminals

could not die on the Cross. When you think about it, with the lack of thousands of years of believers and martyrs who attested to that belief with their lives, it was not only a stumbling block for those lacking faith, it was at times a dilemma for those Christians trying to meet the day-in-and-day-out demands that holding onto the faith required, to believe.

Always problems arising, in the early Infant Church, there were Christians who were not comfortable accepting the concept of God dying on the Cross; therefore they emphasized the *death of the Human Jesus.* And then there were other Christians, who could only conceive the *crucifixion being of God,* and not of man; they refused to portray the Corpus, and elected to hang a simple wooden Cross. The Councils of Ephesus and Chalcedon were called and irrefutably cleared up, once and for all, the issue, by condemning those who insisted the crucifixion was not that of the *God-Man.* Although, with this condemnation, the Councils resolved the issue, there were those within the Church who, lacking the strength to believe, held on to the condemned heretical concepts. And then there were those Christians, *Pride* entering their hearts and minds, who postured themselves above the teachings of the Church, and stubbornly continued to proselytize these heresies condemned by the Councils.

Only Triumph - no Sacrifice

Of course, there was the Triumph of the Cross. Of course, we see it as a Victory, a Victory over death. But early Christians, who, preferring to see the Cross simply as a *Triumph* - Easter Sunday and the Resurrection - chose to ignore the strong argument that without Good Friday and the Passion, there would not have been a Resurrection, and an Easter to celebrate. Showing the Wounded Christ on the Cross would *highlight the Sacrifice,* therefore, the Cross was once again stripped of any sign of the Lord's suffering for our salvation. Only those holding onto the *Sacrificial* part of the Triumph over Death venerated the Crucified Lord on the Cross in the privacy of their homes.

The Church is made legal - and Jesus returns to the Cross

The controversy was to finally come to an end! Emperor Constantine saw an apparition of the Cross in the sky, the Church became *legal;* and the persecution ceased.[11] But that was not the only card God dealt. When God wants something to be known, as the Lord Jesus said on His entrance into Jerusalem, Passion Sunday, *"Even should My disciples be silent, the stones would cry out."*[12] And so, God brought about a miracle which would have the greatest impact on belief and veneration of the Cross - the discovery of the True Cross by Queen Helena, mother of King Constantine. Fragments of the Cross were dispersed around the Christian world, and with them devotion to the Cross.[13]

The Glorification of the Cross

In the 5th and 6th Centuries, Crosses, magnificently adorned, began to flourish, right up to and including the Middle Ages. Crosses were embellished with priceless jewels, with a fragment of the True Cross majestically placed in the center of the Cross, for the faithful to venerate. The Cross, truly a *Glorious Cross*, was now the antithesis of the somber wooden cross of the early Church.

Lamb of God

Carrying on the tradition of Our Lord's victory over death, and through Him and His Sacrifice on the Cross, our victory, the ornately decorated Cross of Triumph was joined by a new Image appearing in our churches, a Lamb carrying a Cross. Our churches, from the beginning - a classroom for the faithful, by depicting a Lamb carrying a Cross, they brought to life the *Agnus Dei*[14] we recite before receiving Our Lord Jesus in the Eucharist:

Lamb of God Who takes away the sins of the world, have mercy on us.

---

[11]But more on that in a later chapter
[12]*cf*Lk 19:40
[13]But more on that in a later chapter
[14]Lamb of God

Lamb of God Who takes away the sins of the world have mercy on us;

Lamb of God Who takes away the sins of the world, grant us peace.

Mother Church introducing The Lamb of God carrying a Cross, brings to the faithful the same unspoken hope that Mother Mary brought in Knock in 1879 - Our Lord's triumph over death - the Lamb of God Who through the Cross takes away the sins of the world! What a reassuring sign, in a sometimes dark and hopeless world, a world which has forgotten how to love and be loved.

The Cross - one of the most loving, lasting signs...

Of all the symbols used in the Church, one of the oldest, most prominent and endearing signs in the Church has been the Cross. Although we find the Cross first being used during the Mass in the 5th Century, it would be centuries later, before the Cross would be widely used during the Sacrifice of the Mass in the Western Church.

Now over 2000 years have passed, since Our Lord gave up His Spirit on the Cross and it has not lost its reality to those taking part in the Mass[15] - *This is the Last Supper and Jesus is about to come to us, Body, Blood, Soul and Divinity.* When we wrote our chapter on the Mass,[16] the three priests editing it were of one mind and one heart - They could not think of celebrating the Sacrifice of the Mass without our Crucified Lord on the Cross, on the wall of the Sanctuary, reminding the faithful what was coming about, and on the altar to remind *them* what *The Mass* was really about - *The Ongoing Sacrifice of the Cross.*

The plain wooden Cross, first placed on the Altar in the 13th Century, was soon replaced by a Crucifix with a Corpus of Our Lord crucified. In the Roman Missal of Saint Pius V[17] in 1570,

---

[15]who know what is really happening during the Mass

[16]*This is My Body, This is My Blood, Miracles of the Eucharist* **Book II** by Bob and Penny Lord

[17]Read more about Saint Pius V in Bob and Penny Lord's book:

we find it obligatory to have the Crucifix on the Altar. The Crucifix may be suspended above the altar; in fact it is preferable it be hanging on the wall above the tabernacle, in back of the priest, when he is celebrating the Mass facing the people, or in front of him when he is facing the East -*ad orientum.*

The Cross becomes the Crucifix

Although displaying the Cross in the churches began in the 5th Century, it was not until the 13th Century that the *reality* of Christ's Passion was to be graphically brought to the faithful. No more Triumph at the cost of belittling the Crucifixion that brought about the Triumph. Whereas in the Fifth Century, the Cross was resplendently embellished with brilliant jewels, signifying Good Friday was a day to celebrate, as it was on this day, on this Cross, that our freedom was purchased, in the Thirteenth Century, the Church felt it important that the faithful recognize the *Suffering aspect* of that Cross. It was His Passion on the Cross that brought about the Triumph over death by Our Lord and Savior on Good Friday, which subsequently brought about the glorious Day of Resurrection - Easter Sunday.

No Passion, just Resurrection

In the 20th Century, Modernism[18] infiltrating the Church, we find the capitulation of the Corpus on the Cross with Jesus' Five Precious Wounds to a spotless white Jesus adorned with resplendent priestly robes. As such, the Cross emphasized the *Resurrection* and the *Celebration aspect of the Mass* at the sacrifice of the *Sacrificial aspect of the Mass,* the *Ongoing Sacrifice of the Cross,*[19] thus ignoring the fact there would not

---

Defenders of the Faith.

[18]a heresy surfacing in the early 20th Century, condemned by Pope St. Pius X and an Ecumenical Congress. For more on this and other heresies, read Bob and Penny Lord's book: *Scandal of the Cross, and Its Triumph, Heresies throughout the History of the Church.*

[19]Declared at The Council of Trent in the 16th Century. For more on the Council, read Bob and Penny Lord's book: *Treasures of the Church, That which makes us Catholic.*

have been the Resurrection, if there had not first been the Sacrifice of the Cross. As one of the areas this change compromised was the Sacrifice aspect of the Mass, it would follow, they would remove the bleeding, wounded Corpus on the Cross in favor of gold and silver crosspieces, or just a huge Risen Christ. Again, we go back to Archbishop Fulton J. Sheen, when he cried out, *"They will believe anything, only no Cross!"*

The Processional Cross

The Processional Cross dates back to at least the late 6th Century. As soon as the Infant Church became legal, in Rome we see the dawning of the Processional Cross! It was carried at the head of a procession, as well as when praying before each of the Stations of the Cross.

To bring it additional fame and importance, in the year 800 A.D., after having been crowned Emperor of the Holy Roman Empire by Pope Leo III, Christmas Day, Charlemagne, gave the Pope a gift of a Processional Cross.

The use of the Processional Cross extended to before the commencement of the Mass, a procession would approach the doors of the Church, with priests and acolytes (altar servers) following an acolyte carrying the Processional Cross.

In the 13th Century, Pope Innocent III declared that, after approaching the Altar, the Processional Cross was to be placed on the Altar. But it was not until the next century that the Cross became a Crucifix, truly preparing the faithful for what was to transpire on the Altar - the Sacrifice of the Mass, the Ongoing Sacrifice of the Cross.

The Consecration Crosses

In the Middle Ages, the Church began painting 12 consecration crosses on the walls of a new church, on the 12 areas, where it had been anointed by the Bishop. This custom has continued to this day, only in varied ways, like in *The Shrine of the Most Blessed Sacrament,*[20] they appear as 12 small raised

---

[20]The Shrine of the Most Blessed Sacrament, founded by Mother

golden consecration crosses.

The Blessing of the Cross and Indulgences connected with it

The Roman Missal speaks of three blessings of the cross: one in a field where it will be placed, and the other two solemn blessings of the cross or crucifix performed by a Bishop, preferably; but in case of the absence of a Bishop, permission may be delegated to a priest.

The following Indulgences can be placed on a Cross or Crucifix: *Apostolic Indulgences*, the *Indulgence of the Way of the Cross*, the *Indulgence of a happy death.*

The Cross and the Mass

Do we understand what we are doing, every time we make the Sign of the cross?

In the Name of the Father and of the Son and of the Holy Spirit." Before the Mass begins, and we make the Sign of the Cross, do we know what we are really doing? We are calling upon the Holy Trinity - the Father, and the Son and the Holy Spirit - the Triune God, Who was there the day the world stood still, and Jesus triumphed over death - on the Cross. Before we begin the ongoing Sacrifice of the Cross - the Sacrifice of the Mass, we are calling Those Who were there at Calvary, giving full assent to the Sacrifice which would open the Gates of Heaven. One of the other greetings which is so powerful is:

The grace of Our Lord Jesus Christ, and the love of the Father and the fellowship of the Holy Spirit be with you all.

"Many of our newer, more traditional priests, before they begin to pray the Mass, preface it with, *'As we should begin all things, let us begin in the Name of the Father and of the Son and of the Holy Spirit.'"*[21]

Angelica and the Poor Clare Nuns of Perpetual Adoration, can be visited in Hanceville, AL

[21]Taken from the chapter on the Holy Trinity in Bob and Penny Lord's book: *Treasures of the Church.*

In the Name of the Father, and of the Son...

"As we should begin all things..." Do we begin all things inviting our God in Three Persons into our lives, into our every day lives? When we awaken, is making the Sign of the Cross the first thing we do, joining spiritually those Angels and Saints who watched and wept, as our Lord cried out, *"Father, do not hold this against them; they know not what they do?"*[22] And in so doing, do we pause one minute and reflect on what happened back, thousands of years ago, in the Garden of Eden, when even as His first creation was disobeying the Father, He set about His plan for our salvation, with that Cross we just made?

Do we thank Our Lord Jesus for the sorrowful suffering He endured on the Cross, and His Father for watching His Most Precious and Only Son die so horribly; and for whom? For those who often have no time to praise Him, to visit Him in the Tabernacle, to attend reverently the ongoing raising of the Cross, and Him on it, at Mass? Do we know what we are saying, when, as we make the Sign of the Cross, we pray, *"In the Name of the Father and of the Son and of the Holy Spirit?"*

Devotion to the Cross down through the ages

The Lord said to Moses, *"....lift up your staff and with hand outstretched over the sea, split the sea in two, that the Israelites may pass through it on dry land."*[23] With that motion of the staff, as God had dictated, the Israelites were freed from slavery. But God desired a more complete freedom for His children and so once again wood had to be raised, only now a staff in the form of a Cross! The freedom of the Israelites was only a temporary reprise, but this staff upon which Jesus hung would split open the curtain, freeing God's children from slavery eternally.

God the Father kept speaking to His children, only in veiled language. Once again God the Father wanted to save His children, once again with wood - the Ark of the Covenant. In

---

[22]Lk 23:34
[23]Ex 14:16

Genesis, we read:

"When God saw how corrupt the earth had become, since all mortals led depraved lives on earth, He said to Noah, 'I have decided to put an end to all mortals on earth; the earth is full of lawlessness because of them. So I will destroy them and all life on earth.'"[24]

God then instructed Noah how to save himself, his family and his livestock, instructing him to *"'Make yourself an ark of gopher wood" Wood!* Again, we see God trying to save His children from dire disaster, with *Wood!* Although God told Noah He would destroy all life, He promised Noah for his faithfulness and obedience he would spare him and his family.

The Cross, O Holy and Precious Cross...

Weep not, dear Angels of God, your Lord has not died in vain! His Cross will not be hidden. Your cries will not be stilled. From every church, His Cross will hang. From every church, the bells will resound, the faithful will bend their knees, and the procession will begin; Mother Mary will be awaiting her children at the foot of the Cross and, taking you by the hand, will mend your wounds and remind you there is a God and He died for you.

And so, as you will see, as you read on, *the Wood of the Cross, the Wood of Salvation,* although often obscured and embellished beyond recognition, refused to be hidden. Satan and his fallen angels could *never* still the thunderous roar of the Angels. Crosses which refused to be silenced, began appearing everywhere. As you walk through the villages throughout Europe, those which wars and bombings could not obliterate, there are, on the corners of buildings, on homes, churches, parks, wayside chapels, everywhere the eye can see - Our Lord present on the Cross, reminding them and us how very much He loves us. ***Salvation comes through the Wood of the Cross!***

---

[24]Gen 6:13

Above:
Miraculous Crucifix that survived dynamite blast at Our Lady of Guadalupe Shrine in Mexico City in November, 1921

Above:
The Cathedral in Mexico City

Right:
The Miraculous Crucifix inside the Cathedral in Mexico City An enemy of the Church placed poison on the Feet of Our Lord on the Crucifix. As the Bishop went to kiss Our Lord's Feet, the Lord raised His Legs out of reach.

The Cross Protects
Our Lady of Guadalupe

Our Lord Jesus protects His Mother Mary

We know that Jesus and Mary love each other as no other people in the history of the world or of the Church. Why then do we find it so amazing that Jesus would do anything to protect His Mother, even to the degree of creating a Miracle? Or should the question be, *"Are there any situations where Our Lord Jesus would not give us a Miracle to protect Mother Mary?"*

In this book, we believe that you will be given the privilege of experiencing many Miracles by the Son for His Mother, or by God the Father for His Daughter, or by the Holy Spirit for His Spouse. Or for that matter, we shall see Miracles performed through the intercession of the Angels for the benefit of their Queen, Mother Mary.

It is no secret that the Apparition of Our Lady to Blessed Juan Diego was a true gift from the Lord, which gave us the family that makes up our dear neighbors to the south, Mexico. Our Lady's appearance also prevented a major blood bath, which was about to take place between the natives of Mexico and the Spanish conquistadors. In addition, through this miraculous apparition, we were gifted with 8,000,000 converts in a period of seven years, A phenomena the Church has not experienced to this day. It was truly a great outpouring of the Holy Spirit on these beautiful people.

But we have to understand what these dear people were up against, both Indians and Spanish. Originally, the expedition which brought the Spanish people over to this continent was done by the Catholic Queen, Isabella, in thanksgiving for having freed her people from the clutches of Spain's arch enemies, the Moors.[1] For more than seven hundred years of captivity, the

---

[1]moor - a member of a Moslem people of mixed Arab and Berber

55

Name of Jesus was not allowed to be spoken under pain of imprisonment or worse, death. This country was not able to worship Our Lord Jesus openly.

The Spaniards sent over a group of Franciscans to convert the Indians to Christianity. There was a common ground between our Faith belief and the teachings of an Aztec god, Quetzalcoatl. Their tradition says he was a great prophet who appeared at Cholula in 700 A.D., and taught the people a civilized religion along the lines of Catholicism. Legend has it that person was the Irish Saint Brendan, who traveled up and down the coast of Mexico, evangelizing. When Cortez and his troops came to Mexico, the natives recognized the black cross on the sails of their ship. Many were ready to go over to the new religion. The Indians who converted to Christianity were able to live in peace and harmony with their rulers, but there were too few, and time was running out.

After ten years, the situation had come to a head just about the time when Our Lady chose to appear to Juan Diego on Tepeyac Hill. The Indians were at the point of organizing a revolution, to massacre every European in their land. History tells us that it was almost the eve of the revolution when Our Lady came. It's been determined that at the time of Our Lady's appearance, the Aztecs were capable of killing every European in Mexico. There was a great need for God to bring these two peoples together. He chose His Mother as the perfect instrument, as He had done fifteen hundred years before, at the Annunciation in Nazareth.

It was important for Our Lady to come to the Indians. In that way they would embrace Christianity, and the Spaniards would accept the Indians as fellow human beings, rather than strange, mystical animals. The apparition at Tepeyac Hill was the catalyst that brought them together. We had lost 6,000,000

---

descent living in NW Africa; a member of a group of this people that invaded and occupied Spain in the 8th Century. (Webster's Dictionary)

Catholics in Europe, and through the Mother Of God, our Mary we would gain in the course of 7 years, **8,000,000** Indians converted to the Catholic Faith. Nothing like that has happened, before or since, in the history of our Church. What had been wholesale massacre became wholesale conversion. The Holy Spirit filled the land on a much greater scale than in Jerusalem on the day of Pentecost. Reconciliation between the Spaniards and the Indians came about. Peace came to Mexico.

Our dear Pope John Paul II declared Our lady of Guadalupe *Patroness of the Americas* (North and South), uniting us as one people. And She will protect us with her mantle; and She will bring peace once more to our land.

As for the miraculous tilma of Juan Diego, critics and enemies of Our Lord Jesus and His Mother Mary have spent the last 450 years trying to disprove this was a work of Heaven. The cloth on which Our Lady chose to have her image imprinted is Cactus cloth, which has a life span of no more than 20 years if it is not painted on. If it is painted on, it lasts about 6 years. This cactus cloth, which was used by Juan Diego for many years prior to Our Lady's visit from Heaven, has never decomposed, more than 470 years later.[2]

Those who do not believe in the power of God or in Miracles, could never accept that this was a miraculous occurrence. At one time, authorities in the art field tried to simulate the circumstances of how the tilma might have been painted by human hands. Investigations began as early as the middle of the sixteenth century, using whatever tools were available to the artistic and scientific communities of the day. It has continued till today, with the latest scientific and computerized equipment available. They would try anything to disprove the authenticity of the Tilma.

---

[2]For more on Our Lady of Guadalupe and other authenticated Apparitions of Mother Mary, read Bob and Penny Lord's book: *The Many Faces of Mary.*

Jody Brant Smith (a Non-Catholic) wrote a book[3] a few years ago, in which he and a colleague, Dr. Callahan, (a Catholic) performed extensive experiments on the Image of Our Lady, such as infra-red photography, ultra violet photography, and computer-enhanced black and white photography. They were trying to determine if a sketch had been made underneath the painting, which would have proven that the painting was done by human hands. They were also trying to determine what kind of colors and pigments were used in the painting.

Prior to issuing the findings, the author **(Remember, a Non-Catholic)** made the following statement:

"Some may find it ironic that in our skeptical age the tools of science have been used not to disprove but in some degree to authenticate miracles of the past. Our discovery of the absence of under sketching in the image of Guadalupe and our inability to account for the remarkable state of preservation of the unsized cactus cloth as well as the unfading brightness of the paints or dyes used in the original parts of the painting put Dr. Callahan and myself firmly in the ranks of those who believe the Image was created supernaturally."

With all the information they were able to gather from the use of the sophisticated equipment at their disposal, they were not able to determine what pigments or dyes (if any) were used to make the portrait. They were easily able to rule out thousands of possibilities, but were never able to make definite conclusions as to *what was used.*

So now, with all of the above, we think you will agree with us that Satan had to be *super-angry*, so angry he'd do anything to get rid of the Tilma. A new plan was hatched. If he couldn't discredit the Tilma, he'd destroy it. In 1791, a minor attempt was made to obliterate the Image. A cleaning lady in the Basilica spilled nitric acid, which was used to polish the silver and gold of the frame, across the middle section of the Image on the cloth.

---

[3]*The Image of Guadalupe - Myth or Miracle*

Remember, this is cactus cloth, a vegetable substance. Virtually nothing happened to the Image. There was just a watermark on the cloth. But in an effort to avoid anything like that in the future, the Image was given a protective plate of glass some years after this accident. But it was not to protect the Image from anything like the devious plot Satan had planned for her. It was to protect Our Lady more from the oil from the hands that continually touched the Tilma over the years, and from candle wax.

However, it proved to be providential, because in November, 1921, a major attempt was made to desecrate this beautiful gift, God had given to the people of Mexico and to the world. Satan whispered in the ears of a deranged person to destroy the Image of Our Lady of Guadalupe. He planted hatred in the man's heart. He planted the seed which became the poison needed to spur the man on. On November 24, the deluded man walked into the old Basilica, which was beginning to sink, even at that time. To the naked eye, he appeared very reverent and loving towards Our dear Mother. He carried a bouquet of flowers, supposedly to offer to Mother Mary. He went to the main Altar, above which was the beautiful, miraculous Tilma of Juan Diego. He gently placed the beautiful cluster of flowers on the Altar. To any of the Faithful in the Basilica, he would have appeared to be just another of the loving Mexican men who adored their Mother. But inside the bouquet of flowers was a bomb! He made sure to place the flowers strategically under the Tilma, at the foot of the large, very heavy brass Crucifix.

We believe that he either left the Basilica, or went to the back very quickly. Because it was not very long after, that an explosion of gigantic proportions rocked the aging building. It was ear shattering. The building shook to it's rafters. Blocks of marble were dislodged. All the windows in the Basilica were blown to smithereens. The glass blew out onto the street below. Pilgrims inside the Basilica were strewn all over the church from the force of the blast. Fearful the church would surely collapse, they ran to safety outside, in the great Plaza of Our Lady of Guadalupe.

To explain the Miracle of the Cross in the eyes of Faith, we would have to say that Jesus on the Cross expanded, at least to the height of the Tilma, and, arms outstretched, blocked the impact of the explosion. He threw His Body in front of His Mother, protecting her from the onslaught. He took all the punishment on Himself, rather than have His Mother, or this Image, so important to the people of Mexico, be destroyed. The brass Crucifix twisted and distorted. It actually twisted around, so that the Corpus was at the back of the base, turning, as it were, to look at His Mother, to be sure that she was all right.

There was a great deal of damage done to the Basilica. It took months to repair it. But the area around Our Lady, the Altar, the frame of the Tilma, and the Tilma itself, were not marred in any way. The Miraculous Crucifix is with us to this day. It has been put on display in a special place inside the new Basilica of Our Lady of Guadalupe. Jesus is there to help us. He loves us the way He loves His Dear Mother. Would he block you with His Body if you were in danger? What do you think He did for us on the Cross? Keep your eyes on the Cross. Jesus is there for you. He will give you your own personal Miracle of the Cross.

Jesus on the Cross saves a life
Miracle of the Cross, Mexico City

The Spaniards came to Mexico City in 1521, ten years before Our Lady Guadalupe appeared there on a hill to a new convert, an Indian named Juan Diego. In order to help in the evangelization, and ultimate conversion of the natives, a church was built in 1524 by the Franciscan missionaries. Four years later, in 1528, a Papal Bull was issued by Pope Clement VIII elevating the church to the awesome title of *Cathedral.*

When that same year Juan de Zumárraga was appointed Bishop, he proposed to the Spaniards the construction of a church worthy of that honor, explaining as well that the first church built by Cortés was damp and too small for the growing population. A Canon was sent to Spain to obtain permission to build. It was agreed construction would commence in 1536. A choice piece of property was chosen and excavation began immediately. However they could not proceed until they received permission from King Philip in 1552. Completion of the Cathedral was not realized until 1813.

What with the influx of over 8,000,000 convert natives flowing into Mexico City to venerate their Queen, Our Lady of Guadalupe, the first Cathedral soon became too small to accommodate all the pilgrims and consequently it was torn down as soon as the Sacristy was built in 1623. There they would celebrate Mass and hold all services until *that* got too small. So we can see the Hand of God prompting His children to build the large Cathedral you see today, when you visit Mexico City. On one of our numerous pilgrimages to Mexico for the celebration of the Feast of Our Lady of Guadalupe, upon entering the Cathedral we were fascinated by a black crucifix in the right nave of the Cathedral. When we inquired, the custodian told us the tradition that has survived 400 years!

The Cross of Poison

In the year 1602, this crucifix was in a Dominican church, used by seminarians, called *Porta Coeli* (or Heaven's Gate). Only the Crucifix was *white marble!* As it was next door to the Cathedral and used by the seminarians, it was the Archbishop's custom to celebrate Mass there daily. It was also his custom to kiss the Feet of the Crucified Lord on the Crucifix, before beginning the ongoing Sacrifice of the Cross, the Holy Mass. Now not everyone was happy with the conversions that had come about, especially those who had profited from the natives, like the medicine men who were now out of business. And then there were those who liked the status quo of the human sacrifice of over 20,000 innocents each year.

One day, a man who hated the inroads the Bishop and the Church were making, decided to poison him. Carefully observing the Bishop's routine, he placed poison on the Feet of Our Lord on the Crucifix. As the Bishop began his ritual for the morning Mass, and went to kiss Our Lord's Feet, the Lord raised His Legs out of reach. The Bishop did not kiss the Feet and consequently did not die; but Our Lord once again saved a child of His from the venom of one of the Church's enemies, as the poison went through His Corpus on the Cross turning the statute black. The Crucifix was taken to the Cathedral where worshippers could come, and visit, and pray.

Till today almost 400 years later, the faithful come and venerate the statue of their Lord, which miraculously saved the Bishop. Every Friday at twelve noon, Holy Mass is celebrated in this Chapel of the miraculous Cross of Poison. The official Feast Day of this miracle falls on the 3rd Friday of October. Multitudes come to Mexico City and the Cathedral, to celebrate this miracle and supplicate Our Lord to have mercy on them.

When the Archbishop saw this miracle take place, he realized he had been miraculously spared and instituted this Feast Day and the celebration of the Holy Mass every Friday at twelve noon, the hour Our Lord was placed on the Cross on Calvary

2000 years ago.

When we meditate on this miracle and all the circumstances surrounding it, we can once again see God's Hand. The name of the church where the miracle manifested itself (through the Will of God) was *Porta Coeli* or Heaven's Gate. Do we not consider the Church Heaven's Gate, as it is within its holy walls we find the Sacraments of Salvation? It was not by mere chance or a coincidence that this miracle took place in this church - Heaven's Gate. Is the Lord not once again telling us that it was through the Cross that we were saved, that we were redeemed?

Beloved cousins to the South, Holy Mexico, precious bouquet of mixed flowers in God's garden, what a legacy you have, what an everlasting heritage of faith and faithfulness, right to martyrdom when necessary, do not allow anyone to rob you of your Treasure; it has been hard-earned.

Right:
Crucifix that dodged a cannon ball during the battle of Lepanto

Below:
Banner used during battle

Above: ***Don Juan of Austria, Supreme Commander of Catholic Fleet***

Above: ***Battle of Lepanto - permission***
www.nafpaktos.com/battle_of_lepanto.htm

Miracle of the Cross of Lepanto

One of the most rewarding events in the history of the Catholic Church was the Battle of Lepanto, which took place in 1571, forty years after Our Lady had appeared to Juan Diego on Tepeyac Hill (what is now the famous shrine of Our Lady of Guadalupe in Mexico City). We, the people of God, have always been blessed and rewarded for the trust we have had in Our Lord Jesus and His Mother Mary. Whenever we have prayed the Rosary, They have granted us the power to overcome the enemy.

We were in the days of the greatest of challenges to Christianity, with the fiercest battles fought and at times won and others lost. But they were important times! Battles decided whether the people of the land would continue to be Christian or follow Islam. So to say they were Holy Wars would not be far from the truth. Strangely enough, nothing has changed in these last 500 years.

We were in the 16th Century. Militant followers of Islam were attempting to destroy any vestige of Christ and His Church they could find. The annihilation of the entire Christian civilization was their aim and getting control of the Mediterranean shore an integral part of that strategy. They would, as they had at other times at other shores, subject the faithful to slavery and to heresy. Upon learning of this, the Holy Father Pope St. Pius V summoned all Christians to form the Holy League.

Pope St. Pius V could see the need of a new Crusade against the Moslems. They had been successful in threatening Christianity by sea in the Adriatic, by land in the Balkans, they were now attempting to split Europe in two by taking control of the Mediterranean. A meeting was held on September 10, 1571, of the Christian coalition of commanders on Don Juan of Austria's ship. It was brought to the Pope's attention that their fleet was outnumbered by the Moslems by 268 ships to the

Catholic fleet of 208 ships. Caution and prudence was advised. *"Let cooler heads prevail"* was the thrust of the warning. But one of the captains intervened, and recommended they act immediately, even at the cost of their own lives. Moved by this encouragement, Pope Pius V gave his blessing for the plan to begin immediately. Part of the final preparation for the mission was for every one involved to receive Confession and Communion. The armada fasted for three days. Before departure, a Jesuit gave Don Juan the Pope's final message, *"Hesitate not to engage in battle, for, in God's name, I assure you of victory."*

The formation of a powerful Navy was immediately instituted under the command of Don Juan of Austria. What followed was a fierce battle with the Moslem Navy at Lepanto Bay on October 7, 1571. This day would be dedicated to the Holy Rosary in thanksgiving for the Rosaries said, which ultimately brought about victory for Don Juan and his Navy.

Don Juan had an Image of the Crucified Christ placed in the Royal Galley, as inspiration and symbol of the Church and her Founder Jesus Christ. Their eyes on their Lord they would do battle and bring about victory. A ferocious and bloody battle ensued. It appeared all hope was futile! The Moslems were known for their zeal and willing death for victory. In addition they had 120,000 soldiers to Don Juan's Navy comprising 80,000 Christians. Everything looked bleak for the Christian forces. But they would fight to the last man and die, if need be, to defend the Faith. A banner of the Image of Our Lady of Guadalupe, who had appeared just 40 years before, was placed near the Crucifix.

At about this time, without having any definite information on the progress of the battle, Saint Pope Pius V turned to the entire Christian world and asked them to begin a Rosary Crusade! And the result? Out of the 170 enemy galleys (ships) only 40 escaped! 130 were either sunk or captured. The Christian forces lost 15 galleys and they were able to free 13, 000 Christian slaves.

At one point, it was reported that, during the heat of the battle, a vision of Our Lady appeared in the sky, visible to the Moslems. She terrified them with her queenly presence. She projected to them the omnipotence of the God of the Catholics. It was the main turning point of the battle.

Witnesses of the battle testified to the following:

The first one, daughter of the Moslem Admiral Ali-Baxa wrote to Don Juan of Austria,

"...how grateful I am to you for giving freedom to...after the death of my father...After the defeat of our Navy my brothers were taken into captivity by your Forces and I beg you to set these poor orphans free."   Signed *Fatima Cadem*

Then from a mutilated soldier of Lepanto, *"The Armless of Lepanto,"* Miguel de Cervantes wrote:

"At this moment I was standing
with my sword in my hand held
and with my blood gushing from the other.
"My breast was wounded with a deep sorrow
and my left hand was already severed.
"But the joy was so great
that it reached at the depths of my heart
the joy of seeing the destruction
of the cruel infidel by the Christian one,
which did not even have the time to see my wounds..."

In another place he writes:

"(It was) the best days the Centuries have witnessed."

Then there was the letter from Don Juan, Admiral of the Holy League to His Majesty the King Felipe II, in which he wrote::

"Petala, 8th of October, 1571....the great success of the battle must be attributed to God's Grace."

During this time, our Saintly Pope Pius V was in Rome, trying to conduct the business of the Church, and at the same time, pray constantly for the well-being of his troops, out in the Gulf of Lepanto. A heavenly vision informed him of the victory, at the very moment it was taking place. The Pope went to the windows of the Vatican, opened them and listened for a time, as if in ecstasy. Then he turned with tears in his eyes and a smile on his face. He spoke to those with whom he was holding his meeting. *"This is not a moment to talk business,"* he told them, *"let us give thanks to God for the Victory He has granted to the arms of the Christians."*

The Vicar of Christ on earth, His Holiness the Pope St. Pius V announced the victory himself adding:

"Your Right Hand, Lord, has wounded the enemy."

The reports read, *On October 7th, 1571, the troops of Selim II, Sultan of the Turks, were thoroughly destroyed in a disastrous naval defeat near the harbor of Lepanto.* The victory was credited to Pope Saint Pius V and was mentioned in his canonization. As we mentioned before, a Rosary campaign had been started. A procession of the faithful reciting the Rosary, marched toward the church of Minerva. At the same time, the Pope was in a meeting, with his cardinals, when suddenly he stopped speaking and went to the window. He threw it open and stood there transfixed, as if in a trance. When he returned to these Princes of the Church, he gave thanks to the Mother Of God and Her Beloved Son Jesus. Just as he was saying these prophetic words *"It is now time to give thanks for the great victory which has been granted to the arms of the Christians."* The records show the Christians were claiming victory over the infidels. But the real proof came from prisoners taken in battle. They testified with indisputable confidence that they had seen Jesus Christ, Our Lady of Lepanto, St. Peter and Saint Paul, accompanied by an army of Angels, swords in hand, fighting against the Turks, blinding them with smoke.

The Miracle of the Crucifix of Lepanto

But the greatest and most tangible witness to this miraculous victory was the Miracle of the Crucifix, which not many people know about, but which is still with us to this day. The Lord left us a sign using the twisted Image of Himself on the Cross. A Crucifix, the Image of Christ on the Cross, was placed on the galley, as an inspiration for the troops, to reassure them that God was with the Christians defending their land and their Faith. An enemy shell was fired directly at the Crucifix, hoping to shatter the faith and hope of the men on the Christian ship. As the shell sped toward the Crucifix, the Image of Jesus twisted His Body, and avoided being hit by the shell. The original Crucifix is there till today in the Cathedral in Barcelona, Spain, for the procession of faithful coming and asking Jesus on the Cross for His intercession and also in thanksgiving for favors received here for more than 400 years.

God does not desire wars; but all wars help God's Providence. A perfect example would be what has transpired since those heartless attacks on innocent people in the Twin Towers, the Pentagon and in Pennsylvania. The enemy wanted to bring us down on our knees; and he did! Only it was not the way he planned it. Those who believed in God suddenly remembered that *victory could only be gained on our knees - praying!* And so, God is back where He belongs - in our hearts and in our minds. As in Lepanto, God is the victor; and He will be again.

No one is bad, except those who want to be so, those who would enslave or kill their brothers. In this situation, the Bible tells us it is lawful to defend oneself. And God will help us, as He did when the Red Sea opened up and allowed the Israelites to pass through and then closed the Sea, drowning the Egyptian captives who would enslave them. God is with us; He always has been. It is always wrong to cause harm to one of God's creations, except in the case of self-defense. May the Lord continue to bless our country and grant us His Peace.

Moses and the Bronze Serpent

Our God is such a good God. He has always been faithful to a completely unfaithful people. The children of Israel groaned over their bondage, and cried out to God for help. He heard their cries and remembering His covenant with Abraham, Isaac and Jacob,[1] opened the Red Sea and led them to freedom from captivity by the Egyptians. And how did the Israelites show their gratitude? With the first hardship, they complained - the water in the new land was bitter! Our ever patient Lord told Moses to place a tree in the water; he did so and the water became sweet.[2]

"on the fifteenth day of the second month after they had departed from the land of Egypt, the whole congregation of the people of Israel murmured against Moses and Aaron in the wilderness, saying, 'Would that we had died by the Hand of the Lord in the land of Egypt, when we sat by the fleshpots and ate bread to the full; for you have brought us out into this wilderness to kill this whole assembly with hunger.'"[3]

What does the Lord do? Our ever-loving God appears and tells Moses to speak this to His ever complaining, never satisfied children, *"I have heard the murmurings of the people of Israel; say to them, 'At twilight you shall eat flesh, and in the morning you shall be filled with bread; then you shall know that I am the Lord your God.'"*[4]

The Lord told Moses that the people could gather food for six days, but the seventh, the day He had declared a Sabbath of solemn rest, they were to keep holy and not go out in search of food. What did His children do? They gathered all they could eat for six days and then instead of resting on the seventh, they went out again to gather food. They found none! The Lord told Moses, *"How long do you refuse to keep my commandments and*

---

[1]Ex 2:23
[2]cf Ex 15:22
[3]Ex 16:1
[4]Ex 16:12

my laws?"[5] Moses turned to the people, *"The Lord has given you six days to cook and prepare your food; on the seventh day you must rest."*[6] Finally, they got the message and the people rested the seventh day. For His part, God continued to rain down Manna from Heaven, feeding the Israelites the forty years they spent in the desert seeking the Promised Land.

The Lord continued to instruct Moses, and he in turn passed the Lord's Word to them. Now it came to pass that Moses was delayed in coming down from the mountain. The people became impatient and turned to Aaron to make them gods. Aaron responded by asking of them their rings made of gold. They did as he asked; then he melted the gold and made a golden calf. Upon beholding the pagan calf, they cried out with one voice, *"These are your gods, O Israel, who brought you out of the land of Egypt!"*[7] Aaron for his part built an altar in front to the calf, and proclaimed that the next day, they would celebrate a feast day to their god, the molten calf. God upon seeing His children worshipping the golden calf, told Moses to return quickly to his people as they had corrupted themselves. God was going to deliver his wrath upon His people, but Moses once again pleaded for them, and God repented of the evil[8] He had planned for them; once again giving them another chance.

God had given them chance after chance, and they continued to mess up. Never giving up on them, the Lord dictated the Ten Commandments to Moses, to be passed on to His children. Everything seemed to be going well; then there was not enough water for the community. The people turned on Moses and Aaron, *"Why have you brought the assembly of the Lord into this wilderness, that we should die here, both we and our cattle?"*[9] Moses and Aaron went into the tent and prostrated themselves

---

[5]Ex 16:28
[6]cf Ex 16:29
[7]Ex 32:4
[8]*cf*Jon 3:10
[9]Nu 20:5

before the Altar to the Lord. The glory of the Lord appeared and the Lord said to Moses *"Take this rod, and assemble the congregation, you and Aaron your brother, and tell the rock before their eyes to yield its water..."*[10] Moses took the rod and struck the rock twice and water flowed.

God led them victoriously through villages that were hostile. When the Canaanite king heard the Israelites were coming, he fought against Israel and took some of them captive. Israel once again turned to the Lord, now with this solemn vow, *"If Thou will indeed give this people into my hand, then I will utterly destroy their cities.*[11]*"* The Lord did as they asked and turned over the Canaanites, into their hands, and Israel destroyed them and their cities. The Israelites continued on their journey and traveled by way of Edom. As it proved long and tiresome, the Israelites once again turned against Moses and God with their old tiresome song, *"Why have you brought us out of Egypt to die in the desert? For there is no food and no water, and we loathe this worthless food."*[12]

Well, I guess the Lord finally had His fill of these stiff-necked, ungrateful people and He sent serpents to bite them, causing the death of many. Knowing they had gone too far, the Israelites came to Moses, *"We have sinned, for we have spoken against the Lord and against you; pray to the Lord, that He take away the serpents from us.*[13]*"* Never giving up on them, Moses once again prayed; and the Lord once again answered him, *"Make a fiery serpent, and set it on a pole; and every one who is bitten, when he sees it, shall live."*[14] Moses did as the Lord dictated, he made a bronze serpent, and anyone who had been bitten, when he looked upon it, lived.

The bronze serpent, the prefigurment of Jesus on the Cross

---

[10]Nu 20:8
[11]Nu 21:12
[12]Nu 21:5
[13]Nu 21:7
[14]Nu 21:8

St. John in his Gospel tells us, *"And as Moses lifted up the serpent in the wilderness, so must the Son of Man be lifted up, that whoever believes in Him may have eternal life."*[15] In the desert, the people of God consistently sinned against God; and each time He forgave them and gave them another chance. God never gave up on His people, from the very beginning. Even as Adam and Eve were betraying Him, by listening to the serpent in the Garden, God was executing His plan to save them and those who would follow. But now only the raising up of a new Adam, His only begotten Son, would satisfy the sins and offenses committed against God the Father.

The pattern is the same. God delivered the Israelites from the yoke of enslavement, and they turned against Him. His Son came to deliver sinners from the slavery of sin, and they killed Him. In the Old Testament, we see serpents biting and killing the people of God, and God comes once again to their rescue, through a bronze serpent lifted high on a pole (or tree). In the New Testament, as in the Old Testament, people were sinning against the Father, and loving Father that He was, He wanted them delivered from the tentacles of sin. The only way was by lifting Jesus high on the Cross, so that those who looked upon Him and believed, would be saved from the venomous bite of sin.

The key word here is life. God asked the Israelites to look upon a serpent, which had symbolized death to them, and He gave them the Miracle of the Cross - life. God asks us to look upon Jesus on the Cross, a symbol of the worst form of execution of its day, and we will experience that same Miracle - life. Doctors use the image of the bronze serpent as their symbol, the serpent which caused death as the symbol of the Hippocratic Oath which was until recently, the standard bearer of life, again the contradiction.

We know Jesus was more dead than alive, before He was lifted high on the Cross. The knowledge that His being lifted high on the Cross was the only acceptable sacrifice needed to

---

[15]Jn 3:14

satisfy His Father, gave Him the strength to live through the scourging, the mockery, the rejection, the abandonment, the weight of the Cross on His already badly bruised shoulder, the pain of seeing His Mother's suffering at the foot of the Cross. To repeat the quotation from John's Gospel: *"And as Moses lifted up the serpent in the wilderness, so must the Son of Man be lifted up, that whoever believes in Him may have eternal life."* Look at your Savior on the Cross. Choose the Miracle - choose life.

The Cross, past and present
- a Sign of Controversy

The Cross bars the way, the way to hell!

The Cross of Triumph, the Cross that saved and continues to save, has been a *Sign of Controversy*, from the very beginning. How could a Man give His Life for those persecuting Him, those rejecting Him, those denying Him not once but three times; and then those following *in time memoriam*, inflicting hurt upon hurt, wound upon wound?

No sooner had Our Lord been taken down from the Cross that He had willingly embraced and offered to the Father for our Redemption, than new Pharisees and Saducees, wearing different name tags, cropped up among the early Christians, and with them heresies that threatened to topple the Infant Church which had recently flowed from the Heart of Jesus on the Cross.

Satan, furious that Christ would not come down from the Cross, began his *modus operandi of dissent and division!* Because the Apostles originally began preaching in the Synagogues, *The Judaizers,*[1] an early sect of converts from Judaism to Christianity, insisted that Christianity was a mere offspring from Judaism and belonged strictly to the Jews. If Gentiles wanted to become part of the early Church, they would have to follow the Law of Moses and submit to circumcision.

Always true to His Promise, Jesus raises up a Saint. Saul, zealot of the Jews became Paul, Apostle to the Gentiles. It was a bleeding, wounded Jesus Who spoke to Saul, and pleaded, *"Saul, Saul why do you persecute Me?"* It was a persecuted, sacrificial Lamb Who opened Saul's eyes, mind and heart to the Truth, the Way and the Life Who is Our Lord Jesus Christ. It was a Savior, Who passionately suffered, Who pleaded with Saul. And it was because of the Lord, Who died on the Cross, that Paul, no longer

---

[1]More on this in Bob and Penny Lord's book: *Scandal of the Cross and Its Triumph, Heresies throughout the History of the Church.*

Saul, passionately waged battle against those persecuting his new-found Lord.

Jesus said that *whatsoever we do to the least of His children, we do unto Him.*[2] In wielding the *two-edged sword* against the heretics, Paul fulfilled the mandate Jesus gave him, thus becoming the instrument Jesus would use to bring about unity.

Whenever Mother Church is faced with a heresy, she not only dispels it, she proclaims a Dogma (on a truth already accepted in the Church). Young and brave, the blood of her martyrs flowing in the arenas, Mother Church fights her first heresy; she calls her first council. At the First Council of Jerusalem in 40 A.D., the heresy of the Judaizers was dispelled and a dogma proclaimed, clearing the way for the Gentiles to be part of the Church.

The Cross has always been a bone of contention.

Possibly one of the most far-reaching, destructive arguments put forth by the Judaizers was that the Cross was not necessary to bring about our Salvation, only obedience to the Law of Moses, clearly negating and demeaning the sorrowful suffering and sacrifice offered to God the Father, by and through the death of His Son Jesus Christ on the Cross. If Salvation came about through the Law of Moses, why do the Jews offer sacrifice till today;[3] and why are they awaiting a Messiah? Why was Jesus born and why did He go to the Cross? Were they saying that God the Father would have His Son crucified for no reason? To say this lie is true is to proclaim that Jesus' Suffering and Death on the Cross was to no avail; what a cruel Father would have His Son die so horribly for no purpose. As parents, grandparents and great grandparents, we find that appalling! Now, how in God's Name could they call themselves followers of Christ and believe that His death on the Cross was not needed to free them, and all who followed, from the slavery of the sins of our first parents![4]

---

[2] *cf* Mt 25:45
[3] On the Day of Atonement - *Yom Kippur*
[4] Adam and Eve

What were the two deadly sins committed by Adam and Eve? One - that of *Pride* - you can be like God. And the other - *Disobedience* - I will not serve! Like so many heretics, throughout the history of the Church, these early heretics liked the Mystical Body of Christ that had formed after the Death of the Savior. As heretics and dissidents after them, for the last 2000 years, they wanted the Army of Believers, not that which they believed in, lived and died for the first 300 years. They wanted the *organization* of the Church, but not the *Church*. Heretics and dissidents wanted, and have always wanted the flesh, but not the soul; the shell but not the heart. Without the soul, we have a band of wild animals running amuck, the flesh seeking and grabbing until it destroys itself and all around it.

In the Old Testament, it is taught that the truth enters through the mind, but goes out through the heart. Without the head fully functioning, a human can live (possibly on life supports), almost indefinitely; but when the heart stops beating, there is no life and you are dead. It is the head which receives, but the heart which answers, transmitting love.

Never satisfied, the enemy always looking for a crack in the structure, a branch of the Judaizers, **the *Ebonites*** taught that Jesus was not Divine, but a mere man. So the Ebonites denied His Divinity and another band of heretics, the Simonians denied His Humanity. Now it follows if Jesus was not human, then He did not take on our sins and die for us on the Cross - we are lost!

Moslems till today say they cannot believe that God died on the Cross. We Christians believe and teach that the *God-Man* Jesus Christ died on the Cross. Scripture tells us that God was not satisfied with burnt offerings and sacrifices. The Father had put up with His unfaithful children long enough. In order for the Gates of Heaven to fly open, there had to be the Ultimate Sacrifice, that of His Only Son. And because all was lost through the act of one man (Adam), all had to be redeemed and saved by the sacrifice of another Man (Jesus). Ergo, the God-Man we adoringly call Jesus Christ.

In this world where bad is good and good is bad, where there is no sin, no Heaven and no hell, we need to Lift High the Cross! The hymn that we always sang, in a little Roman Catholic country church in Pearl River, Louisiana, will not go away. The words hauntingly resound as sweet notes in the air, reminding us who we are and why we were born. The little church, with its holy priest and parishioners will not stay locked away gathering dust, but is persistently cropping up in the photo album of our hearts.

Lift High the Cross

Lift High the Cross, the love of Christ proclaim,
till all the world adore His sacred name.
Led on their way by this triumphant sign,
The hosts of God in conquering ranks combine.
Lift High the Cross, the love of Christ proclaim,
till all the world adore His sacred name.
Each new born servant of the crucified
Bears on the brow the seal of Him Who died.
Lift High the Cross, the love of Christ proclaim,
till all the world adore His sacred name.
O Lord once lifted on the glorious tree,
As Thou hast promised draw the world to Thee.
Lift High the Cross, the love of Christ proclaim,
till all the world adore His sacred name.
So shall our song of triumph ever be:
Praise to the Crucified for victory.
Lift High the Cross, the love of Christ proclaim,
till all the world adore His sacred name.

Our dear brothers and sisters, as never before, it is of paramount necessity we acknowledge the Cross and lift it high! God is back! That we might know a new world of His Peace and Joy, we must be willing to lift the Cross and carry it to our own Calvary, if need be.

Lift high the Cross for all the world to see!

Salvation through the Wood

Salvation has always been through the Wood. Let us begin with:

Noah's Ark

St. Anthony reminds us that in Genesis we read, God told Noah to build *"an Ark of polished wood, and cover it inside and out with pitch."* So important was this to God for His people, He carefully instructed Noah,

"This is how you shall build it: the length shall be three hundred cubits, its width fifty cubits, and the height thirty cubits."

St. Anthony goes on to speak of the parallel between the farmer who sowed seed in Luke's gospel and Noah; both were figures of the Christ Who came to save the people of God. Saint Anthony uses the parallel of God's mandate to Noah to that which He gave to His Son:

"The Ark is the Church. As Christ `went out to sow some seed,' He went out also to build His Church, `of polished wood,' that is, made up of Saints, pure and perfect, and He `covered it inside with the pitch' of mercy and love, and `outside' with the pitch of good works.

"The Ark is `three hundred cubits in length' ...the three classifications of faith found in the Church, prefigured by Noah, Daniel and Job, symbolize the prelates (or bishops), the continent, and the married.

"The width of fifty cubits symbolizes the penitents of the Church, for it was fifty days after Easter that the grace of the Holy Spirit came down upon the Apostles, and in Psalm 50 (The Miserere: Prayer of Penitents) we find the promises given to penitents - forgiveness of their sins.

"The height of thirty cubits also refers to the faithful of the Church because of their faith in the Trinity.

"Christ then `went out' from the Father and came to this world `to sow some seed,' that is, to build His Church in which

is preserved the incorruptible seed which will last throughout all ages. "1

Saint Anthony goes on to say that:

"As the Ark of Noah saved the people who took refuge in it, so too does the new `Noah's Ark,' the Church, save us through the waters of Baptism.   It is in the Church that one finds salvation, mercy, love and forgiveness." Salvation through the Wood - the new Wood, the new "Noah's Ark," the Church! As we travel through this book and you may have noticed through all your journeys through other books we have written, the overpowering theme is the Church! Everything and everyone points to the Church, the Church which flowed from the Pierced Side of Jesus on the Cross, the Cross of Wood, the Church which came forth from the very Heart of Jesus, making us one with Him for all eternity. Oh how He loves our Church! Oh how we love our Church!

Jesus' Podium of Wood

When we look at a boat, we see it is narrow in the helm and aft,2 and wide in the middle. This not only gives the boat balance, but aids the boat to cut through the water smoothly, bringing it safely ashore (our Home in Heaven). Again, when we look upon the boat, we see in the narrowness of the front (of the boat) the words of Jesus that the path to the Kingdom is narrow; the middle (of the boat) is wide to hold all God's children, as Jesus prayed in John 17. And once the family of Christ is inside the boat of the Church, the Church strengthens them with the Seven Sacraments, enabling them to triumph over the storms of life, which threaten to capsize the boat and drown them.

*"Jesus got into one of the boats, the one belonging to Simon, and asked him to pull out a short distance from the shore; then, remaining seated, He continued to teach the crowds from the boat."*3

1Saint Anthony
2front and rear
3Saint Anthony

In this Scripture reading we see Jesus teaching from the boat, the boat of Wood. This has a two-fold teaching. Jesus has chosen the boat, a vessel of *wood* as His podium. He will later use a new podium of wood, the Cross and then the Bark of Peter and the Church. Because He made a promise to be with us until the end of time, He did not allow His Word to end in Galilee. He would continue to teach from the Wood, the Bark of Peter, His Vicar on earth.

When we think of the boat, remember how all his disciples were frightened when the storm became fierce! Jesus was sleeping peacefully, fully confident in the Will of His Father. But being compassionate and patient with those lacking faith, he rose at their cries rebuked the winds and sea, and stilled the waters and wind:

"And behold, there arose a great storm on the sea, so that the boat was being swamped by the waves; but He was asleep. And they went and woke him, saying, `Save us Lord, we are perishing.'"[4]

Do we not turn to Our Lord, when we think we are drowning, perishing at the hands of the enemy? And where do we go; if we are smart? We run to the Church and to the Lord Who dwells there in the Tabernacle. *Help Lord, we are perishing,* we cry out, and a peace comes over us, for He has heard us and is rebuking the forces who are attacking us. *Turn to the Lord!*

"And getting into a boat He crossed over and came to His own city." Again, we see the Prefigurement of Our Lord bringing us to His own city, Heaven, through the boat of Wood, the Bark of Peter, the Church!

Another time, when Jesus heard the news that His cousin John the Baptist had been beheaded, He stepped into a boat and went to a quiet place to pray. Was He speaking to His Father? Saint Teresa of Avila says that (mental) prayer is speaking to Someone Who loves you. We do not hear that the God Jesus grieved over the horrible beheading of his dear cousin, the one

---

[4]Mt. 8:23

born to herald His Coming, but the Man Jesus, Who was like us in all but sin, had to have cried out, *Why!*

Seeing those who had followed Him, His Heart was moved to compassion. He began to teach the multitudes, give them a how-to-live sermon on the Mount. Then His generous Heart, understanding His children's needs, and seeing they were hungry, Jesus multiplied the loaves and fishes, feeding over 5000 men (probably more like 15,000 as they did not count women and children in those days). They were all amazed and lauded Him. But soon later, when He will give them the dissertation on the Bread of Life, they will leave Him. Yet, never giving up, He will go to the Wood of the Cross and die for them.

Another time, in another *boat*, the disciples were fishing, when they saw a figure coming toward them, walking on the water. Recognizing Jesus, Simon Peter enthusiastically went toward Him, jumping in the sea; he in turn began walking on the water. All was going fine, while Peter kept his eyes sealed on Jesus, but the moment he looked down, away from the Lord, he began to sink. The Wood has always been a podium of learning! In Jesus we can do all things, our eyes meeting His, His strength and love giving us the power to do at times the impossible. More often than not, Our Lord is asking us to look at Him on the Cross and learn from Him. When we do so, we can walk on water! Better yet, we can live for Him, and if need be die for Him!

Jesus will later deliver His greatest teaching, the most important of His whole ministry on earth - from another piece of wood - the Cross, the Wood of the Cross! Today, is the Church not on the Cross; is Jesus still not on the Cross, Arms outstretched, reaching out to us to love us?

'The boat is a symbol for the Church of Jesus Christ, entrusted to the guidance of Peter. The Church needs a competent guide, not one who is incompetent. The Church needs a leader who can defend it from dangers, not one who would work havoc upon it. "[5]

---

[5]Saint Anthony

Saint Anthony would have us end this section on the Wood of the Boat with his words:

"Dearly beloved, let us ask the Lord Jesus Christ Himself
to make us board the boat of Simon Peter
with the virtue of obedience.
May He steer our boat away from worldly things
toward the heights of contemplation.
May He help us cast our nets
that we may retrieve a great catch of good works
and attain You, good and great God.
May He Who lives and reigns throughout all ages
grant us these things. Amen."[6]

Abraham and Isaac - Prefigurement of The Father and Jesus

"God tested Abraham and said to him, ... `Take your son, your only son Isaac, whom you love, and go to the land of Moriah and offer him as a burnt offering upon one of the mountains which I shall tell you.' So Abraham rose early in the morning, saddled his ass, and took two of his young men with him and his son Isaac; and he cut the wood for the burnt offering, and arose and went to the place of which God had told him.

"Abraham took the wood of the burnt offering and laid it on Isaac his son....Isaac called out to his father! And he replied, `Here I am, my son.' Isaac said, `Behold, the fire and the wood; but where is the lamb for the burnt offering?' Abraham said, `God will provide Himself the lamb for a burnt offering, my son.'

"When they came to the place of which God had told him, Abraham built an altar there, and laid the wood in order, and bound Isaac his son, and laid him on the altar upon the wood.

"Then Abraham put forth his hand, and took the knife to slay his son. But the Angel of the Lord called to him from Heaven.... `Do not lay your hand on the lad or do anything to him; for now I know that you fear God, seeing you have not

---

[6]Saint Anthony

withheld your son, your only son, from Me.'"[7]

I can never read nor write about Abraham and the sacrifice he was asked to give that I do not feel tears welling up in my eyes, almost blinding me. And then when I think, no, ponder that Our dear Father in Heaven did what He did not require of Abraham, I am afraid to continue, the pain is so intense. Because of the Father's Will, not only He but the Mother of Jesus were party to, and present at, the great Sacrifice of the Son, the Most Precious Son. Oh the pain! We have in our Holy Family Mission a bas-relief[8] of the Trinity carved in marble, depicting God the Father holding His Crucified Son tenderly in His Arms. The look of pain on the Father's face is just the way I have always pictured it. The Holy Spirit is hovering over the Two other Persons of the Trinity. They were all there! God the Father saw His Son suffer! The next time we are tempted to compromise, remember the Sacrifice the Holy Trinity made for us, along with our precious Mother Mary.

The Ark of the Covenant

The Ark of the Covenant or the Sacred Chest of the Ancient Israelites was made of acacia *Wood* - four feet long, two and a half feet wide, and two and a half feet high. The Tablets of the Ten Commandments were placed within the Ark, which explains why it has been called the Ark of the Covenant. It was as well considered to have the presence of God within the Ark's walls. In the same way, in the new Ark of the Covenant, Mary will have God within her walls, the walls of her womb.

As a sign of the Royalty within, the Ark was covered by gold plates with rings of gold through which they placed poles of wood to carry the Ark. The gold plate on top of the Ark read in Hebrew, *kapporet* or mercy seat. Using the Hebrew root *kpr* we find the word *kipper* or atonement. On the *Day of Atonement* or *Yom Kippur*, the Ark of Covenant would play an integral part in

---

[7]Gen 22

[8]Sculpture in which figures are carved in a flat surface so that they project only a little from the background

the ceremony.

At the Jordan, the Ark of the Covenant was in front, leading the Jews out of captivity to the Promised Land. Again we can see the Lord preparing His people with signs, symbols and wonders for the coming of the Lord, His One and Only Son. We Catholics have an Ark of the Covenant, the Tabernacle in which Our Lord Jesus Christ dwells, Body, Soul and Divinity. In our Ark, dwells the Lord Who leads us out of the captivity or slavery of sin into the Promised Land - our eternity with Him in Paradise. And let no one deceive you, there is a Heaven; just as there is a Purgatory and a Hell.[9]

The Ark of the old Testament was taken by the Philistines and then it was returned to the Israelites in "Beth-Sames." It would be David who would bring the Ark to Jerusalem and place it in a tent. Scripture tells us that when David spotted the Ark, he danced with joy. In the New Testament we read that when Mary, our Ark of the Covenant, approached her cousin Elizabeth, the baby (John) within her womb leapt or as in the Greek translation - danced. Do our hearts leap with joy, when we visit our church and kneel before Our God in the Tabernacle? In the Synagogues, only the High Priests could be in the presence of the Ark of the Covenant. In our Church, we are privileged to be in His Presence in the Tabernacle whenever we choose to be. The Ark of the Covenant was taken from the Israelites by the Philistines, and they mourned until it was returned. Are our Tabernacles being taken from us, as they are shoved farther and farther from our sight? That which we take for granted, will there be a day when we too will grieve? Solomon built a temple for the Ark of the Covenant. Are we in the days when Joseph and Mary approached the different inns in Bethlehem and there was no room for Jesus, the Savior of the world, to be born.

In the enormous new churches and cathedrals, no tabernacle to be seen, we cry out, with Archbishop Fulton J. Sheen, *"What have they done with my Lord?"* Why have you hidden Our Lord?

---

[9]Read *Visions of Heaven, Hell and Purgatory.* by Bob and Penny Lord.

We have the Lord Himself in our midst, and we want to be able to walk into His House and talk to Him, listen to Him, bask in the warmth of His Love. We hear some priests and bishops say, the Tabernacle is a distraction during the Mass. For almost two thousand years, our priests faced the tabernacle during the Mass. The Mass is not a spectacle, it is the Ongoing Sacrifice of the Cross. So leave our churches alone.

On Holy Thursday, when Our Lord in the Blessed Sacrament is moved from the church, there is a loneliness; suddenly the church seems empty; there is a deafening silence which overshadows the talking as the faithful leave. We go to where He is in repose before He is brought to the Rectory, and we weep. Easter Sunday we rejoice; He is back! He is risen! Then we go about our day-in-and-day out business of living and we take Him for granted again. Our pastor used to complain on Easter Monday that the Church was empty. *"Where are the people? They were here last weekend. They were here during Lent. What happened to them?"*

Out of sight out of mind. Bring back our Arks, our Tabernacles to the Temple, *please!*

The Living Miracle of
The Hill of Crosses

The account we will share with you is one of the most unusual Miracles of the Cross we have researched. In order to explain the Miracle of the Hill of Crosses, we must give you a little background on the Lithuanian people. They are a marvelous people, stronger and more faithful to the Church than most ethnic groups we have ever met. If the term, *"Holy Stubbornness"* ever applied to any group of people, the Lithuanians would be at the top of the list.

They have gone through so many periods of occupation by their enemies, but have never accepted themselves as having been conquered. Russia has always been part of their existence, or rather their cross. From the earliest days, they have battled for their own independence. In the Fifteenth century, they formed an alliance with Poland called the Polish-Lithuanian Commonwealth. This was in an effort to keep Russia out. It had its good points and its bad points. The good points were that they converted to Christianity under their alliance with the Poles. They even accepted the Polish customs and language.

The bad thing was it didn't last very long. Less than fifty years later, the Russians took over Lithuania again. One of the tricks of invaders has always been divide and conquer. That's how they dissipated the power of Poland and Lithuania. Between the Russians, the Prussians and the Austrians, they divided the country into three parts. Lithuania and Poland set up guerrilla forces against the Russian despots, but they never had enough strength.

When the Bolsheviks overthrew the Tsars, Lithuania thought they had a chance at self-government, but then the German Army took over the country during World War I. As soon as it ended, Lithuania felt she had an open window of opportunity. She took it, and declared Lithuania an independent country. Almost immediately, the Bolsheviks came in and took over the country.

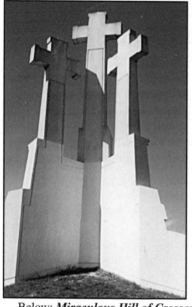

Left:
Lithuania - Land of Crosses
Lithuania has always been noted
for its love for the Cross of Christ.
These three Crosses are on a hill
near Vilnius, the capital of
Lithuania. The Communists at
one point took dynamite and
destroyed them but soon the
faithful Lithuanians rebuilt them
at the same location. These
Crosses can be seen from all over
the city of Vilnius

Below: ***Miraculous Hill of Crosses in Lithuania - The Communists***
would destroy them and they would miraculously re-appear. There are
tens of thousands of Crosses of every size, shape and type.

The provisional Lithuanian government went into exile in Kaunas, and has been in exile in one form or another from that time on.

After Adolph Hitler came to power in Germany in the 1930s, Nazi Party propaganda agitated Germans to rise up against Lithuania over the territory of Memel, located on the Baltic coast. Largely Lithuanian-inhabited Memel was part of Germany before World War I, but the Allied Powers put it under Lithuanian administration, and in 1923 Lithuania annexed it to gain a seaport. In March 1939 Hitler reannexed the territory. Nazi Germany attacked Poland in September, 1939, marking the outbreak of World War II. This Hitler did, after signing a non aggression pact with the USSR. The pact contained a secret codicil which assigned Lithuania to the German sphere of influence; however, later that month the pact was amended to add most of Lithuania to the territories assigned to the USSR. The upshot of all this was the USSR was able to take over Lithuania without this little country having a word to say about it.

In June 1940 the Soviet Red Army invaded Lithuania, and a new pro-Soviet government was installed. Only the Communist Working People's Bloc, a party organized and led by Soviet Communists, was allowed to participate in the parliamentary elections held in July. The following month Lithuania formally became the Lithuanian Soviet Socialist Republic (S.S.R.), a constituent republic of the USSR.

However, the United States and other democratic powers refused to recognize the legality of the Soviet annexation. This was when Lithuania officially became a nation in exile, with all the major countries accepting Lithuania on that basis. This lasted for almost 60 years. When the Soviet Union finally crumbled in 1989, the only country they insisted they maintain control of was, you guessed it, Lithuania.

How have the Lithuanian people held on, with one invader after the other lusting after this seaside country and its resources? If Poland was a corridor between Russia and Germany, Lithuania was the carpet they crushed as they lusted, lunged and tried to liquidate. What her invaders did not know was the real treasure, the real resource they could never own, and that was the Lithuanian people.

We knew such people! There was a family living in our parish in Southern California, who spent their every waking moment, telling whoever would listen, the plight of the Lithuanian people under U.S.S.R. occupation; they showed photos and videos of a Holy Stubborn people who would not be conquered. What was God's reward? Their son became a priest and is now serving under the Archbishop Sigitas of Kaunas, Lithuania.

Another example of the power of this people to resist all forms of threats and torture is this same Archbishop, who spent five years in a concentration camp in Siberia, celebrating Holy Mass clandestinely, at the risk of his life and those of the prisoners participating. He would save what little rations of bread he had and use it for the Mass. He would not allow the prisoners to sacrifice what meager provisions they received. When we interviewed him for EWTN, we asked him to speak to the priests in the world. He called his brother priests and bishops to be holy Priests and bishops, as they are called to be holy as God is holy, victim-priest in communion, one with the Victim-Priest - Jesus Christ.[1]

Enough said, if you want to know the Lithuanian people you need only to go to Siauliai, Lithuania, to the Mount of Crosses. As you approach this mount, the breathtaking image of suffering - the mass array of crosses lining the mount, the evidence of the relentless faith of the people, hits you and you find yourself a fan of the faithful of Lithuania, forever. There are tens of thousands of crosses of every size, shape and type, or should I better say, crucifixes; because their Lord is on the Cross, on every Cross. He has been their strength and their hope; what else did they

---

[1]Call Journeys of Faith and inquire how you can buy the video of this powerful testimony for your priest.

need! Holy Scripture tells us if only we had the faith of a mustard seed, we could move mountains. This Mount of Crosses and its story is a contrast in faiths, faith in the One and Only God and its antithesis - faith in the forces of the anti-Christ.

These crosses are made of wood, cast or forged iron, some are inlayed with precious amber, others embroidered or knitted, there are those towering crosses mounted in concrete and smaller ones perched in a bottle. They range from the quite primitive to the magnificently sculpted; from the barely visible to the majestic monuments looming high into the blue sky framing them. It is truly an awesome sight. From a short distance it almost appears to be a small planet crowned with crosses. Whether you view the Mount gleaming brightly in the light of the sun's rays or see her haunting beauty framed by overcast skies - the rain cascading down from the heavens as if the Angels were spilling their tears on it, it is truly God's wonder.

Lithuania - Land of Crosses

The struggles of the Mount of Crosses so closely parallel those of their motherland, Lithuania. When you look at the Mount of Crosses, it is like opening a history book; between its pages - hope and helplessness, victories with subjugation close by; but never once do you read despair or defeat in those crosses nor in the hearts of the Lithuanian people.

As in other European countries, from the very beginning of their acceptance of the Church in Lithuania, there have been wayside chapels with the Suffering Christ. Villagers would pass by and don their caps, make the sign of the Cross and pray! So the love of the Cross has always been paramount in the hearts of the Lithuanian people. As History has destined from the very beginning that the road for Lithuania is to be marked by crosses, the faithful place these crosses in prominent places. Is it perhaps to remind them that they are not alone, that He Who walked the Way of the Cross, walks beside them always?

How did the Mount of the Cross begin?

No one can accurately document when the custom of placing

the crosses on the Mount began, but allow us to pass on some accounts gathered over time.

According to a historian of the Nineteenth Century, the Mount was originally used to worship pagan gods. A sacred fire, attended by young priestesses, was burnt there. With the arrival of Christianity, the pagan traditions gave way to those of the Christians; hence the crosses.

The locals told him that the first crosses were put up after the uprising of 1831. Relatives of the fallen insurgents, ignorant of the burial place of their dear ones and afraid of persecution by the tsarist authorities, should they discover they were related to the patriots, would put up a cross in their loved ones' memory on the Mount. The tradition continued after the Uprising of 1863 and 1864. Old photos show crosses placed only on the top of the Mount. *"Now the Mount looks like a forest of trees; there are so many of them. I counted some 130 on the top. Besides there is a little church there."* wrote the historian.

In 1914, when they excavated the Mount, they discovered stone articles, lime and bricks. In 1991, when historians were permitted to explore parts of the Mount, they excavated artifacts of ornamental ceramics, a silver broach, knives, chisels and an arrowhead. The historians attributed the finds to the 13th or 14th Centuries. Life on the Mount was peaceful and for the most part uneventful, except for the times when raiders attacked the settlement.

The Mount of Crosses guards some of the deepest secrets of Lithuania's history. A monumental battle raged nearby. Then in more modern times, Lithuanian patriots fought against the Bermont gangs (Bermont was a Russian general who defected and joined the German Army). So in Lithuania, like in Poland, if it was not one oppressor, it was another.

With the passage of time, more and more crosses were placed on the Mount. It has always been a place of prayer and like the Cross it so gloriously honors, it has always been looked upon as a living monument of faith and hope.

Other accounts include:

A great battle raged in Lithuania, with many brave hearts falling trying to defend their country. Mourning relatives built the Mount in three days and nights and in their memory buried their loved ones there.

Then there is another account where there was a villager who fell sleep while trying to nurse his ailing daughter out of danger. As he slept, he dreamt of a woman wearing a white robe, who told him if he would place a cross on the Mount, his daughter would be healed. A deeply devoted man, he scaled the hill and placed a cross upon it. On the way down who should he encounter but his daughter, well, completely healed!

Another publication writes, there was a priest who wanted to discover what was inside the Mount. Now as the Mount, from the very beginning was shrouded in mystery, the people were more than reluctant to dig. But the priest, being very forceful, persuaded some villagers to dig and make a hole on the top! As he was digging, one of the men cried out, *"I see the roof of a buried church!"* With that, he climbed down into the hole and emerged carrying lanterns. That evening the priest had a dream of someone cautioning him to return the lanterns. Disregarding the warning, the priest joined the others and continued digging. Suddenly one of the men cried out in pain! He had a cramp in his leg and could do nothing to relieve the excruciating agony he was suffering. It was as if a bell went off in the priest's head, or was it in his heart; in any event, he ordered the digging stopped and the lanterns returned. The afflicted worker encircled the Mount over and over again, vowing to continue praying until he was healed. He recovered completely!

There is an account dating back over six hundred years ago, when Lithuania first entered Mother Church. There is a saying that France is the Church's eldest daughter. Well then Lithuania must be called the most reluctant daughter, waiting till the last to join the Church because she feared the influence and assimilation of powerful, Catholic Poland next door. Now although the country was officially Catholic, there were those who continued to worship pagan gods. There was a certain man who would spy on converts, speaking about their true belief, and then report what they had said. This got back to villagers and they lured the poor deluded man to the Mount, where they hit him on the head and he collapsed. On his grave, a cross was inscribed, *"You needed a cross. Have it."*

If you were to ask the faithful of Lithuania how the Mount of Crosses came about, there are probably as many stories as there are crosses. But one truth remains triumphant - the belief in the value of the Cross and the faithfulness of the faithful to the Mount through occupation after occupation by enemy forces.

During the last occupation by the U.S.S.R., placing crosses on the Mount was forbidden, with the threat of a death sentence if discovered. The Mount became a symbol of resistance to violence, humiliation and genocide. Lithuanians returning from Siberia would put up crosses to thank God for the opportunity to walk the lands of their motherland and to breath her fair air, once again. Pilgrims after pilgrims were persecuted, but that did not stop the holy stubborn Lithuanians from honoring and giving praise and thanksgiving to their Lord. During the endless years of occupation and persecution, the Mount stood as a powerful symbol directing the hearts of Lithuanians toward hope in a rebirth of their country and their Church in Lithuania. They believed that the crosses were there to announce to the world that the nation of Lithuania is not dead!

When we brought our pilgrims to the Mount of Crosses, we discovered from the Primate's representative that as the faithful would place crosses, the soviet soldiers would knock them down. Not to be discouraged by this little setback, the faithful returned at night and not only placed the fallen crosses back, they brought additional ones. And all of this with the sword of death hovering overhead, ready to strike!

Atheists were hell bent on wiping out the Mount. They made their first move on April 4, 1961. The wooden crosses were ripped down, broken and burned. The iron ones were taken away for recycling. Roads and paths were blocked by soviet soldiers and the KGB. The Maple tree planted to mark Lithuania's independence was uprooted; only to return to the Mount as a cross. Ashes covered the countryside, in evidence of the evil that fills the heart when you turn your back on God. The Lithuanians cried, but did not stay down long! At night they returned and put up new crosses! One was inscribed: *"Jesus, do not punish the villains for they do not know what they are doing."*

Despite the threats and intimidation, crosses continued to appear. The Red army said, *Fear won't stop them; then block the roads.* They bring crosses at night? Dig a ditch across the road leading to the Mount, so that no one can pass. Not to be deterred, the faithful floated crosses up the river to the Mount. As the heart will not be stilled, but beats to the drum of the Master, so as more and more crosses were torn down and destroyed, more and more appeared. April, 1973, the soviets were once again at their game of destruction and devastation. The faithful put up a cross in memory of Romas Kalanta, a Lithuanian martyr who publicly set himself on fire in protest to Soviet occupation.

Midnight, May, 1973, a procession formed, carrying a cross 3 meters long (or 9'9") to the Mount of the Crosses. The moon lighting their way, marchers silently, solemnly marched toward the Mount. A Nun, Sister Gema cried out, *"It is entrusted to me!"* lifted the cross on her frail shoulders, and carried it to the top of the Mount. As for the organizer of the procession, when he returned to his home, the KGB was waiting for him. He was tried, found guilty and sentenced. Years later, he was to receive a special blessing from Pope John Paul II, whose mother was Lithuanian.

One plan to kill the spirit of the people by taking away the crosses from the Mount, after the other failed. The Soviets tried everything; but the results were always the same. The hearts of the faithful would not be silenced; their country and Church were under siege, but their oppressors could not conquer their wills. And so, crosses continued to come; persecution followed, and crosses continued to come.

When Lithuania was at last freed from the clutches of the oppressors, crosses began to come from many parts of the world, in as many different languages as there were different sentiments. Lithuanians came back home to their motherland and the Mount! It was a somber but uplifting experience to see the many Lithuanians returning from Siberian imprisonment to place their crosses, proclaiming to the whole world, *Lithuania still lives; they could not kill our spirit.* Crosses began coming from across the Atlantic Ocean. One man brought a cross by boat from Baltimore, Maryland, thousands of miles and a continent away. In 1990, the crosses were once again counted and there were more than 40,000!

The Miracles of the Cross, the Power of the Cross. What is there in the Cross that gives people, like the faithful of Lithuania the courage to not only be willing to die for the Faith but to live for it?

Miraculous Cross of Genazzano

Genazzano is one of the most beautiful Shrines to Our Lady in the world. It is in a little town less than 40 miles from Rome, and would you believe, that in the 25 years we have been traveling all over the world, we had never heard of it, or gone there. But it is so powerful, we should have told you about it years ago. We're just thankful the Lord has allowed us to visit it now, so that we could tell you about it. Unfortunately, we don't have the space to get into great detail about this miraculous apparition. But we must give you at least a short version of what happened here, because everything about the Shrine is miraculous. It is truly an extraordinary place to visit. But don't let us forget to tell you about the Miracle of the Cross which took place here. It's as remarkable as the account of the Translation of the Image of Our Lady which came here.

We will begin at the beginning. It was in the year 1467. The Ottoman Turks[1] were threatening all of Europe for the second time in a thousand years. The small country of Albania, which was very Christian, was under the rule of one of their own, Scanderberg, whose very name instilled fear in every follower of Islam. He had defeated them in battle for over 23 years. The Turks constantly outnumbered his troops by at least four to one, but Scanderberg always asked for the protection of Our Lady of Scutari, symbolized by a fresco of Our Lady which, according to tradition, was brought over to Albania from the Holy Land by the Angels at the same time the Holy House was transported to Yugoslavia. Our Lady never failed him or the people of Albania. She even extended her protection to Rome and the princes of Italy.

But alas, in 1467, Scanderberg died, and the Moslems rejoiced. They planned a major attack on Albania, knowing that

---

[1]Ottoman Turks are ancestors of the Saracens, who attempted to destroy every sacred place of Jesus in the Holy Land, and predecessors of the Islamic militants of our time.

Above: ***Miraculous Bleeding Image of Our Lord at the Shrine of Our
Lady of Good Counsel of Genazzano, Italy***
Below: ***The sword that struck the Image above bent,
as shown in the photo.***

without the strength of their leader, the soldiers would fold. It was at that time that two soldiers, Giorgio and De Sclavis, were praying at the little church of Our Lady of Scutari. They pleaded with the Madonna to tell them what to do. Should they stay in Albania, and die for the cause of country and Faith? Should they do what most of the Albanians were doing, run for safety in another country? Both men prayed at the same time. They felt the overpowering presence of Our Lady in the room with them. They were given an inner locution to go home. They would be told what to do as they slept.

Both men went home, overjoyed that they would be receiving an answer to their dilemma from Our Lady as they slept. That night, in his sleep, Our Lady appeared to Giorgio. He knew it had to be her, because, although she looked the same as the image of Our Lady of Scutari, she was so much more beautiful; she was breathtaking. She spoke to him in the apparition. She told him that he and De Sclavis were to prepare to leave Albania for good. When they had everything ready, they were to meet at the chapel of Our Lady of Scutari. She would then tell them what they were to do.

As soon as Giorgio awakened, he ran to tell his friend what Our Lady had instructed them to do. However, Our Lady had beat him to the punch. She had appeared to De Sclavis as well, and had given him the same instructions. The two prepared for their final journey, then returned to the church. They knelt in prayer. They were deep in prayer, alternately gazing at the beautiful image of Our Lady on the wall of the church, and then going back into prayer. All of a sudden, they saw the fresco detach itself from the wall. It was then surrounded by a white cloud; Angels positioned themselves all around her. The entire entourage began to move slowly out of the Church. The two soldiers followed, not really believing their eyes, but trusting in Our Lady.

They followed her slowly from the church through the town in the direction of the Adriatic Sea. Did anyone see them? We don't know. There's no mention of their coming in contact with anyone as they followed Our Lady on that nineteen mile trip to the sea. At last, they arrived at the shoreline of the Adriatic Sea. They had to wonder what was next, but again, they had complete trust in Our Lady. So they just continued to walk, right into the Adriatic Sea. They were not in a trance or anything of the kind. They *knew* they were walking into the water. They didn't know for sure what would happen, but they kept going. As with the Jews crossing the Red Sea, or Peter on the Sea of Tiberias, they were allowed to walk on the water. They looked down as they put one foot in front of the other. As each foot would touch the water, it stepped onto what became a small solid diamond, like slate, which held their weight. Then as that foot would raise up, the little diamond would disappear and another would form as the next foot touched the water. This continued all the way from Albania to Italy, a distance of just over 190 miles, coast to coast.

There's no mention of how long it took for the journey to Italy. An interesting point to note is that all the while they were walking over the sea, they had the sun during the day to guide them, and the moon and stars at night. They never felt cold at night, or hot during the day. They never tired, although this trip had to take days, at least. They never felt hungry or thirsty, for the entire time they were following Our Lady. After they arrived on land in Italy, the journey continued on land in the direction of Rome. At a given point, the soldiers could see the towers of the churches of Rome. They were sure that this was where Our Lady wanted to go. But she was full of surprises. At a given point, just when they ventured near the gates of the city of Rome, the image of Our Lady, with the cloud and the Angels, disappeared. She was gone. They were shocked. This was the only reason they were here. What would they do now? Now they found that they were exhausted, in need of sleep, and famished. They realized they had not eaten in days. They went in search of food and shelter.

Our Lady goes to Genazzano

Our attention switches to Genazzano, a small village in the province of Latium, not more than 50 kilometers (31 miles) from Rome. Therefore, Rome would exert a major influence on the little village, especially where it came to morals or lack of them. Genazzano was very much like Rome, only on a much smaller basis. It had degenerated into a haven for corruption, moral decay, idol worship, sexual permissiveness and on and on. But there was a widow, a holy lady, named Petruccia de Nocera. She was a third order Augustinian. In the town of Genazzano, there was a broken-down church named after Our Lady of Good Counsel. At one time, it was a place of great spiritual renewal, but with Renaissance, churches took a back seat to secular humanism and paganism, and so this little church in honor of Our Lady was in great disrepair.

But the Augustinians wanted it rebuilt. Petruccia had been given inner locutions from Our Lady for many years, telling her she wanted the church rebuilt. At one point, Our Lady told her that she wanted the Image of Our Lady of Scutari to leave Albania. Petruccia understood what she was being told. Our Lady wanted this little broken-down church to house the Image of Our Lady of Scutari. So she spent all the money she had, attempting to rebuild the church, even to the point of selling her home to donate the money towards the building of the new church. But she was pretty much alone in her quest to do the work of Our Lady in this way. As a matter of fact, she had become the town joke. She spent all her time around the church with only one wall up, which was only about three feet high. This was all Petruccia could afford to build. Every one knew she had put all her money into this venture, and it looked like it was never going to happen.

That is, until the 25th of April, 1467 at 4 p.m. There had been a town market in the piazza that day, and so many local people, as well as some from outlying areas, were in the town square, buying and just enjoying the day. All of a sudden, there were sounds of what seemed like a choir singing. But there was no choir in town that could sing as beautifully as the sounds that were coming to the people. They looked all around them. The sounds became louder, and more distinguishable. They were hymns to Our Lady. Petruccia, who had her head down in prayer, lifted her eyes in the direction of the beautiful singing. There, in the sky, not 50 meters away, was the white cloud, with the Angels surrounding the Image of Our Lady of Scutari, being carried to the church of Our Lady of Good Counsel.

Now, the entire town, in addition to Petruccia, could see the Heavenly entourage approaching the little Church. Everyone watched as the fresco floated down, down, down until it stopped in front of the one three-foot wall of the church. And there it stayed. At first, there was silence. This was followed by soft voices of people in awe, which was then followed by cheering and shouting. Petruccia was in tears of joy; Our Lady had come. The townspeople, who had not had a thought about Our Lady for years, all of a sudden were crying out *"Madonna,"* singing *"Salve Regina."* It was truly a miracle.

Word traveled all over Latium and the surrounding provinces. It was abuzz in Rome. People were flocking to the little church, from all over Italy. The two soldiers, who had been in prayer since they lost Our Lady, heard about what had happened, and rushed to Genazzano to see if it was truly Our Lady of Scutari who had come to that place. When they arrived at the church, and saw their Lady there, they fell down on their knees in tears. They were truly home. They remained in that town for the rest of their lives.

As soon as this miracle had taken place, money began to pour in for the construction of the little church. A new, beautiful Shrine was built in a period of three years. It was completed in 1470, the same year Petruccia died. She had lived long enough to see her dream, and the mandate she had been given, fulfilled. There has been an ongoing controversy over the years as to whether the Image in the Church in Genazzano is actually the

Image from Scutari, Albania, despite the testimony of the two soldiers and Petruccia. Some think it came directly from Heaven as a means to convert the sinners of Rome and the Latium. But all evidence points to the account given by the soldiers and Petruccia.

There is another aspect of the Miracle of Genazzano which defies explanation. The fresco, which is actually a piece of the wall of the church in Scutari, never adhered to the wall of the Church in Genazzano, not to this day. It is suspended in mid-air. It floats about six inches from the wall of the church. Sadly, a large frame has been placed around it so that one cannot see the space between the fresco and the wall. However, this does bring to mind the Holy House of Loreto, which does not sit on the ground. It rests about an inch above the ground. It defies logic, but not miracle. With the miraculous, anything is possible.

There are so many miracles attributed to devotion to Our Lady of Good Counsel here in Genazzano, it would take three more chapters to tell you everything. One thing we can say, in the first 110 days after the fresco of Our Lady came to Genazzano, 161 recorded miracles took place. They were all documented and accepted. Miracles continue to occur for those who pray for the intercession of Our Lady of Good Counsel. We're told that even copies of the image of Our Lady, when placed in different parts of the world, have yielded miraculous results. Our Lady of Good Counsel is a very special title of Our Lady's. She is there to help us through our Pilgrimage of Life. Talk to her; she will answer you. Look at her image; ask for her help; don't be surprised if she smiles at you.

The Miracle of the Cross of Genazzano

Although the account of Our Lady's journey to her Shrine at Genazzano is such a powerful story in itself, the real reason we wanted to include it in this book was because we thought it was so important to share with you this incredible series of Miracles of the Cross. To be given the gift of having one Miracle of the Cross is a true blessing, but to learn about three Miracles regarding the same Cross is a triple blessing. Let us tell you about it.

Pope Martin V was born in Genazzano, and so naturally, he had exempted his home town from taxes. However, his successor, Pope Paul III was not native to the town; therefore, he didn't feel the same way as Pope Martin V. This new Pope began levying heavier and wider taxes. Many provinces resisted, fighting against what they considered to be high-handed tactics. Perugia rebelled, as well as other provinces, and Genazzano joined the revolt. Consequently, Genazzano was occupied on March 25, Feast of the Annunciation, 1540, by Papal troops. The Miracle of the Cross happened during this time. The story was narrated by an Augustinian Priest, who had extremely high credentials. He was Sacristan of the Pope, and founder of the renowned *Biblioteca Angelica at Sant' Agostino* in Rome. This is his account of how the miracle occurred:

"During the occupation of Genazzano by the papal troops, a soldier, who had been playing cards in the piazza, and who had lost badly, began cursing blasphemies against Our Lord Jesus and His Mother Mary. The soldier was under the influence of too much wine in addition. He stormed into the Church, and with his sword, he violently struck the forehead, chest and legs of the image of Our Lord Jesus Crucified, which was above the altar. To his complete shock, Blood gushed from the parts of the Body of Christ which had been struck." This was Miracle # 1! But in addition, we have Miracle #2: *"A supernatural force took hold of the sword, used by the violent soldier, twisted it so badly it came out of the soldier's hands and fell to the ground."*

During the investigation which took place after the event, it was determined that the sword was twisted by Divine Intervention, because for it to be so badly twisted intentionally, it would have taken great strength and a tremendous amount of work.[2] Another startling finding of the investigation was, where the body of Our Lord Jesus was struck, there was discoloration

---

[2]See Chapter on the Miracle of the Cross of Guadalupe.

on the fresco which remains there to this day.

In remembrance of the Miracle of the Cross, and also of the blasphemous nature of the offense, the twisted sword was kept right next to the Miraculous fresco to show the power of the Lord. But that's not the end of the story. We now have Miracle # 3. About a hundred years after the fact, in 1640, the patriarch Colonna (of the family of Colonna)[3] ordered that the sword which had caused the sacrilege, be straightened. The local blacksmith, Andrea Barbarano, under duress, obeyed the command of the patriarch. It took more than a full day of working on the sword with fire and a hammer, but he finally straightened the sword. As he was about to present the newly straightened sword to the Patriarch, it began to tremble spastically, and twisted right back to the position it had taken right after the violent attack on the fresco of Our Lord Jesus Crucified. The miraculous sword is next to the miraculous fresco to this day. No one has dared to make any changes to it, till today.

"Silence them!" they shouted to Jesus. And He replied, *"Even if I should silence them, the very stones would cry out.*[4]

No matter what man tries to do to kill the love we have for God, our very souls cry out for Our Savior, at one time or another in our lives. The human heart will not be stilled! And so it was with this and other Miracles of the Cross.

---

[3]The Colonna family were instrumental in the Popes being forced to leave Rome in 1307, because of the threats they presented to the safety of the Papacy there. This brought about the Avignon Popes, who stayed away from Rome for 68 years and eventually caused the Western Schism.
[4]*cf* Lk 19:39

The Way of the Cross
and how it began

When you enter a Roman Catholic Church, your eyes first go to the Altar and the King Who dwells there. The Altar of Sacrifice is there in the Sanctuary, ready for the next Sacrifice of the Mass, the ongoing Sacrifice of the Cross. As your eyes and heart travel, on the walls you see the truth of what is going to happen during not only the next Mass, but during every Mass, before and after, for the last 2000 years - the Stations of the Cross.

Fourteen stations in all, they too often graphically represent, in a too gentle manner the horrific truth of the price paid for our Redemption.

The First Station begins with Jesus being condemned by Pilate. When you stand before this station, do you enter into the moment and what really happened? Jesus was sold out by His own people, those He came to save! The all too few shouted and either coerced or frightened the many into standing idly, helplessly by, while He Who they had called the Messiah was being condemned to death. Little or no attention was paid to His Mother, as, obedient to the Father's Will, She stood by and saw a murderer chosen over Her Beloved Son.

The Second Station, we see Jesus, with love and sorrow for those unwittingly participating in this moment of infamy, willingly opening His Arms to accept the Cross of Redemption. Jesus begins the Way of the Cross! His Body wracking in pain from the scourging He had received, more dead than alive, He begins the fight to reach the Cross on Calvary. The wounds inflicted were enough to have killed Him, but with every ounce of strength He could summon He walked on, knowing that since it was by the wood[1] we were lost, it would have to be by the

---

[1]When Adam and Eve disobeyed the Father by eating from the Tree of Knowledge

wood (of the Cross) we be saved.

We have reached **The Third Station** and Jesus has fallen for the first time, from the weight of the Cross. Oh Lord, how much pain did we inflict, when you carried the Cross laden down by our sins? His Skin hanging from His Precious Body, more often than not, exposing His Bones to the cruel elements, Jesus told Saint Brigid the greatest physical pain He endured was that on the Shoulder on which He carried the Cross.

If the pain and sorrow were not enough that Both had to endure, Jesus meets His Mother at **The Fourth Station** of the Cross. What transpired between Mother and Son? When He was condemned, She was there, standing silently by, never once uttering even the smallest cry, lest She make Her Son's resolve to obey His Father's Will, more painful. Now She was being called to say Yes, once more. Their Eyes met. What did you want to do, Mother Mary? There before you stood your Son. Not even your worst nightmare could equal what you saw. The hours He had spent in the dungeon were a terror relived. Were you remembering how frightened You and Saint Joseph had been, before finding Him preaching to the elders in the Temple, your relief turning to a stab in the Heart when You heard Him speak for the first time of doing His Father's Will? Dear Mother Mary You said Yes! Tears You didn't dare to shed, lest He suffer even more, Your Immaculate Heart which so loved Him, breaking; sorrow muffled, silent screams ripping away all your defenses, how did You do it?

As you walk the Way of the Cross, you too soon realize you are walking beside not only the Son, but the Mother, and how deeply you love Her. One year, we went to Oberammergau, to see the Passion Play. Although the actors only spoke German, we had the booklet to help us translate their words into English. At this station, translations were hardly needed. When Mother Mary saw the soldiers roughly pushing Her Son, away from Her, to His final degradation - the Cross, in the play She screamed, *"Not Him, do it to Me!"* Oh Most Precious Mother, did you want to cry out? Were these words locked within your heart? Oh what did it take to not cry out, to not beg to take Your Precious Perfect Son's place!

How many times have we reluctantly, grudgingly carried the cross handed to us? We have arrived at **The Fifth Station** of the Cross, and Simon of Cyrene will go from an uninvolved spectator, willingly or not, to an involved member of the drama, as the soldiers place the Cross on his shoulders. We have to pause a moment and reflect. Whenever we have been in the Holy Land and walked the Way of the Cross, bystanders have mocked us, store owners have tried to entice us into going into their stores; to them it was an opportunity to profit from what they judged a ridiculous tradition at best. And so it was with Jesus and the time He walked the Way of the Cross.

So often we are accused of being a patriarchal Church, a demeaning Church toward women. As we have researched the lives of the Saints and written about the many powerful women Saints, we have often wondered what Church they are talking about. Surely it cannot be the Church Jesus founded, where women, starting with Mother Mary have played such an integral part!

Here we are at **The Sixth Station** and Veronica dashes out from the crowd of women following the Savior once again, only now to the Cross. Now, the Cross and its ramifications so frightened the Apostles, they ran away; all that is except John. The women accompanied Jesus and His Mother. What did it take for this woman, Veronica, to bravely step out and wipe the bleeding Face of the Lord! Surely they could have killed her, or at best placed her in jail. Today, in our more enlightened times, women stepping out and trying to prevent innocent unborn babies from being crucified in their mothers' wombs have suffered unmentionable indignities, to the point of incarceration. What could have happened to Veronica! When we think she is our sister, I find myself hanging my head down and crying. What would I have done?

Veronica, when you wiped our Savior's Face, did you see how weary He was? We have come to **The Seventh Station**, and Jesus has fallen for the second time. Were the spectators making bets how long before He would collapse? You find yourself wanting to cry out, with the women following Jesus, Don't get up, Lord! No more, Lord, have You not suffered enough?

Some women step out, their babies and children in their arms. They can no longer just follow Him. It is **The Eighth Station** and Jesus is approached by the women of Jerusalem, who have been following close by. They have seen His suffering and they are crying. The Lord gently says, *"...do not weep for Me, but for yourselves and for your children."*[2] He is trying to warn them of impending strife and suffering in times and generations to come. He had wept over Jerusalem and predicted its destruction, which came to pass in 70 A.D. He continues to weep, seeing us today rushing to our ruin. He has sent us warning after warning, and we have either ignored His pleading that we change, or like St. Augustine, we have sent Him an empty promise, One more day, and then I'll convert.[3]

The end must have seemed interminable, Lord, as You struggled to carry the Cross. We are at **The Ninth Station**. Now weary beyond human understanding, Our Lord falls for the third time. When we were in Lourdes, videotaping the Way of the Cross, and came to this point in the Stations of the Cross, we could not take our eyes from Our Lord's Face. Face down in the dirt, weighed down by our sins, He looked up. It was as if His dear Eyes were looking at us, saying I did it all for you. He looked so weary, so worn from the battle He waged to stay alive. So very tired, His Eyes sad beyond description, I wanted to reach out and touch Him, tell Him it was all right, He didn't have to get up. I wanted to cry out; Please don't get up; haven't you had enough suffering? Instead I just cried!

---

[2]Lk 23:28
[3]cf St. Augustine

We have reached Golgotha and the time has come. Possibly, for me, one of the most painful stations is **The Tenth Station**. When the centurions, made enough sport of Him, they placed a cloak on His brutally beaten Body. Now they stripped Him of this cloak, taking His Precious Skin with it, leaving Him only the pain to accompany Him to the Cross. They dared to strip God, to strip He Who with one word could strike them dead! But He did nothing but obey His Father. This was His Will, and all Jesus had to do was obey! All during this, His Beloved Mother stood by, her strength carrying Him through the inhuman ordeal, saying Her last Yes! They offered Him gall to drink, to allay some of His excruciating pain; but Jesus refused, choosing instead to offer full reparation to the Father, for the Redemption of our sins.

And now the time has come! We are at **The Eleventh Station!** Jesus is nailed to the Cross. Whenever we walk the Way of the Cross, whether at Lourdes, or at San Giovanni Rotondo (Padre Pio), on the Via Dolorosa in Jerusalem, we can feel the pain of the nails piercing Our Dear Lord's Hands and Feet. The centurions were meticulous, choosing blunt-edged spikes, the more to render Him excruciating pain. I can still remember the cries uttered by an actor, during a Passion Play on Good Friday, and they haunt me. We were at a church in Louisiana and the parishioners were putting on their yearly Passion Play. At one point, the actor playing Jesus cried out, His pain piercing the silence of the church, and tears involuntarily spilled down everyone's face. Lord, with You, it was not a reenactment, it was a reality. But You did not cry out! Like Your Mother, You held in Your grief, right up to the last moment.

It is time! We are at **The Twelfth Station!** They raised Him up on high, Cross and all. To each Side, hung a criminal - one would be with Jesus in the Kingdom and the other condemn himself to eternal damnation. Holding on, Jesus, Your Lungs collapsing from the strain of hanging on the Cross, when You beheld Your Mother and the one You loved at the foot of the Cross, You gave Your Mother to Him (St. John) and to us, *"Woman, behold your Son."*[4] And then to His Beloved Disciple John, *"Behold your Mother."*[5] How can we but love this Mother the Lord so generously gave us, one of His last moments on the Cross! Then Holy Scripture tells us, *"After this Jesus, knowing that all was now finished, said, `I thirst.'"*[6] Yes Our Lord thirsts, He thirsts for souls, the same souls he suffered and died for on the Cross. Our Lord drank the bitter vinegar they handed Him; and when we sin are we not handing Him a sponge filled with bitter sins? After receiving the vinegar, Jesus cried out, "It is finished." Yes, it was finished; the price had been paid and accepted - no more need for sacrifice; the Father was satisfied! Oh victorious Cross! On this Cross we were saved; all our sins had been paid for. All we had to do was to sin no more; just as Jesus had directed Mary Magdalene. But Jesus knowing the weakness of His children and the lure of sin and evil which pervades the world, left us Disciples, Priests who would be able to absolve us of our sins through the Sacrament of Penance.

The centurion, having pierced Jesus' Side with his sword, Blood and Water flowing from His Heart, the Church was born! Jesus would live forever through that Church! He would keep His promise to be with us till the end of the world! He would commune with us and we would never be the same! We are now at **The Thirteenth Station** and Jesus is taken down from the Cross and placed in His Mother's Arms. Now, He and She are alone in Their love and grief. If we look carefully, we can never forget the look in Her eyes as She looks up to Heaven, Her final Yes given, Her Son would no longer hold Her in His Arms; She would not see His Smile, feel His tender embrace, hear Him speak; He had gone to the Father. And so She held on, for as long as they would allow Her to do so. Night was fast

---

[4]Jn 19;25
[5] ibid.
[6]Jn 19:28

approaching, and as the Sabbath was about to begin, they would have to bury the Body before sundown. Mother Mary, did you say, Oh Son, the years flew by so quickly!

We are coming to the end of our Journey to the Cross. It's **The Fourteenth Station** and Jesus is laid in the Tomb. To the foolish that was the end. What had begun so gloriously was ending in hopelessness and despair, to all but His Mother. She had trusted the Father from Her first Fiat. She had trusted Her Son and Lord, while He walked the earth those thirty-three years. He had said He would rise and His Mother knew He would. She knew no tomb could hold Him, and so when the ladies, with Mary Magdalene among them, went to the tomb, Mary stayed behind and, as on the day of the Incarnation, she prayed. Pope John Paul II joins us, saying he believes it makes sense; of course the first one Jesus would appear to would be was His own Blessed Mother.

And so, we come to what some churches have - **The Fifteenth Station** - the Resurrection. Jesus had to rise, in order for His children to know that all He had told them was true. Although we were saved on the Cross, Jesus, by His Resurrection, has given us the hope and promise that we too shall rise. We hear St. Paul saying,

"If Christ has not been raised, your faith is futile and you are still in your sins. Then those also who have fallen asleep in Christ have perished. If for this life only we have hoped in Christ, we are of all men most to be pitied."[7]

How The Way of the Cross began

It is believed that the tradition of walking the Way of the Cross began with Jesus' Mother. After He ascended into Heaven, Mother Mary followed Her Son's steps to the Cross, kissing each spot where Her Son shed His Blood. She prayed, pausing at each station, where Her Son had walked and suffered, reliving the price He had paid. We became aware of this through

---

[7]1Cor 15:17

a vision St. Brigid had, where this was revealed to her by Mother Mary.

St. Jerome and other historians write that following the Way of the Cross, as an act of piety, began in the early centuries of Christianity. As early as the Fifth Century, stations were set up outside the Holy Land, in Europe, in the church of San Stefano in Bologna, Italy. But it would not be until the Twelfth and Thirteenth Centuries that widespread devotion to the Passion of Jesus would begin in Europe.

Now the Crusaders had originally gone to the Holy Land to protect Christians, who were given the choice by the Saracens to either accept the teachings of Mohammed and follow Islam, or be killed. In addition, the Crusaders set out to prevent the Shrines from being desecrated and ultimately destroyed. They visited the places made holy by the presence of Jesus and Mary, and followed the agonizing footsteps of Jesus, as He walked the Way of the Cross.

They failed in their pursuit to protect the various Shrines dedicated to the life of Jesus and Mary, and their crusade ended in them having to return to their respective countries. But Jesus had made an indelible stamp on their hearts. The Crusaders, upon their return from the Holy Land, began promulgating devotion to the Way of the Cross. They went about erecting plaques in their homes, representing the different places Jesus had walked to His Death in the Holy Land. In so doing, devotion to the Passion of Christ began to grow. But it was not generally the practice until the Fifteenth Century, when the erecting of Shrines dedicated to the Passion of Jesus in Europe would begin to really spread.

Now in the Holy Land, the Saracens were not able to erase all traces of Jesus, as they had planned. In 1342, the Franciscan Friars came to the Holy Land, and became custodians of the Shrines. They carefully excavated areas in Jerusalem, Nazareth, Mount Tabor, Capernaum, Bethlehem, Shepherd's Field and etc. Now St. Helena had traced sites where the Holy Family had lived, where Jesus taught, where He was condemned to die and ultimately where He was crucified. She placed mosaic floors at each of these holy sites. Wherever the Franciscans found these floors, they built Shrines. This grew! In keeping with their focus to bring alive the circumstances surrounding Jesus and His life, they eventually set up signs at the places along the Via Dolorosa, where Jesus had walked and bled. With this devotion, the Way of the Cross began to spread.

It became a general practice to have Stations in monasteries, in Franciscan friaries, priories, chapels and churches throughout the world, wherever Franciscans served.

When God wants something, He raises powerful men and women to do His Will. Why are the stations so important to the Father? There has always been a battle for men's souls, the world expending fortunes and endless effort to lure men and women away from Jesus and His Sacrifice. You see, the enemy of God knows if we realize how very much the Father loves us that He would allow His Son to pay the price for our Salvation, and if in turn we come to terms that when we sin we wound the Lord because He loves us so very much, and lastly that whatever we do the Holy Spirit is with us, never leaving us, loving us even when we are committing the most heinous of sins against Him, then we will be called to change, we will rebuke Satan and his false promises. The Way of the Cross is the reliving of the Passion, the Passion the Holy Trinity suffered for us and our salvation.

In the Eighteenth Century St. Leonard of Port Maurice spread devotion to the Way of the Cross so zealously and successfully, he became known as the "Preacher of the Way of the Cross." He set up more than five hundred and seventy two Stations of the Cross between the years 1731 and 1751.

Indulgences

At one time, in order to gain indulgences one had to visit the Holy Shrines in Jerusalem. As this was not financially possible for most, in 1686, Pope Innocent XI granted the Franciscans the privilege of placing Stations in all their churches. He further declared that all indulgences heretofore granted to the faithful devoutly visiting Shrines in the Holy Land pertaining to Christ's Passion and Crucifixion, would be passed on to those making the Stations of the Cross in their churches and in any churches affiliated with the Franciscan Order.

In 1694, when Pope Innocent XII succeeded Pope Innocent XI, he granted the continuance of the privilege. Then in 1726, Pope Benedict XIII extended the indulgences to all Catholics making the Stations, whether in Franciscan churches or in their respective parish church.

Today, anyone making the Stations of the Cross with a contrite heart, may gain a plenary indulgence. Should one receive Holy Communion the same day as they piously pray the Stations of the Cross, they would gain an additional plenary indulgence.

Furthermore, if one receives Holy Communion at least once during that period, he would get an additional plenary indulgence upon reception of Holy Communion.

Should one not be able to complete praying the Stations, he would receive a partial indulgence of ten years for each Station made. It is important to not interrupt praying the Stations for more than a few moments, except to hear Mass, go to confession or receive Communion.

The conditions for gaining an indulgence are:

(1) The person making the Way of the Cross must be in a state of grace.

(2) He must meditate on the Passion of Christ

(3) He must proceed from one station to the next.

(4) The Stations are not to be interrupted (except for Mass, Confession or receiving Holy Communion).

Usually the prayers of the Way of the Cross are led by a Priest or a religious. Either the Priest will go from Station to Station saying the prayers out loud, while the faithful are following at their pews, or as in the case of outdoor Stations the faithful will process with him from Station to Station, joining in, saying the prayers.

To gain an Indulgence, it is only required that one move from Station to Station, meditating on the Passion of Christ. But it is traditional (although unnecessary to receive an Indulgence), to say one Our Father, One Hail Mary, and One Glory Be to the Father for the Pope's intentions. In many instances, you may pray other prayers as well, but they are not required to receive an Indulgence.

Indulgences through the Station Crucifix

One can gain the same Indulgences from venerating the Crucifix as from walking the Way of the Cross. This practice began in 1733 in Rome. The Pope bestowed upon the Franciscans the privilege of blessing the Crucifix for the ailing, for pilgrims and for prisoners. From April 2, 1933 to this day, the Custodian General of the Franciscans has been granted the privilege to delegate his friar Priests to bless the Crucifix in this way that it would contain all the Indulgences gained through praying the Stations of the Cross. According to Church Law, other Priests may gain this privilege through an Apostolic Indult. Presently the requirements for gaining the Indulgences through venerating the Crucifix are:

(1)The person must be hampered in some way from praying the Stations of the Cross.

(2)One must say twenty Our Father, Hail Mary and Glory Be to the Father.

(3) While praying, he must be holding the Crucifix in his hands.

(4) He should be meditating on Christ's Passion.

Something to remember is that the Indulgences are gained through the Figure of Christ on the Cross and not the Cross.

As I am writing about the Way of the Cross, I find myself desiring to run, not walk but run, to the nearest Catholic church and make the Stations of the Cross on my knees. I often wonder if we understand the true meaning of what we are doing! The

Stations are a reenactment of the first Way of the Cross!

I remember our first Pilgrimage to the Holy Land (which turned out to be more a tour than a Pilgrimage. It was then that we determined we would never go out with a tour company again). From the very beginning, we were suspicious of our guide, as he never removed his hat when he entered a church, nor did he stop smoking, not even during Mass. Nothing we could say would convince one of the priests with us that he was definitely not Christian. In addition to this obvious lack of respect for all that we believe, this guide kept telling all the pilgrims to wait to buy from his cousin (everyone is their cousin), as he would give us good deals.

The time came to walk the Way of the Cross. By the time we arrived at the Ninth Station, we were deeply, emotionally involved in the suffering of Our Lord. It was as if we were really there. All we could think was, He walked here; His Blood fell on this ground making it holy; He suffered here. The pushing and shoving of passerby's, the snide remarks from taunting bystanders made us feel kind of good. We were really walking with Our Lord! We arrive at the Station, where Jesus falls the third time. And the guide stops us! Pointing to a shop, he calls out, "Here, everyone, is my cousin's shop. This is what you have been waiting for." The young priest we had been trying to warn about the guide turned to us, shocked and more than a little upset. Bob merely said, *"What's the matter, Father? It's just like at Jesus' time - business as usual! We know who he is, but half our group has followed him!"*

Christ came that man might change and be saved; and man keeps fighting the program!

How long, Lord; how long! If we have eyes to see and ears to hear, what we read in Holy Scripture has to make us tremble!

"....there followed Him a great multitude of people and of women who bewailed and lamented Him. But Jesus turning to them said,

> `Daughters of Jerusalem, do not weep for me, but weep

for yourselves and for your children. For the days are coming when they will say, Blessed are the barren, and the wombs that never bore, and the breasts that never gave suck! Then they will begin to say to the mountains, Fall on us; and to the hills, Cover us. For if they do this when the wood is green, what will happen when it is dry?'"

Do we hear what Jesus is trying to tell us? Where will we be when He comes again? Where will our children, and grandchildren, and great-grandchildren be when He comes again? Will we hear Him, or will the din that pervades our world, overrunning any sense of sanity and decency, stifle His Cry, His invitation to Heaven? I look at the world around me, the world He died to save, and I too cry!

Saint Agnes of Montepulciano
Saint of Saints

During one of Catherine of Siena's ecstasies, she exclaimed, referring to St. Agnes of Montepulciano: *"I give you thanks oh my Lord, for showing me the place that will be mine (in Paradise), next to my sister Agnes."*

Who is this Saint (virtually unknown in our country) that a powerful Saint and Doctor of the Church - Catherine of Siena should say this of her?

We're about Holy Clusters again. God is bringing us to Tuscany, once more, ancient Tuscany filled with a history of the greatest Saints and most deplorable sinners. Agnes, one of the great Saints was born in 1268, in a hamlet three miles from Montepulciano, named Gracciano, in the "Villa di Gracciano Vecchio." A Dominican like Catherine, Agnes would die April 20, 1317, thirty years before Catherine of Siena was born. Again, the Church is in crisis; again God sends us powerful men and women Saints!

Agnes was born into the nobility. At age nine, she would ask permission from her parents to enter a monastery of Nuns living a very austere life, in Montepulciano. They were called *Le Suore del Sacco,* Sacchine or Sisters of the Sackcloth, because of the coarse material of which their habits were made.

Seeing her rapid growth in spirituality, an older Nun, Sister Margaret, steeped in holiness, took over her formation. Agnes was wise beyond her years; so it comes as no surprise that at age fourteen she was asked to be housekeeper. When word came that a Nun was needed to take over a new monastery that was being formed in the town of Proceno, Sister Margaret was chosen. She in turn chose Agnes to be her assistant. The Nuns in Montepulciano were heart-broken, as she had made such a powerful impact on their lives; but they obeyed. Soon Nuns were asking to be sent to the new convent in Proceno, and before long Agnes was asked to become Abbess. Now this needed

Above:
Saint Agnes of Montepulciano
Saint of Saints
An Angel appeared before her,
offering her a Consecrated Host.
Below: ***When St. Catherine of Siena***
came to venerate Saint Agnes' body,
and went to kiss her feet, St. Agnes'
left foot rose to meet her lips.
Right: ***Jesus spoke to St. Agnes***
from this Crucifix

Above: ***Saint Agnes of Montepulciano***
levitates to the Crucifix.

special permission, as she was so very young. Pope Nicholas IV granted a special dispensation to allow the fifteen year old to be elected Abbess. This is just one example of the many gifts our Saint was given at an early age. She attracted people to her by her spiritual insights and her profound holiness.

The Lord blessed St. Agnes with many miracles during her life. Because of time and space, we will just mention a few, some of the most powerful that occurred in front of the Crucifix.

The Miracle of the Holy Water

Sister. Margaret and Sister Agnes set out with all due haste for Proceno and the new monastery. It was autumn and they were dressed in their coarse habits. They had crossed the Paglia River on the bridge of Centeno, and were climbing up a small hill, densely filled with wild brush. What with the intense noon heat and the difficulty laboring through the thick brush, they began to feel tired. They had an urgency to get to the monastery; they wanted to run, at least keep going. They were so close, they could see through the trees the short distance they had to travel before arriving to their final destination. But the fatigue was greater than their desire. It was above all, Sister Margaret the older Nun, who felt the need to sit down, to regain some new energy. And obedient as always, the younger nun, Sister Agnes, agreed to the older Nun's request.

They were almost there, tired, but happy to be coming to the end of their journey. Feeling a bit parched, they sat down on the trunk of a tree, and Sister Margaret put her hand in the wicker basket and withdrew the straw covered wine bottle. She went to take a sip of water, and to her utter dismay, found it was empty. Agnes noticed this and seeing in the face of the older nun, an expression of disillusionment, without saying a word she took a few steps away from Sister Margaret, knelt down on the dirt, and started to dig with her hands. Scarcely a few seconds had gone by, when a spring of water began to flow. At first it was muddy water then clean and fresh. Agnes took a sip; then invited Sister Margaret, who could not believe her eyes, to come close to the spring to quench her thirst.

The spring no longer exists, nor does the small church built by the people of Proceno over the place where the miracle took place. All that remains, to show the first miracle of St. Agnes, is the name of the place "Acquasanta,"[1] and a statue of the Saint which guards the entire village.

Prayer and Ecstasy

The life of the Sisters of the Sackcloth of Proceno was serene, lived in prayer and the various daily duties, and work that the Nuns did to try bring in funds to cover the expenses of the monastery. A life of poverty, which was the rule of the Nuns, was a testimony of Sister Agnes, who lived for 15 years with no food other than bread and water, slept on the bare dirt floor, using a stone as a pillow. The Saint ceased this hard regime of penance only when illness debilitated her body so much that the doctors ordered her to cease.

Agnes dedicated herself with passion to prayer, finding through prayer the most appropriate means to feel united to her Divine Spouse, a mystical union which became always more intimate. She was blessed with many extraordinary ecstasies, visions and apparitions. Numerous were Agnes' ecstasies, during which she was taken from this world to enter into a supernatural world. As confessor and spiritual director of the Sisters of the Sackcloth in Montepulciano, Blessed Raymond of Capua[2] speaks of the many ecstasies Agnes had in front of the Crucifix, which is still kept and venerated in her Shrine.

Mother Mary shares the Baby Jesus with Sister Agnes.

On the evening of the Feast of the Assumption, Agnes kneeled before the Crucifix and prayed to Our Lady, expressing her desire to be able to see Jesus. Whereupon she had an extraordinary apparition:

---

[1]Holy Water in Italian
[2]Blessed Raymond was also the confessor and spiritual director of St. Catherine of Siena

"There was a glimmer of light never seen before; rays abounded around the light; and in the middle of the light, there appeared, dressed with the sun and crowned with stars, the Queen of the Universe, with the Son of God, the Baby Jesus in her arms, nestled against Her Holy Breast. Blessed Mother was breast feeding the Baby Jesus. Then Our Lady walked over to Agnes and placed the Baby in her arms. Shaken and a little confused, Agnes took the Baby and embraced Him, drawing Him closer and closer to her. She was overwhelmed with indescribable joy and immersed in a sea of bliss."[3]

At the end of the vision, Our Lady came close to Agnes, to take back the Baby; but Agnes, inebriated with joy from her encounter with the Baby Jesus, wanted that moment to last an eternity. Rather than relinquishing Him to His Mother, she held Him all the more closer, so tightly Our Lady had to almost literally pull the Baby from her hands with force. But as she was resignedly letting go of the Divine Infant, Agnes succeeded in grasping a small Cross which, attached to a thin thread, was hanging from around His Precious Little Neck. The Vision disappeared, but the Cross remained in the hand of the Saint, leaving Agnes in such a state of exhilaration that the sisters, who ran at the sound of her cry, found her prostrated on the ground, unconscious.

Agnes and her Eucharistic Christ

During the life of the Saint, the Church was emphasizing the theology of the Sacraments, thanks to the great masters of theology most in demand during the Saint's lifetime, St. Albert the Great, St. Bonaventure, and Saint Thomas Aquinas. In particular was the Eucharist which was (and is) the center of worship of the faithful, stressing above all, the Real Presence of Our Lord Jesus in the Consecrated Host and Chalice. Only a few years before the Saint was born, the Miracle of the Eucharist of

---

[3]Blessed Raymond of Capua

Bolsena[4] (not far from Montepulciano) occurred. It is almost a
sure thing that the young Agnes knew about this Miracle, which
strengthened her faith and devotion to the Eucharist.

Blessed Raymond of Capua writes about one Sunday at
dawn. The Saint was in the monastery's garden, kneeling before
the Crucifix, away from everyone, immersed in prayer. She went
into such a deep state of ecstasy, that way into the night, she was
still on her knees in the olive garden. Now the sisters never
dared to interrupt her while she was in prayer. They had tried a
couple of times, the first year, but Agnes had reproached them,
very decisively admonishing them never to disturb her prayer for
any reason whatsoever.

The sun was setting when Agnes finally came out of the
ecstasy and remembered that it was Sunday. Now her soul was
devastated!   She was profoundly remorseful for not having
participated in the Holy Sacrifice of the Mass. But as she was
weeping, there appeared before her an Angel offering her a
Consecrated Host. Jesus, Whom she had kept company all day
in prayer did not wish to deprive her of Himself in the Eucharist.
This Miracle repeated itself exactly the same for ten consecutive
Sundays.

*"Agnes, whom God wanted to guide to perfection, deserved
to receive the Body of Christ from the hands of an Angel many
times."*[5]

The sisters gave testimony to this miracle, just as it has been
related. They also testified they heard Agnes talk about it as if
she was talking of the Divine world; and although the Saint
spoke about it obscurely, the sisters from her time related the
event very clearly.

---

[4]more on this Miracle and other Miracles of the Eucharist in Bob and
Penny Lord's book: *This is My Body, This is My Blood, Miracles of the
Eucharist, Book I*

[5]Blessed Raymond of Capua

Miracles of the Cross

Throughout the life of the Saint, Our Lord Jesus would come alive on the Cross during St. Agnes' ecstasies. It was during these times that He would reveal to her matters which were of great importance to her regarding her own spiritual walk in the community life, or in the Church. Very often, she would levitate to the Cross during her ecstasies. And it was to this Crucifix, which in a state of ecstasy the Saint levitated, embraced and placed her lips on Jesus' Side.[6]

A Chapel of the Crucifix was built in 1557 in her church in Montepulciano, and in it was placed the Crucifix that had been in Saint Agnes' chapel during her lifetime. It was this Crucifix that spoke many times to the Saint.

The Foretelling of Illness

Agnes had been in Proceno nearly fifteen years, when she became enraptured in one of her frequent ecstasies, listening to Jesus as He spoke to her from the Miraculous Cross. At this time, He prophesied a long and painful illness, which she would have to endure.

As Sister Agnes continued to kneel before the Crucifix, Blessed Virgin Mary appeared to her seated on a high throne, surrounded by an army of Angels, forming a crown. The angels were singing in a marvelous harmony the Marian sequence *"Vernans rosa, spes humilium, propitia..."*[7] While contemplating the Vision, her heart filled with indescribable joy, the Saint's attention was suddenly drawn to the surprising demeanor of some of the Angels! They were fanning Our Lady's face, so as to give her relief from what appeared to be some kind of extreme heat. Agnes struggled to understand the significance of the Angels fanning Our Lady, since the Virgin Mary in the glory of Paradise certainly would not feel suffering or physical discomfort like cold or heat.

---

[6]from the Chronicles of the Monastery
[7]Spring rose, hope of the humble, benevolent, compassionate,.

Shortly after this mysterious Vision, Agnes began to notice the first symptoms of an illness *"which was affecting her limbs, and most especially her head."*[8] This illness and pain would be her companion the rest of her life until her death.

The Saint came to understood the full meaning of the Vision, especially the part about the Angels, which had left her perplexed: God, by allowing her to see the fanning of Our Lady's face, seemed to be endeavoring to tell her:

"You will have to sustain the grief of a grave illness, but will have the sweet comfort of My Grace; you will suffer serenely each adversity, without the affliction of impatience."[9]

The sudden appearance of the illness deeply disturbed the doctors, who, immediately attempted to impose on Agnes, an end to the harsh penance to which she had been subjecting herself for some time. Only the orders of the doctors and the insistence of the Nuns convinced her, although unwillingly, to abandon the exhaustive fasting, and instead of resting on the bare dirt to do so on a real bed. Only the understandable consolation of the Nuns, who awaited her quick healing helped her carry out their wishes.

Life of Charity

It was not mandatory for the Sisters of the Sackcloth to be cloistered, so there are various testimonies speaking of Agnes and the Sisters maintaining a good relationship with the people in town. Whenever their presence was needed they would always be there to offer a word of comfort and whatever type of assistance they could offer. The monastery was visited not only by benefactors and relatives, who brought offerings in the form of monetary donations and food; but also by many poor people with whom the Sisters willingly shared the gifts which the Good God in His Providence never allowed them to be without.

The first biography of the Saint recalls that numerous times in the monastery the bread bin was empty, the oil jug dry, and they

---

[8]Bl. Raymond of Capua
[9]taken from her biography by Bl. Raymond of Capua

had no funds. Certainly it had nothing to do with lack of donations that were given to the monastery. In addition, some of the sisters came from rather wealthy families, as well as the nobility. These conditions existed because of the great generosity of the Sisters who never sent anyone away empty-handed nor poor pilgrims without food.

Agnes trusted in the infinite and boundless abundance of Divine Providence, and every time the provisions were about to run out, God's help always came to their aid.

One winter day, some hermits, who lived in a hermitage not far from Proceno, and were known for their holiness, were passing by the town. They wanted to meet the Prioress about whom they had heard so much. They visited the monastery; whereupon Agnes received them and spent a considerable amount of time teaching them about the mysteries of the Faith and how to follow the road to holiness. At the end of their visit, she invited them to eat something and she sat with them at the prepared table. The guests observed with curiosity that while their plates were served full of food, the plate belonging to the Prioress was empty. But they did not dare say anything regarding this. Besides, they did not want to stop the edifying power-charged conversation. Suddenly on Agnes' plate a rose appeared, a full-blown rose of sweet perfume and a rainbow of colors.

The hermits were amazed and shared their awe and wonder. The Saint became aware that the Miracle was being attributed to her merits. She quickly put that to rest. In the midst of painful embarrassment, true humility made her promptly share the following explanation:

"Our omnipotent and merciful Lord, graciously has willed to send, now that is cold and winter, a summer flower, fresh and fragrantly perfumed, because you, with the fire of your charity, have inflamed our hearts with your love of God and because of your adoption of the Saints' examples of holiness, have strengthened and affirmed the teaching of chaste life, which you

have kindly dwelled upon. You all have said that is not for you,
but it is to you that Our Lord has sent the rose.'

"They all agreed that they had to, with all of the strength of
their hearts, give thanks and praise to God, Author of all
Miracles."[10]

Agnes was always prompt to assist anyone in need. One
time she went to give assistance to a relative, who was possessed
by the devil. As soon as the Saint arrived and was in the
presence of the possessed, he began to have tremendous
convulsions, and the devil using his voice yelled: *"I cannot*
remain here anymore, because the virgin Agnes has entered."
Then after a few moments the body of the poor man fell onto the
ground and remained motionless, freed from the presence that
had overtaken him. After awhile the relative was revived and
wanted the Saint to remain so that he could show his gratitude;
but after inviting everyone to give thanks to God from Whom all
Miracles come, and cautioning them not to attribute the Miracle
to her, Agnes returned in a hurry to the monastery.

The people of Montepulciano were anxious for their famous
daughter to return to their town. And when she was approached,
she gladly consented to have them build a convent for her and
some of her Sisters. Though they had been living the
Augustinian Rule, she felt, for the permanence of the
Community, she and her Sisters should be part of an Order and
so she chose the Dominican Order. The convent was finished in
Montepulciano and Agnes left Proceno. Upon her arrival at the
new convent she was immediately installed as Prioress, a
position she occupied until her death. Miracles, prophecies and
cures came about through the Saint. Although she was in
excruciating pain for most of her later years, it did not interfere
with her apostolate and the convent flourished under her
direction.

Before her crippling illness, an Angel appeared to her one
day, and bringing her over to an olive tree, offered her a drink

---

[10]Blessed Raymond of Capua.

from a chalice, instructing her: *"Drink this chalice spouse of Christ; the Lord Jesus drank it for you."*

Agnes submitted to all sorts of cures, in response to her Sisters' pleading; but finally, mercifully, it was time to go *Home*! She addressed the weeping Nuns around her bed:

"If you loved me, you would be glad because I am about to enter the Glory of my Spouse. Do not grieve over my departure; I shall not lose sight of you. You will find that I have not abandoned you and you will possess me forever."

Saint Agnes was forty-nine years old, when she died.

Countless pilgrims have venerated the Saint's incorrupt body, over the centuries, including such as St. Catherine of Siena and King Charles the 5th.

When Saint Catherine came to venerate Saint Agnes' body, and went to kiss her feet, St. Agnes' left foot rose to meet her lips; and it is still raised for all to see, hundreds of years later. Another time, when St. Catherine came to pray before her body, Saint Agnes showered down white Crosses, not unlike manna from Heaven. Miracles upon miracles abounded through the Saint's intercession, and the Church in Montepulciano is filled with ex-votos thanking the Saint for favors received.

King Charles the 5th came and knelt before the body of Saint Agnes. But as he had not converted, as yet, she told him to visit a priest and convert; then come back

Saint Agnes was canonized in 1726. She was truly a role model, a Saint's Saint. Saints wanted to be near her, to absorb some of the holiness she radiated. Kings wanted to be close to her; rank and file, brothers and sisters like you and me want to be close to her. Why? Because she illuminated the love of, and power of, Our Lord Jesus to all who came to her. She is one of many role models in this book, and among the many other Saints about whom we have written. There is one there for you, and for me. Embrace your role model. Follow him/her to the Kingdom of Heaven. Jesus will be waiting to welcome you Home.

The Shadow of the Cross
according to Saint Anthony

Saint Anthony's canonization came about one short year after his death, unheard of in the History of the Church. Shortly after, his friars, looking through Saint Anthony's writings, discovered an incident which powerfully revealed our Saint's deep devotion to the Cross and his firm belief in its power.

Saint Anthony's Brief

He writes, one evening; while he lay sleeping, the devil appeared! He leapt toward Saint Anthony; then pouncing on him, he grabbed our Saint by the throat and began choking him. He applied such excruciating pressure, he was about to overpower him, when summoning his last ounce of breath, our Saint rebuked him. He invoked the name of the most precious Virgin Mary! Then making the **Sign of the Cross** on his forehead (by so doing, calling upon the Blessed Trinity - the Father, the Son and the Holy Spirit), he sent the enemy of mankind plummeting down into the pits of hell. The spirit of death gone, Saint Anthony felt immediately relieved, the pain was gone, and God, once again wasting nothing, turned a negative into a positive!

Finding this incident in the Saint's life led to a practice, down through the ages, of devotees of Saint Anthony, praying and carrying Saint Anthony's Brief with them wherever they went. So powerful was the impact this had on the Church, Pope Sixtus V had *Saint Anthony's Brief* inscribed on the obelisk in front of St. Peter's Basilica.

Saint Anthony's Brief

Behold the Cross of the Lord!
Be gone you enemy powers!
The lion of the tribe of Juda,
the root of David has conquered, Alleluia!

The Brief of Saint Anthony says: *"Be gone you enemy powers."* The Truth speaks the Truth, to those who desire to hear the Truth, and pass on the Truth. We hear in our Saint's

Below:
Basilica of St. Anthony of Padua
Many pilgrims come here to visit
this great Saint's tomb and venerate
his relics.

Above left: *St. Anthony of Padua - Teacher of Christian life*
Saint Anthony's Brief - "Behold the Cross of the Lord! Be gone you
enemy powers! The lion of the tribe of Judah, the root of David has
conquered, Alleluia!" Pope Sixtus V had this Brief inscribed on the
obelisk in front of St. Peter's Basilica.

Above: *Jesus appears in the arms of St. Anthony of Padua*

words his deep faith in the power and saving Grace of the Cross of Jesus. As all who love Jesus will keep His Word, if we go back to the letters of Saint Paul to the Corinthians, we hear again the ring of truth we hear in Saint Anthony's words:

"The message of the cross is complete absurdity to those who are headed for ruin, but to us who are experiencing salvation it is the power of God."[1] The Cross is the Power of God, the Power through which He chose to redeem us that we might once again be heirs to the Kingdom!

Power and Salvation in the Shadow of the Cross

On the Feast Day of the Discovery of the Cross,[2] Saint Anthony's sermon was on the *Power of the Cross,* the Power that is found in the Shadow of the Cross, the Shadow which helps us when we are feeling alone and weak. In quoting from these two Bible passages, he helps us to better understand the Shadow of the Cross and its place in our lives:

"I delight to rest in his shadow, and his fruit is sweet to my mouth."[3]

And then again we read:

"The anointed one of the Lord, our breath of life, was caught in their snares, he in whose shadow we thought we could live among the nations."[4]

As with much Old Testament Scripture, we can see Jesus and His Passion being foretold. Saint Anthony points out that *The shadow* referred to in the above passages is the Shadow of the Cross that was to come, and *The anointed one of the Lord* is the Messiah, Whom they were awaiting (and some Jews are still awaiting) - Our Lord Jesus. Jesus is the *Breath of Life*.

Author's Note: It is amazing how brilliant our ancestors were, quoting Scripture without knowing chapter and verse, and in

---

[1]2 Cor 1:18

[2]It is believed the Cross was discovered September 13, between the years 325 and 334

[3]Song of Songs 2:3

[4]Lam 4:20

addition often not realizing it was Scripture.   Their mothers, fathers, grandmothers and grandfathers had passed on these gems of wisdom and they in turn passed them on to us - the next generation.   For example, my ancestors, from the tiny island of Sicily, had an expression: *sciatu* (pronounced shatu) that was only used as a word of endearment reserved for your closest loved ones. *It means Breath!*

Another expression - one meaning the person is the very finest of human beings, the very essence of all that is good and honorable, someone to look up to is: *pezzo di pane* meaning piece of bread - Jesus is the Bread of Life; He comes to us and we are able to receive Him, Body, Blood, Soul and Divinity in the Eucharist at every Sacrifice of the Mass.

So again we see a people steeped in love and deep knowledge of Jesus in their lives, often without knowing they are referring to their Lord.   We have an expression in our community, *Scratch a Catholic, no matter what he calls himself and he bleeds Catholic.*

Again referring to Amos, Saint Anthony explains that when Amos uses the expression: *His Shadow,* he is prophesying the Shadow of the Cross that was to come - the Shadow that saves.

The *snares* Amos speaks of are those in which Jesus allowed Himself to be caught.   Because of Jesus, the Breath of life, Who allowed Himself to be caught in the snares set for Him, we were freed from the *snares* of sin, and under His Shadow, the Shadow of the Cross we can *live among the nations.*

"When the heat of the sun, that is diabolical temptations or concupiscence of the flesh, afflict a person, he should immediately hurry to sit under the shadow of that precious tree (from which Jesus hung) and humble himself. Only there will he find refreshment from the heat and remedy against temptation. The devil having lost all power over the human race because of the Cross is terrified to approach it."[5]

---

[5]St. Anthony's sermon

The Tree Saint Anthony speaks of was the Tree of Death,[6] upon which hung our sins through the sacrifice of our precious Savior. Through His sorrowful suffering the Tree of Death (Tree of Forbidden Fruit) became the Tree of Life. As it was through a tree we were first lost, it had to be through a Tree that we would be saved.

One night, I couldn't sleep; I was recuperating from an operation and it seemed no matter how or where I placed my body, I was wracked with pain. I couldn't sleep and so I prayed! Suddenly my thoughts left my pain and I was with Jesus, witnessing *His* Pain. *Oh my Lord nowhere to rest Your bruised bones; Your flesh echoing every stripe You suffered for our sins.* I began to weep. *Lord, have I taken for granted Your suffering? Have I taken for granted the pain You endure each day, as we look the other way when You are being persecuted? I stand in the shadow of Your Cross, and I weep. Forgive me Lord.*

As I sit at my desk and type, as I gaze at You on the Cross, all that has appeared at times almost hazy comes into focus and I can see - It is You! You are inviting us to come close, to enter into the Shadow of Your Cross, and in so doing rest awhile away from the cares and fears of the world, for as You have so often reminded us, You are with us to the end of the world. I can see! Everything is in true perspective, now. It is Lent. Soon Good Friday will come and go; Easter Sunday will follow, and it will be business as usual. Fools that we are, we cry out, We did our penance, what more could anyone one want! But Lord, You remind us of Your Cross, so that we will not be afraid to stand in the Shadow of Your Cross, running away from its Wounds and rejections, its derision and consequences, as Your other friends, the Disciples, did. You do not ask us to carry Your Cross; but instead to stand in the Shadow of Your Cross.

---

[6]In another chapter we will speak more about the connection with the Tree of Knowledge in the Garden of Eden (Genesis)

Symbols of the Cross

In one of his sermons, we hear Saint Anthony once again preaching on the Cross as he quotes Matthew:

"He (Jesus) *entered a boat, made the crossing, and came into his own town."*[7]

St. Anthony makes the connection between the *boat* which Jesus crossed into His own town (Capernaum) and the *boat* (the Cross) with which Jesus will carry us to His own Town (Heaven). Now for just one moment let us set the stage! If we dare go to our Bible and to chapter and verse preceding this crossover to *His town,* we see Jesus subjecting Himself to the temptations of the devil in the desert for *forty days.*[8]

He bears the loss of his cousin Saint John the Baptist, the one who baptized Him, who opened the way for His coming. After Jesus gave His chosen people the miracle of the multiplication of the loaves and the fishes, they abandon Him when He gives them the mandate, *"Amen, amen I say to you, unless you eat the flesh of the Son of Man and drink His Blood, you do not have life within you."*[9] Still He is ready to forgive and bring them to *His own town - Heaven.*

He preaches; He teaches; He heals; He gives the blind sight and the deaf hearing; He forgives their sins and brings them the Good News! They reject Him, they abandon Him; they blaspheme Him; and yet He, like His Father (when Adam and Eve betrayed Him), continues to prepare the way for their Salvation and for the generations to come. What an awesome God we have!

The boat as a symbol of the Cross Jesus ascended

In another sermon, Saint Anthony spoke of the boat as a symbol of the Cross on which Jesus willingly ascended, hung and died, whereupon Life triumphed over death. He wrote:

"The boat is a symbol of the Cross Jesus ascended. This is

---

[7]Mt 9:1 here Matthew is referring to Capernaum, as we read in Mt. 4:12
[8]Mt 4:1
[9]Jn 6:53

the reason He said 'and I, once I am lifted up from earth, will draw everyone to Myself.'"

And how would He draw everyone to Himself - *by the hook of the Cross!* ..As we read in Amos (8:2): *'Amos, what do you see? And I (Amos) said: 'A hook to draw down the fruit. Then the Lord said to me (Amos): the end has come to my people Israel; I will not pass by them anymore.'"*

Saint Anthony uses the hook as a symbol for gathering fruit:

*"Notice the **fruit** has three qualities: **taste, color** and **fragrance**. Fruit is a symbol of righteous people in whom are found the **taste** of contemplation, the **color** of holiness and the **fragrance** of a good reputation. The Lord daily draws this fruit to Himself with the **hook** of the Cross."*

My dear Lord! When we think of the Lord drawing us close to Himself with the hook of the Cross, upon which He died for us, it brings tears to our eyes, to have such a loving, ever faithful God Who loves us so, right to death on the Cross and is now raising us up on that Cross, just as we are writing this book and you are reading it, all He asks of us is to be a righteous people. And the sad truth is that even when we slip and fall, He is waiting by our side ready to pick us up and start all over again to draw us to Him with the Hook of His Cross. If you ever feel lonely and unloved, go to the Crucifix and adore this Lord, Who with all to live for, opened His precious Arms wide and giving up His Spirit, died for you, that you might live eternally. Contemplate what He was feeling those three days prior to His merciful end of the Passion, for it was you He saw.

When the prophet Amos said: *the end has come to my people Israel,* Saint Anthony explains he (Amos) was prophesying that the ascent of Jesus on the Cross would be the end of Israel's *pitiable and sinful state.*[10] Do you remember how at the Presentation of Jesus in the Temple, *"Simeon told Mary, 'Behold this child is destined to be the rise and fall of many in Israel.'"*[11]

---

[10]St. Anthony
[11]Lk 2:34

When he beheld the Baby Jesus, being a holy and righteous man, he was blessed by the Lord to see Amos' prophecy fulfilled, laying there sweetly in his arms."[12]

When the Lord said to Amos: *"I will not come pass by them anymore."* Saint Anthony explains the passage as meaning *"He will make us pass with Him (Jesus) into glory!"* To bring about this point, he quotes Holy Scripture: *"Before the feasts of the Passover, Jesus realized that the hour had come for Him to pass from this world to His Father."*[13]

Jesus came to free the chosen people, and the builders (the chosen people) rejected the Stone; He became the Cornerstone, and the inheritance passed on to the last laborers[14] (the Gentiles).

"Jesus said to them, 'Did you never read in Scriptures:

'The stone that the builders rejected has become the cornerstone; by the Lord has this been done, and it is wonderful in our eyes?'"[15]

In his Sermon for the Third Sunday after the Octave of Epiphany again we hear St. Anthony drawing an analogy between the Cross and the boat. Going to Matthew (8:23), he quotes: *"He got into the boat and His disciples followed Him."* Again Saint Anthony repeats: *"The boat which the disciples got into is the same boat or Cross of Jesus Christ which transports us to the shores of our heavenly home."*[16]

Saint Anthony goes on to compare the Cross to the boat in which Jesus fell asleep:

"Behold a great tempest arose in the sea, so that the boat was covered with waves, but Jesus was asleep."[17]

"When Jesus slept the sleep of the death on the Cross, His disciples, having rejected the Cross, fled because of their lack of

---

[12]St. Anthony
[13]Jn 13:1
[14]*cf Mt.* 20:16
[15]Mk 12:10
[16]St. Anthony
[17]Mt 8:24

faith, but when they ardently desired Resurrection, they awakened Him. He rebuked them saying 'O foolish and slow of heart to believe. Was it not necessary that the Messiah should suffer these things and then enter into His glory?'"[18]

In both instances the disciples were frightened. In the first instance, on the Sea of Galilee, with the sea threatening to drown them, Jesus was asleep. They called out to Him; He chastised then for their lack of faith; but He saved them. When we see the disciples at the end of His ministry on earth, they are once again frightened, a better word would be terrified. The centurions had taken their Lord, the One they thought was the Messiah and He had not resisted, He had not struck them down! In their humanness they had doubts, and the doubts led to crippling fear. But Jesus never gives up on us! To those whom He chooses, He sends the Hounds of Heaven, filling them with that longing that only He can fulfill. Those same disciples who panicked in the boat and then ran from the Cross will nobly die rather than deny their Lord and Savior Jesus Christ.

Lift high the Cross

The Cross - the Passion of Christ on the Cross becomes the Power of the Cross!

"Because the people complained, the Lord sent saraph[19] *serpents as a punishment. The Lord said to Moses: 'Make a bronze serpent and place it as a sign. If anyone looks at it, he will recover.'"*

Again God's children are misbehaving, unfaithful to their ever faithful God.

As our God is a generous God and always gives us a bake shop when we ask for a cookie, so his servant Anthony uses this word from God to teach us *two-fold*. Not only does this scripture bring to light the saving, compassionate power of the Cross, but

---

[18]Lk 24:26

[19]Saraph: the Hebrew name for a certain species of venomous snakes; the word probably signifies "the fiery one," these snakes being so called from the burning effect of their poisonous bite.

to those whose faith is lacking and, like the disciple Saint Thomas, need to place their fingers in the Wounds of Christ, it brings sharply to light the two Natures of Jesus Christ - the God-Man. Saint Anthony writes:

"The bronze serpent symbolizes Christ, God and Man. The bronze signifies His Divinity, since bronze is durable and does not deteriorate with age (He Who is, was and always will be).[21] *The serpent on the other hand, symbolizes Jesus' Humanity, which was raised on the wood of the Cross as the sign of our salvation."*

Our Saint concluded   his sermon   with this poignant reflection:

"Let us raise our eyes
and `keep them fixed on Jesus'[22]
the Author of our Redemption.
Let us contemplate our Lord
pierced with nails and suspended from the Cross."

Saint Anthony quotes Deuteronomy (28:66) to bring across a point:

"Your life will hang before you, and you will not believe your life?"

The important words here are *"your life."* He did not just say *"life"*, but *your life!* Ask anyone in danger, on his death bed, or suffering an incurable disease. Ask a mother whose child has a 106° fever how precious *your life* is, for your child's life is even more priceless than your own life. Not just *life* but *your life.* Whether it be your own life you are praying for or for that of a loved one, *your life* is beyond cost, a golden treasure, a pearl beyond price. But Saint Anthony carries this truth further to He Who is Truth, He Who is *the Way, the Truth and the Life,* when he writes:

"The soul is the life of the body; Christ is the Life of the soul."

---

[21]inserted by author
[22]Heb 12:2

Now, if what Anthony and the Church teach - that Christ is the life of the soul - and hundreds of thousands have died martyrs' deaths defending that truth, then the life we should be protecting is the eternal life given to our soul by *He Who is the Life of that soul.* The flesh and its demands are waging constant battle with the soul and its Life, Jesus Christ. When the flesh wins, and the soul is vanquished, the enemy of God has us in his filthy hands and leads us, deluded and lost, into everlasting damnation with him. Why have the martyrs given their lives, for the last two thousand years? They all treasured life on earth, but not to the loss of eternal life in Paradise. And as Jesus said,

"Whoever loves his life loses it, and whoever hates his life in this world will preserve it for eternal life."[23]

Then in Matthew, we hear Jesus again speaking of the importance of *your life,* only now He is referring to the error of saving the flesh at the cost of the soul, as He teaches:

"For those who want to save their life will lose it, those who want to lose their life for My sake will find it."[24]

Lest the disciples did not understand and the church Saint Anthony was preaching to did not as well, Anthony goes on to quote Jesus, once more:

"Without Me, Jesus said, you can do nothing."[25] Again is Jesus not saying that He is the Way, the Truth and the Life? Again is He not saying without *His presence* in your life you are not alive, but dead? When we studied and wrote about the Miracles of the Eucharist,[26] we learned that the Eucharist is the Heart of the Church. Without the heart there is no life in the human body and we are dead; without the Eucharist there is no Heart in the Church and we are no less dead.

But you ask, How can I know when I am giving into the flesh

---

[23]Jn 12:25

[24]Mt 10:39

[25]Jn 15:5

[26]Bob and Penny Lord's books: *This is My Body, This is My Blood, Miracles of the Eucharist* Books I & II

at the cost of the soul? Go before Jesus on the Cross. If you really want to hear and feel Jesus, go, no, rush to the nearest church whose Crucifix shows Jesus suffering, before His time had come to go to the Father. Look in His eyes! Look into your heart! Open your Bible, perhaps to Lamentations (1:12):

"Come, all you who pass by the way, look and see whether there is any suffering like my suffering."

One day, I was sitting in a hospital with a beautiful soul who has since gone to the Father; she was worried because her husband was undergoing a serious operation. Knowing there was no consolation I could give, I opened my Bible and began to read silently a scripture I didn't remember having read before (having just returned to the Church a short while ago), Psalm 22:7:

"...I am a worm, hardly human,
scorned by everyone, despised by the people.
All who see me mock me;
they curl their lips and jeer
they shake their heads at me:
You relied on the Lord - let Him deliver you;
if he loves you let him rescue you."
Yet you drew me forth from the womb,
made me safe from my mother's breast.
Upon you I was thrust from the womb;
since birth you are my God.
Do not stay far from me,
for trouble is near,
and there is no one to help."

Look upon Our Lord crucified; He will lead the way. Look at His Eyes. What pain can equal His pain! Do you want to cause Him anymore pain than He already suffered? Then you will know what to do! Saint Anthony says:

"Your very Life hangs on the Cross."

And he, and we, ask:

"How can you not suffer with Him? How can you not partake in His sufferings?"

We were once at a Trade Show, when we were still in the world. Each show, members of our parish would help us set up our display. This one day, one of them hit his thumb with the hammer. I instinctively called out: "Offer it up to the Lord!" An exhibitor across the aisle said, *"It has been so long since I heard that expression; we Catholics know the value of suffering - the value of the Cross!"* How can you love Jesus more; how can you soothe His wounded Body and Heart, at times? Pick up your Cross and follow Him.

Look into the Mirror - do you see the Cross of Jesus?

It is said that the eyes are the mirror of the soul. If we agree with Saint Anthony that *Christ is the Life of the soul,* and we agree that the eyes are the mirror of the soul, then when we look into the mirror, we should see reflected back to us - Jesus Who is the Life of the soul. And when we look into the mirror, which Jesus do we see, or rather which Jesus do we choose to see? Is it Jesus with His flowing robes - teaching, healing, bringing the Good News that God loves us, the Jesus everyone followed, hung on His every word? Or is it the Crucified Christ on the Cross, rejected and abandoned by all but His Mother, Mary Magdalene, John the Beloved and a few women, His Arms outstretched - welcoming us to share in His Passion for the sins of the world, His Hands that healed and Feet that tread the roads in search of souls mercilessly pierced, His Sacred Heart run through out of love for us, His five Wounds spilling His precious Blood? Whom do you see? What is the reflection that stares back at you? Can you bear to see it? Have you thrown His Cross back at Him? He has forgiven you! Have you, like Simon of Cyrene reluctantly accepted the cross? He has forgiven you!

Do you ever stop to wonder why Jesus had to bleed in order to redeem us for our sins? When you look at Jesus on the Cross, do you ever stop to ponder on how grievous our sins must have been for this to be the only accepted sacrifice the Father would accept. *"How serious were your wounds which could not be healed by any other medicine except the Blood of the Son of*

God?"[27] Saint Anthony goes on, *"...if you pause to reflect on this matter seriously, you will realize how sublime is your dignity, how precious your worth, which demanded such a price that is Jesus' agony on the Cross."*

And why do we dare to lift our eyes to the Cross and why is Our Lord pleased when we do? Does He want us to suffer? The very opposite. Jesus wants us to know His Peace and Joy in this world and the next. Saint Anthony tells us that in the Cross, we *"will learn how to deflate our pride, mortify the desires of the flesh, to pray to the Father for those who persecute us, and to commend our spirit into God's Hands."* This is the reflection we need to work toward seeing in the mirror of the Cross.

To bring this to a close, we again quote Saint Anthony who quotes Saint James:

"A man who listens to God's word but does not put it into practice, is like a man who looks into a mirror at the face he was born with; he looks at himself then goes off and promptly forgets what he looks like."[28]

Saint Anthony draws an analogy between this and the Cross:

"Similarly, we look at the Crucified and see the image of our Redemption. Perhaps this sight will produce in us a certain amount of suffering, albeit[29] *small. However as soon as we look away, we divert our hearts to other things and return to vain worldly amusements."*

The Summit of Christ's Wisdom revealed on the Cross

It is the Feast of the Chair of Saint Peter and Saint Anthony draws a correlation between Jesus on the Cross and David and King Solomon. First with David:

"David sitting on the throne was the wisest chief among the three, he was like the most tender little worm of the wood."

Saint Anthony in his sermon commenting on this reading,

---

[27]Saint Anthony
[28]Jas 1:23
[29]although

tells us that *"David whose name means "handsome to behold" is Christ, Who, with His Hands nailed to the Cross, defeated the powers of the air"*[30] just as David triumphed over Goliath.

Speaking of *the three,* Jesus and the two thieves on each side of Him, *"Christ was also the wisest among the three."*

Like David, Jesus was *"handsome to behold,"* Saint Anthony tells us, because the Angels desired to look at the beauty of His Face, as recorded in Revelation (1:16), *"His Face shown like the sun at the brightest."*[31]

We read in the Book of Kings, *"sitting on the throne was the wisest chief."* Christ was the wisest because as He sat on the throne, *the throne of the Cross,* although in the eyes of the foolish He appeared humiliated, He was the Victor because being one with the Father, He was doing the Father's Will and, with the Wisdom of the Father, He knew the final story - the Redemption of the world. Being one with the Father, He had the Wisdom of the Father, therefore *as He sat on the throne, He was the wisest.*

Saint Anthony compared Christ on the Cross with Solomon, again quoting from the Book of Kings (5:9,13):

"God gave Solomon wisdom and exceptional understanding and knowledge. He discussed plants, from the Cedar of Lebanon to the hyssop growing out of the wall."

When Jesus walked the face of the earth, He taught, using things and examples familiar to the people He was trying to reach. He did not speak in veiled language but in terms they could understand: When he wanted them to know they could depend on God and God alone, and not things of the world:

"Therefore I tell you, do not worry about your life and what you will eat, or about your body and what you will wear. For life is more than food and the body more than clothing. Notice the ravens; they do not sow or reap; they have neither storehouse nor barn, yet God feeds them. How much more

---

[30]Saint Anthony
[31]Saint Anthony

important are you than birds![32]

To bring about the point of God's unconditional and everlasting faithfulness, Jesus spoke of the lilies in the fields:

"Consider how the lilies in the field grow; they neither toil nor spin, yet I say to you that not even Solomon in his glory was arrayed like one of these. But if God so clothes the grass which flourishes in the fields today but tomorrow is thrown in the oven, how much more you, O you of little faith!"[33]

Trying to reach His children, He used the following to speak of His unfailing, ever-faithful, eternal love. He promised, even should a mother forget her child (as something incredulous) He will never forget us.

"Does a woman forget her baby at her breast, or fail to cherish the son of her womb?

Yet even if these forget,

I will never forget you."

See I have branded you on the palms of my Hands..."[34]

"Jesus said to them, Amen, amen, unless you eat the Flesh of the Son of Man and drink His Blood, you do not have life within you."[35]

When he said this in Capernaum, He knew full well what the Jews would think. He knew they would run away; but even though it meant losing them, as He is the everlasting Truth, He had to speak the truth, the whole uncompromising truth! But make no mistake about it, He was speaking their language. They understood, but did not have the faith to follow Him, and so they wait. They listened to Solomon and yet here was Jesus before them, He Who created Solomon, and they knew Him not. When Jesus asks us to share His Cross, do we know Him or know Him not. Saint Anthony writes,

"Like Solomon sitting on his ivory throne, Jesus sat on the

---

[32]Lk 12:22-24
[33]Lk 12:27,28
[34]Is 49:15-16
[35]Jn 6:53

Left:
*The tomb of
St. Anthony of Padua
The tomb of this most loved
and favorite Saint is one of
the most visited sites in all
of Europe.*

Right:
*Chapel of Relics
Basilica of
St. Anthony of Padua
This reliquary contains
many relics from St.
Anthony including his
lower jaw, tongue
and voice box.*

Above: *Our Blessed Mother appears to St. Anthony*

wooden throne of the Cross. "

Saint Anthony goes on to say:*"The* **summit** *of Christ's wisdom was revealed on the Cross; when Jesus defeated the devil, as mentioned in Job (26:12): Wisdom has struck the proud one."* We read in the Catechism of the Catholic Church, that... *"The Eucharist is the Source and* **Summit**[35] *of the Christian life."*

One of the hardest pills of obedience the devil had to swallow was that Jesus, only begotten Son of the Father would agree to become a creature, below the Angels; and then to compound things further, to spring from another creature - Mary; and, to further enrage him, whom he (the devil) would have to honor as his Queen. Pride consuming him, he could not obey and took one third of the angels with him. In the Garden of Eden we see how this one act of Pride and Disobedience would lead to another and through our first parents - Adam and Eve - to another, and another, and another in time memoriam.

Obedience carried the Cross, and in so doing defeated disobedience. Suffering on the Cross, *Humility* opened the gate to Heaven which Pride had closed.

"The Cross brought peace to the world ;
               and it must bring peace to our hearts. "[36]

A woman once said, *"We cannot expect to end abortion through legislation; it can only be done by changing men's hearts. "* Brothers and sisters, when that comes about we will see the end of the merciless slaughter of innocent unborn babies, the Church will be richer with holy religious allowed to come into the world, our country will be united under the God under Whom we were created; and the world will know peace because as our dear Pope John Paul II pleaded, we *"the moral leaders of the world*[37] will change men's hearts and then with one head, one heart and one Spirit we will know peace!

---

[35]bolded by author

[36]St. John Mary Vianney - the Cure of Ars

[37]Pope John Paul II told the people of the United States that we are called to be the moral leaders of the world, in St. Louis, Missouri, 1999.

Jesus speaks to Thomas Aquinas

Thomas Aquinas is one of the greatest minds Our Lord Jesus gave to the Church. He was a tremendous logician, using an uncanny gift for cutting through jungles of verbiage to come to a simple conclusion, especially about our Faith. This was needed sorely in the Church of his time, and possibly moreso in the Church of our time. Most seminaries, following the teachings of the Magisterium of the Church, use Thomas Aquinas' teachings as part of their curriculum.

Thomas' walk to the Lord was not an easy one. Well, let me rephrase. It was never a problem for him. He knew exactly what he wanted, and what the Lord was calling him to do. The problem was his family's. They never agreed with Thomas' decision to enter the Order of Preachers. They pictured him as spending the better part of his life as Abbot of Monte Cassino, the famous Benedictine Abbey.

To give his family some credit, they were from the upper class. He came from a long line of counts. Of noble lineage, his father was a knight, and his aspirations for Thomas were to follow in his footsteps. It is believed he was born in the year 1225. When he was a child, lightening struck the house during a violent thunderstorm and his little sister was killed, but Thomas was left unscathed. However, it was a very traumatic experience for the young Thomas, which resulted in his being nervous during thunderstorms. Because he was spared, there is a popular devotion to him as Patron of thunderstorms and sudden death.

His family obsessed on the Benedictine community at Monte Cassino. From the time when he was a young boy, it was pretty well decided this is where he would spend his life, and as we told you before, they had great plans for him to spend his years as Abbott in essence a Bishop. So, when St. Thomas was five years old he was entered as an oblate in the Benedictine Abbey of Monte Cassino, and remained there until he was thirteen. From there, Thomas spent five years studying

Left:
Jesus spoke to Saint Thomas Aquinas from the Cross. He was told, "You have written well of Me, Thomas. What would you desire as a reward?" Thomas broke into tears, as he replied, "Nothing Lord. I'm doing it all for You."

Below:
Saint Thomas Aquinas
Defender of the Eucharist
"Angelic Doctor" of the Church
philosopher
and author of the
Summa Theologiae
Tantum Ergo
O Salutaris

the arts and sciences at the University of Naples; and it is there
he became attracted to the Order of Preachers. Friars watching
him highly absorbed in prayer said they could see rays of light
shining above his head. One of them told him, *"Our Lord has
given you to our Order."* Thomas expressed his ardent desire to
join the Preachers, but as his family would object strenuously, he
felt it wiser to wait. Three years passed and at age nineteen
Thomas attempted to join the Dominicans.

Thomas had been right. Although they did not mind him
becoming a religious, they objected rigorously to his becoming a
mendicant[1] friar; the Benedictines were more to their liking. His
mother set out to persuade him to leave the Dominicans. But the
friars took him away before she could come and spirit him from
them. Then his brothers and some soldiers set out to abduct him;
and abduct him they did. They caught him resting by the
roadside and after failing to rip his habit from his body, brought
him to the family's castle. He was refused any visitors except his
worldly sister. During his imprisonment St. Thomas studied a
book by Peter Lombard, memorized a great part of the Holy
Bible, and even wrote a treatise on the errors of Aristotle.

Failing at all their attempts to dissuade him, the family sent a
lady of ill repute to seduce him. When he saw her, he brandished
a hot iron and chased her out of the room. There is another
version, and it is up to you which you believe; but this recounting
tells of his sister coming into the room to persuade him to leave
and he not only converted her, she not much later joined the
Benedictine Order as a Nun and finally became Abbess, which is
very possible, because it would have made the family happy, and
also would have encouraged them to leave Thomas alone.

He was held captive for two years before his family threw up
their hands and gave up. They allowed him to return to the
Dominicans. He was sent to study under St. Albert the Great;
and because he remained silent during many of the disputations,

---

[1]These are Orders which beg for alms and go among the people,
preaching. His family could not envision one of their children doing that.

they conferred on him the nickname, "dumb Sicilian ox." One of the students, feeling pity for him began tutoring him. But one day when his tutor became stumped and could not explain a lesson, St. Thomas elaborated on it so brilliantly the student brought it to St. Albert's attention and the next day he gave Thomas a test in front of the whole student body. His answers were so brilliant, his instructor said, *"We call Brother Thomas the dumb ox, but I tell you he will make his lowing[2] heard to the uttermost parts of the earth."*

But as brilliant as he was, he was that much more pious. When he celebrated the Mass, during the Consecration, he became so enraptured, he was moved to tears. His biographer, William da Tocco wrote *"when consecrating (the bread and wine) at Mass, he would be overcome by such intensity of devotion as to be dissolved in tears, utterly absorbed in its mysteries and nourished with its fruits."*[3]

Although he was sent to Paris where he received his "doctor's chair," they would soon lose him to Rome, where he taught as "preacher general" in the Papal School. His new position took him to many parts of Italy where he imparted his wisdom.

St. Thomas Aquinas was involved in the compelling mandate of the Lord to have a Feast Day instituted in honor of the Blessed Sacrament. Jesus dazzled the world of the Thirteenth Century by giving them a Miracle of the Eucharist which began in Prague, Czechoslovakia, and ended in Bolsena, Italy, to focus our attention for His need and desire for a Feast Day in honor of the Blessed Sacrament.

When Pope Urban IV, could not deny the persuasive message of the Lord, through the pleadings of the followers of a simple Belgian nun, Blessed Juliana of Liege, and the undeniable Miracle of the Eucharist in Bolsena/Orvieto,[4] he issued the Papal

---

[2]bellowing, more like the mooing of a cow
[3]Butler's Lives of the Saints
[4]For more on this and other Miracles of the Eucharist, read Bob and Penny Lord's book: *This is My body, This is My Blood, Miracles of the*

Bull, *Il Transiturus*, in 1264, in which he instituted the **Feast of Corpus Christi**, the Body of Christ. He immediately called on Thomas Aquinas to write the liturgy for that prestigious Feast. Among the beautiful hymns in honor of the Blessed Sacrament, St. Thomas wrote the memorable **"Tantum Ergo"** and **"O Salutaris"**.

You can see how the Lord works in the lives of His Powerful Men and Women. He doesn't just use them once, and put them away in a closet. St. Thomas is a perfect example of this. He became so well-known, especially in his knowledge of the Eucharist, that St. Louis, King of France, called on the Saint, to come to Paris, to speak to the students of the University of Paris. There was a question on which they were totally divided. It had to do with the Real Presence of Jesus in the Eucharist, and they asked Thomas Aquinas to settle it for them.

We find from this, that Thomas was not only a brilliant man, but a very humble man. As well known as he was, he knew that nothing he could say to these young minds, astute in their own rights, could convince them of the Real Presence of Jesus in the Eucharist. So he did the most intelligent thing he possibly could have done. *He prayed and fasted!* Does that sound familiar? We recall that our Lady has been asking us to do that for as far back as we can remember. Well, St. Thomas Aquinas prayed and fasted for three days. During that time, he wrote a treatise, which he laid on the Altar before he presented it to the students. When he finally did present it to them, it was not only accepted unanimously by the University students, but by the entire Church. Thomas gave all credit to Jesus in the Eucharist.

Miracle of the Cross of St. Thomas Aquinas

Later on, when St. Thomas was in Salerno, finishing the third part of his Summa, which deals with the Passion and the Resurrection, he was kneeling before the Altar in ecstasy. He could feel the overpowering presence of the Lord in the room.

He looked up at the Crucifix. It began to glow brightly. Jesus came alive and spoke to Thomas. There is a very special conversation St. Thomas Aquinas had with the Lord, which we have used as a motto for our ministry. He was told *"You have written well of Me, Thomas. What would you desire as a reward?"* Thomas broke into tears, as he replied, *"Nothing, Lord. I'm doing it all for you."* At this point, St. Thomas Aquinas went into ecstasy, and levitated. His entire body floated into the air and hovered over the chapel. All the brothers in the convent came into the chapel where he was praying, and beheld him suspended in the air.

Toward the end of his life, he ceased working on the *Summa Theologiae,* one of the most famous treatises on the existence of God ever written. When the brother who was working with him asked why, he replied *"The end of my labors has come. All that I have written appears to be as much as straw after the things that have been revealed to me."* He had been celebrating the Mass; and went into ecstasy. St. Thomas never divulged what the Lord had revealed to him, but it was enough for this great man to cease working on a treatise he had spent five years developing.

As he lay dying, after he made his last confession and received viaticum, he said,

"I am receiving Thee, Price of my soul's redemption; all my studies, my vigil and my labors have been for love of Thee. I have taught much and written much of the Most Sacred Body of Jesus Christ and of the Holy Roman Church, to whose judgment I offer and submit everything."

Two days later our Angelic Doctor, as he was called, passed to his reward with Jesus His Love. That day, St. Albert, who was in Cologne, cried out, *"Brother Thomas Aquinas, my son in Christ, the light of the Church, is dead. God has revealed it to me."*

Jesus Reveals His Passion to St. Brigid from the Cross

Our Lord has given us such unforgettable gifts in the churches, Basilicas and the Cathedral of Rome. For the purpose of this great Miracle of the Cross, we want to focus in on the magnificent Basilica of St. Paul Outside the Walls. As you approach the grounds from a distance, you are in awe! You enter the beautifully sculpted gardens leading to the entrance into the Basilica and rising before you are the imposing figures of St. Paul with the two-edged sword in his hand and St. Peter holding the Keys to the Kingdom. Then you enter the magnificent Basilica! The first thing to catch your breath is the gigantic mosaic mural in the apse at the front of the Church, depicting Jesus seated, flanked by the four writers of the Gospel. Majestic columns line the center aisle leading to the altar. Your eyes travel up the massive marble walls to a border of Portraits of the Popes of our Church from Peter to our present Pope John Paul II - the 2000 year unbroken succession of our Church!

This Basilica began as a small chapel built over the tomb of St. Paul toward the end of the First Century. When Constantine embraced the Church, and Christianity was accepted as the state religion, the small chapel grew into a small church. In 324 A.D. Pope Sylvester I consecrated the little church. But the church soon became too small to accommodate the overflowing host of Pilgrims flocking to the Shrine of the Apostle Paul. Consequently in 395 A.D. Emperor Theodosius decided to build a large Basilica. He was never to see the completion of his dream. The Basilica was completed under Emperor Honorius. The splendid Basilica survived the Barbarian invasion and the ravages of time. But that was all to come to an end!

Anna Maria Taigi prophesies destruction of St. Paul's

One day Blessed Anna Maria Taigi[1] was praying before the

---

[1]For more on Bl. Anna Maria Taigi, read a chapter on her life in Bob and

Above: *St. Brigid of Sweden - This plaque is located outside the Cave of St. Michael in Italy to commemorate the visit to the cave by St. Brigid*

Left:
Chapel in the Basilica of St. Paul Outside the Walls, Rome St. Brigid of Sweden would spend hours before this Crucifix, adoring her Crucified Savior. Here, she received countless revelations, and the fifteen promises from the Lord.

Crucifix in a side chapel at St. Paul Outside the Walls, when Our Lord appeared to her and told her that because of the sins and blasphemies committed there in the Basilica, He intended to turn it into a heap of ruins. Shortly after in 1823, a fire broke out and the Basilica was almost completely destroyed. Only the apse was left untouched. As always the faithful came forward. Donations flowed in from the four corners of the world and the new Basilica (left true to the original) was consecrated by Blessed Pope Pius IX in 1854.

Now, a natural and normal way to visit the Basilica is to make your way towards the tomb of St. Paul which is directly down the main aisle right in front of you. If you are not careful, and you have a guide who is not knowledgeable about the Faith, you might miss one of the most significant chapels in the Basilica, and a powerful Miracle of the Cross. Let us begin by telling you a little about St. Brigid of Sweden, who is integral to our story about the Miraculous Crucifix.

St. Brigid of Sweden and the Miraculous Crucifix

St. Brigid or St. Bridget of Sweden is one of the most powerful women, who have graced Mother Church with their love and faithfulness. A little brusque at times, or as a dear Bishop once called Penny - a little forthright; she was considered a Prophet to Pope Gregory, as was St. Catherine of Siena. But whereas the Pope himself called her a Prophet, he did not have the fond affection toward her that he had for St. Catherine, who was strong like St. Brigid but gentle.

St. Brigid, like St. Catherine was a Mystic! She had the courage to speak out *strongly* on the need for reform. She boldly attacked the corruption and politics in the Church! Now both powerful women felt the same about Mother Church. But whereas St. Brigid spoke of gloom and doom, St. Catherine called the Church a garden with beautiful flowers having been allowed to grow wild, with weeds in its midst *choking* it. Whereas both desired the Pope return to Rome, it was gentle Catherine who accomplished it. Or could it be that like St. John the Baptist, St. Brigid led the way for St. Catherine?

St. Brigid was born of royal blood June of 1303 - her father a knight and governor of Upland, the principal province of Sweden, and her mother Ingeborg, daughter to the governor of East Gothland.   There   were   mysterious   circumstances surrounding St. Brigid's life from the very beginning. Her mother narrowly escaped death from drowning shortly before she was to be born.   At that time, an Angel appeared to Ingeborg and revealed that the reason she had been saved was because of the child in her womb. The Angel admonished her: *"Bring her up in the love of God, for she is His gift to you."*

Now as she was being born, Benedict, Curate of Rasbo, was praying for her mother Ingeborg to have a safe delivery. Deep in prayer and meditation, he was suddenly encompassed by a brilliant, gleaming, luminous cloud.   From within, Our Lady appeared and told him, *"A child has been born to Birger[2]; her voice will be heard."*

St. Brigid has a Vision of Jesus on the Cross

Brigid got off to a slow start, not speaking until she reached three years old. But once she did begin to speak, her vocabulary and intellect was far advanced to that of other children her age. Early on, Brigid showed strong signs of sensitivity and charity toward all. Her destiny to walk toward holiness, began when she was but seven years old. She had a Vision of Our Lady. Our Blessed Mother offered her a precious crown; she accepted it and Our Lady placed the crown on her head. Brigid never forgot the feel of that crown on her head.

Three years passed and at ten, deeply affected by a homily on the Passion of Christ, the following evening she had a Vision of Christ hanging on the Cross. She heard Him say, *"Look upon Me, My daughter."* To which she replied, *"Who has done this to You?"* The Lord said, *"They who despise Me, and spurn My love for them."* That made such an impression on her that from that

---

[2]St. Brigid's father

time on the Suffering Christ became the center of her life and would remain so, until the end of her life; no amount of pain and rejection would be strong enough to erase that which He told her that day.

Brigid was to know and carry the cross in many ways - the first heavy one being her mother died when she was only eleven years old. After her mother's death, as it was fitting for one of her station to not be without a female chaperone, she was sent off to live with her aunt Lady Katherine.

Now Brigid's heart had belonged to Jesus from the time she was a tiny child, and she later shared, she would have rather die than marry. But nevertheless, when Brigid's father arranged a marriage for her at age thirteen, accepting his wishes as the Will of God, she obeyed.

Well groomed and equally well educated, as was fitting for one of her station, she married Ulf, an eighteen year old, also of royal blood. Their marriage knew joy and holiness mixed with understanding and singleness of purpose; they were of one mind, heart and spirit; it lasted twenty-eight happy years. Although Ulf agreed to Brigid's request they abstain from living a conjugal union for the first year or so, their union finally brought forth eight children. The young couple's prayer that if they should bear offspring they be steeped in virtue and charity, bore fruit: all were distinguished for their holiness, one of whom, their daughter Catherine, was raised to the honors of the Altar, and was canonized St. Catherine of Sweden.

Her husband Ulf proved himself to be highly cultured, gentle, remarkably religious and yet most capable exercising his inherited responsibilities in the affairs of the court. They were well matched; she accepted and carried out her role as a feudal lady on her husband's estate, with the same dedication she had for her role as wife and mother. She not only supervised their children's upbringing, she was gracious to all who visited her and her husband. In addition, she tended the sick and the poor. She counseled girls who had strayed into a life of sin, affording them a new lease on life.

Well known for her wisdom and piety, Brigid was summoned to court by the king, King Mabnus II as principal lady-in-waiting and advisor to him and his bride, Queen Blanche of Norway and Sweden. She held that post for six years. The king proved weak and at times wicked, so Brigid began to assume additional duties, taking an active part in the affairs of the court.

The Lord continued to talk to Brigid; and she would pass on to the kings of different nations, His words. Most ignored her warnings and others began to taunt her with their snide remarks. *"What was the Lady Brigid dreaming about last night?"* became one of their favorite jibes. But she persisted! Her job was to obey. What they did was up to them!

Future Saint and Prophet, Brigid was devoted to reading Holy Scripture, as well as about the lives of the Saints; she was especially fond of St. Bernard. She studied the Early Fathers of the Church. Always hungering for the truth, and in love with Mother Church, she went about getting a complete and thorough formation in Theology, through not only her reading, but by her frequent association with highly distinguished and respected teachers and Bishops.

As in all married life, Ulf and Brigid had their heartaches. Their eldest daughter married a ne'er-do-well noble and had a stormy marriage. Then their youngest son died in 1340. Brigid went on pilgrimage to the Shrine of St. Olaf of Norway, returning with new resolve to try to rectify the problems in the court. Unsuccessful, the grieving couple, now married twenty-four years, in 1342 decided to go on a Pilgrimage to Santiago de Compostela (St. James).

They made a stop in Avignon, where the Papal court had fled, when it became too dangerous for the Pope to remain in Rome.[3] On the way, Ulf became ill, and he received the Last

---

[3]You can find more on this in Bob and Penny Lord's chapter on St. Catherine of Siena in their book: *Saints and other Powerful Women in the Church.*

Rites. Everyone thought it was all over for Ulf, but during a revelation, St. Brigid received word from St. Denis that he would recover. The couple made a vow to no longer be involved with things of the world and dedicate themselves to serving God and Mother Church in religious houses. But before their dream was to begin, Ulf died in a Cistercian Monastery in 1344.

Now Brigid, a widow at all of forty-one years old, remained a caring mother, her eyes and heart aware of her eight children - their whereabouts and welfare. However, she no longer dressed in her finery, but instead began to live a simple and austere life. Her revelations came more and more frequently until she became alarmed, fearful they might be of the devil or a figment of her imagination. But God never leaving us alone and unprotected, granted her the same Vision three times, directing her to seek counsel from a canon who was considered highly reputable. He confirmed that her revelations were of God. We know of them today, because out of obedience, she related them to Peter, Prior of Alvestra, and he wrote them down in Latin and preserved them for posterity.

Brigid founded a new religious order, containing both male and female communities. The order was dedicated to the Divine Savior. She once again warned the King that God would visit His Wrath upon him, his queen, his nobles and the Bishops who were compromising the Faith in his court. The king mended his ways, and gave Brigid a gift of a castle to use for her new order. She'd had a revelation she was to found the monastery for her order at a Castle in Vadstena, and this was the castle she received. The castle had a breathtaking view overlooking the great Lake Vatern, which further enhanced its use as a monastery. And so, along with her many possessions in hand, St. Brigid turned the castle into a monastery.

From the time St. Brigid was in Avignon, she felt that there was something wrong there. It was not like Church. Being from royalty, the Papal Court reminded her of the royal courts she had known in her life. She had a Vision, where she was directed to write to the Pope and tell him the Lord wanted him to return to Rome. She obeyed her Vision by writing a very strong letter to Pope Clement VI, urging him to leave Avignon and bring the Papacy back to the original seat of Peter - Rome. In addition, she begged him to bring about reconciliation between the kings of England and France.

The Pope addressed her second concern, by sending an emissary, who miserably failed to bring about the desired peace between the two countries. Outspoken and determined to right the wrongs she saw, she became out of favor with the Swedish court, but not the people. They loved her. They cheered her, and she on her part went about the countryside bringing about healings. She shared with the people Jesus and His love for each and every one of them, privileged and underprivileged; and before you knew it great conversions came about. In spite of there being no Pope in Rome, she chose to go there for the Holy Year of 1350. Her people wept, as they witnessed their angel leaving them to go to Rome. They would never see her again, as she was to remain in Rome till the day she died.

The Crucifix comes to life and speaks to St. Brigid

Rome became Brigid's home, spending much time there involved in her ongoing search of knowledge, improving her prayer life, making visits to the catacombs and sanctuaries, especially the Basilicas of St. Peter and St. Paul Outside the Walls. It was in St. Paul Outside the Walls, where she would spend hours upon hours praying before the Crucifix, adoring her Crucified Savior, that Our Lord spoke to her. It was before this Crucifix that she received countless revelations. Many were warnings to heads of state.

She is best known for the twenty-one promises and fifteen prayers given to her by Our Lord, before this Crucifix. It was also before this Crucifix that Jesus shared with her His Passion, telling her how many Wounds He suffered, and of the Wounds that hurt Him the most. When St. Brigid begged the Lord to know the number of times He had been struck during His

Passion, He came to life on the Cross and said:

"I received 5,480 blows on My Body. If you wish to honor them in some way, say fifteen Our Fathers and fifteen Hail Marys with the following Prayers (which He taught her) for a whole year. When the year is up, you will have honored each one of My Wounds."

When you stand so close to the Lord and His Passion, you find yourself desiring to share every phase of His Life, especially to soothe His Wounds and many hurts. The Lord accommodated her, by allowing this little servant to undergo trials of every kind, especially those of humiliation and poverty.

In 1364, St. Brigid went on Pilgrimage, with a small entourage of pilgrims to some Italian Shrines, which was to end up in Naples, where she remained until 1367. On her journey of faith, some of the Shrines St. Brigid visited were the Holy House of Nazareth in Loreto, Italy, where she spent much time praying for the guidance and intercession of Mother Mary, and the Cave of St. Michael in the Gargano, near where Padre Pio's Shrine is today.

When you adore the Cross, get ready to endure the gifts of the Suffering Crucified Savior and His Most Precious Mother. How do you wound a mother most deeply? Her children! In 1372, she embarked with her children, among them Charles and St. Catherine, on a Pilgrimage to the Holy Land. Stopping at Naples before boarding the ship, Charles became enamored of and by Queen Joanna, who had a less than enviable reputation. Now, Charles' wife was still alive in Sweden and Joanna's husband in Spain; but she desired to marry Charles and he was no less enthusiastic. No amount of pleading and reasoning would dissuade Charles; and so a mother, St. Brigid began to pray unceasingly to God to handle the situation. And God did! Charles was struck down by an unexplainable fever and after two weeks died in his mother's arms. Grief-stricken, after she laid her son to rest, two pilgrims left for the Holy Land; but the hearts of the mother and sister remained with the loved one they could no longer touch. The account of this mother's heart with regard to the immortal soul of her child reminds us of the trials of St. Rita of Cascia, whose children vowed a vendetta against the people who had killed their father and her husband. They vowed death to the brigands to the last of the family, wife, sons and daughters, and grandchildren. St. Rita prayed that if her sons were to lose their immortal souls in the commission of these horrendous acts, please let her take their bodies *Home*. She even nursed her two boys during their last days on earth, as did St. Brigid.

St. Brigid returned to Rome. In addition to time spent there, adoring and listening to Our Lord, she remained involved in important issues concerning the rulers of her homeland, Sweden, as well as Cyprus and Naples. In addition, she relentlessly worked toward the day the Papacy would return to the Apostolic See of Rome. In a Vision, the Lord revealed to her that the Pope would return to Rome. But her gift of seeing this long hoped and awaited for dream to come true was short lived. Like Moses before her, she would not see it during her lifetime, but would have to salute it from afar. During another revelation she was told by the Lord that she was to go to the Pope and tell him he had a short time to live; and at that time she was to show him the Rule for her order in Vadstena. The Rule was approved and four months later Pope Urban died. Three times St. Brigid wrote to his successor at Avignon, Pope Gregory XI, to return to Rome; four years after her death he finally did. Although St. Catherine of Siena is given credit with having brought the papacy back to Rome, there are those who believe that St. Brigid had a great deal to do with it, even though her methods were at opposite ends of the spectrum from St. Catherine's. St. Brigid was a zealot who told it the way it was, but without the love of Jesus, or so some thought. She had no time for niceties. There was a world to be saved, and she went out to do it.

Her final journey over, God's Will done, this powerful woman of the Church went to her Lord July 23rd, 1373. Her body was kept in Rome for a short time, and then transported by her daughter and her closest friend and confessor, Fr. Peter of Alvastra, as if on pilgrimage, through Dalmatia, Austria, Poland and Danzig, to Vadstena in Sweden, where she had her community of Nuns. Her body rests there to this day. She was canonized less than twenty years later in 1391. She was a powerful Saint whose intercession it would be very much to our advantage to pray.

The Crucifix that spoke to St. Brigid in St. Paul's - today!

The people of Rome have always had a great devotion to the Crucifix that spoke to St. Brigid. They have venerated it faithfully, especially on the first Sunday of every month, and on Good Friday. In addition, the Popes down through the centuries have had a great devotion to the Crucifix, and never enter St. Paul's without praying at the Feet of the Crucified Savior on this Cross. Although the Church was practically leveled in the fire of July, 1823, the Chapel and the Crucifix survived. Be sure, when you go to St. Paul's, to visit this Chapel, which is situated on the left as you face the main altar, and pray before the Crucifix, which spoke to St. Brigid.

Some years ago, there was a well-dressed man who always sat outside the Chapel of the Crucifix and told the following story to whomever would come to the Chapel. He had been away from Mother Church and the Sacraments for twenty-five years. One day he ventured inside St. Paul Outside the Walls Basilica, to study the art and architecture. Being an art expert, he became fascinated with the Crucifix in the Chapel. He told us that when he first looked at the position of Our Lord's Head, how It was bent to the side, he knew and believed that Jesus had to have spoken to St. Brigid, because on all the Crucifixes made prior to and after that time, Jesus' Head was not in this position. It was very clear that Our Lord Jesus had turned His Head to speak to her from this cross. Needless to say, this man experienced a great conversion. He returned to Mother Church and spent the rest of his life telling all who came to the Basilica about the Miraculous Cross.

The Saints live forever. Their memory is deeply steeped in that which they have left behind. Let us close with the promises from Our Lord to St. Brigid.

Promises made to St. Brigid of Sweden

Our Lord made the following promises to anyone who recites the fifteen St. Brigid Prayers for a whole year:

1. I will deliver fifteen souls of his lineage from Purgatory.
2. Fifteen souls of his lineage will be confirmed and preserved in Grace.
3. Fifteen souls of his lineage will be converted.
4. Whoever recites these Prayers will attain the first degree of perfection.
5. Fifteen days before his death, I will give him My Precious Body in order that he may escape eternal starvation; I will give him My Precious Blood to drink lest he thirst eternally.
6. Fifteen days before his death, he will feel a deep contrition for all his sins and will have a perfect knowledge of them.
7. I will place before him the sign of My Victorious Cross for his help and defense against the attacks of his enemies.
8. Before his death, I shall come with My Dearest Beloved Mother.
9. I shall graciously receive his soul, and will lead it into eternal joys.
10. And having led it there, I shall give him a special draught from the fountain of My Deity, something I will not for those who have not recited My Prayers.
11. Let it be known that whoever may have been living in a state of mortal sin for thirty years, but who will recite devoutly, or have the intention to recite these Prayers, the Lord will forgive him all his sins.
12. I shall protect him from strong temptations.
13. I shall preserve and guard his five senses.
14. I shall preserve from a sudden death.
15. His soul will be delivered from eternal death.
16. He will obtain all he asks for from God and the Blessed

Virgin.

17. If he has lived all his life doing his own will, and he is to die the next day, his life will be prolonged.

18. Every time one recites these Prayers he gains one hundred days indulgence.

19. He is assured of being joined to the Supreme Choir of Angels.

20. Whoever teaches these Prayers to another, will have continuous joy and merit which will endure eternally.

21. There, where these Prayers are being said or will be said in the future, God is present with His Grace.[4]

Promises to those who sing "Ave Maria Stella."

During a riot in Rome, a mob came to the house where St. Brigid lived and their leader talked of burning Brigid alive. She prayed and asked the Lord if she should flee to safety. Jesus told her to stay: *"It doesn't matter if they plot thy death. My power will break the malice of thy enemies; if Mine crucified Me, it is because I permitted it."*

Our Blessed Mother added: *"Sing as a group the Ave Maria Stella and I'll guard you from danger."*

St. Brigid was told by the Lord: *"I will send my Angel who will reveal to you the lesson that shall be read by the Nuns of your monastery, and you shall write it as He tells you."* And although Brigid, considered these to be the words of the Lord, she always submitted her revelations to the judgment of Mother Church. She never sought glory or fame, only to do the will of God. Her maid said of St. Brigid, she was "kind and meek to every creature and she had a laughing face."

Pope Boniface IX canonized St. Brigid' October 7, 1391

---

[4]These Prayers can be found in a little blue book with the Pieta on the cover. Your local Catholic Bookstore should have it.

St. Camillus and the Red Cross

Did you ever wonder where the Red Cross came from? Did you ever wonder who came up with the concept of the work to be done by the Red Cross, and the symbol of the Red Cross? Would you be surprised if we told you that it came to us through a Miracle of the Cross? Read on, brothers and sisters.

Over 450 years ago, a baby boy was born in a tiny village in the Abruzzi province of Italy. St. Camillus came into a world of position and wealth, his family being of the nobility. As his mother was well in her sixties, this was nothing short of miraculous; and so she excitedly awaited Camillus' arrival. But her joy was short-lived when she had a dream of giving birth to a baby boy with a cross on his chest. Not only that, in her dream, she saw him being followed by other children wearing the same cross. Highly superstitious, she feared this was a bad omen and some great disaster would befall her family. Her darkest fears were, he would become a leader of bandits and robbers. May 25th, 1550, his mother, Camilla went to Mass, as was her custom. But shortly after arriving in church, she began to experience labor pains. She was still so upset by her dream, she chose to give birth in a barn, thinking that if her child was born under the same circumstances as Our Lord and Savior, surely this would dispel any misfortune that was to come to pass. She was basically covering all her bases. A healthy boy was born and this boy, Camillus was to grow into a towering height of 6 feet 6 inches.

He grew so quickly, his father sent him to school earlier than usual. But he was a restless youngster, often wandering away from home and getting into scraps. People appealed to his father to use discipline on the boy, as he was not only trouble, he led others into mischief. The father feared that his wife's dream was coming true, and that the boy would be trouble for himself and others. As befits someone in his position and since he was such a problem in the village, he was sent away to school. But things were not any better away in school. More disposed to getting

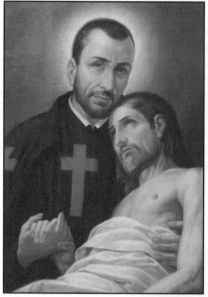

Above:
*Jesus spoke to St. Camillus
from this Crucifix*

Above:
*Saint Camillus de Lellis
The International Red
Cross took its symbol
from the order he
founded.*

Right:
*Jesus speaks to Saint
Camillus de Lellis from
the Cross
"Why are you afraid?
Do you not realize that
this is not your work
but Mine?"
St. Camillus decided to
form a new
Congregation,
The Ministers of the
Infirm.*

into trouble than studying, scarcely had he learned to write, than he was gambling with cards and dice.

His father came up with the solution, it was time to enlist him in the military. Seventeen years old, he was about to leave home with his father to fight alongside the Venetians against the Turks, when his father died. So Camillus set out alone to follow in his father's footsteps and fight the invaders. As was the passion of soldiers of fortune of his day, he soon was gambling and quarreling. He finally lost everything: his sword, his powder flask, his cloak, even his shirt.

Now, don't get me wrong. Camillus was not bad; he was just a product of his time and position. Although he was victim to his shortcomings, principally his addiction to gambling, there is that strain of the spiritual that he inherited from his mother that crops up from time to time. God, never giving up on us, placed him on a ship. One day while serving on the high seas, his vessel was threatened by a violent storm threatening to capsize it. The ship ominously tossing from side to side, Camillus promised God if he would save him, he would take the habit of St. Francis when he arrived home. But as is the case with most of us, when he arrived home, danger past, his promises were long forgotten and set-aside.

But God was not finished with him, yet. No sooner back home, than a serious wound appeared on his leg. As it was beyond the local doctors, Camillus was sent to a hospital for incurables in Rome. Although he begins as a patient, no sooner is his leg healed, he volunteers to work in the hospital caring for the sick. It would seem that God had placed him here to prepare him for the work the Lord would have for him. But nine months hardly passed than he was being dismissed because of his quarrelsome disposition and his ever-haunting gambling habit. More to what he believed to be his nature, he re-enlisted in the fight against the Turks.

Now, during the winter months, the soldiers would be dismissed without pay and had no alternative but to go home or beg. Reduced to begging, Camillus shamefacedly knocked on the door of the church asking for charity. Then, he met a rich man who invited him to work for him, serving the Capuchins. In exchange, he would offer him food and lodging. Now, who should God put in his path but a Capuchin who invited him to turn his back on sin and in so doing avoid temptation. Touched by his love and warm words, Camillus begged the Capuchin to pray for him.

The decadence he had reduced himself to overcomes him and the memory of the vow he made to the Capuchin so moves him, Camillus dismounts his horse and gets on his knees, crying out to God, *"Wretch that I am, why did I not know my Lord sooner?"* This is the day that changes his life. Camillus is 25 years old by this time. He joins the Capuchins, but is soon sent away as his leg has begun to fester once more.

As you see the fiber of his life being woven into place, if you look carefully, you find a very patient God directing his errant little son. Camillus goes to Rome, to the same hospital as before, for the second time. Now, with a completely different mind-set, he offers to serve the sick. And serve he did. This was a completely converted young man. He served them with compassion and gentleness. But after four years, his wounded leg healed, he set out once again to join the Capuchins. He was admitted, only to be dismissed shortly after, as his leg had begun to fester once again.

Camillus returned to the hospital a third time and served so zealously and faithfully, he was made superintendent of the hospital. Sadly many of the people employed by the hospital were not of the greatest character; even criminals were engaged. Camillus was grieving over the decadence and the unscrupulous manner in which the sick were cared for, when one evening, while meditating on the need to serve the ill better, an idea struck him: Form a Congregation of pious men, who would not serve the sick solely for reimbursement but out of love for God, with the tenderness of a mother caring for her ailing child.

Soon five men joined him and Camillus quickly turned a room of the hospital into an oratory, where they would come to pray and do penance. But sadly this idea was not accepted by the guardians of the hospital; jealousy came into the picture and they did all in their power to block Camillus.

Jesus speaks to St. Camillus from the Cross

He was at the end of his rope, at the point of almost despairing and giving up, when Jesus came to life on the Cross in his bedroom and spoke to him,

"Why are you afraid? Do you not realize that this is not your work, but Mine?"

With that Camillus decided he would form a Congregation, but then who would follow a layman? Therefore, under the spiritual direction of his confessor, St. Philip Neri,[1] Camillus began his walk toward the priesthood. To bring this about he first entered the School of the Jesuits, beginning at the very bottom. Considering he was now thirty years old, how very humiliating it had to be studying with the younger men. But persist he did and on the 26th of May, 1584 he was ordained a priest. To his delight, he celebrated his first Mass in the same hospital he had been serving in all those years, among his beloved sick.

Camillus founded a new Congregation, The Ministers of the Infirm. He had a Vision of Our Lady. She, the Heavenly designer, gave him the design of the habit she wanted him to wear. It consisted of a long black cassock with a large red cloth cross in the middle. In obedience to Our Lady, and as a sign of his love for Christ, Camillus asked permission to wear a red cloth cross on his cassock, and it was granted by the Pope. Everything in place, Camillus and his companions adorned their cassocks with the red crosses and they were on their way, working with the sick. One day, showing his red cross to the people, Camillus

---

[1]Read more on St. Philip Neri in Bob and Penny Lord's books: *Defenders of the Faith* and *Visions of Heaven, Hell, and Purgatory.*

proclaimed,

"Look at this cross, which my mother feared was to be the ruin of her house, how God has changed it into the resurrection of many and an exaltation of His glory!"

St. Camillus fights on a different battlefield

His ministry took Camillus and his followers far and wide, setting up communities in all the major cities of Italy, tending the sick wherever the Lord called them. During the Pontificate of Gregory XIV, a horrible famine broke out, immediately followed by such a widespread plague, 60,000 people died in Rome alone. Camillus wasted no time in reaching out to the poor, clothing them, feeding them, offering shelter and administering the Last Rites to the dying.

Camillus traveled by sea caring for those in the hold, and then upon reaching shore buying whatever provisions they needed.

Camillus went back to the battlefield, only now as a soldier of mercy, the red cross on his breast, administering to the sick and dying. His companions went into the battlefields of Hungary and Croatia in the years 1595 and 1601, and formed the first *military ambulance*.

He was so successful organizing assistance to the wounded on the battlefield, that the International Organization for assisting the sick would later adopt the Red Cross as its symbol and name.

Christmas 1595, the Tiber River overflowed inundating the streets and houses, as well as dragging men in its wake. Camillus and his men had been working all night in the hospital, but when they saw there were men, women and children in the water not able to get out, they waded in and remained there until they were able to help the last one out. St. Camillus said,

"I wish I had a hundred hands so that I could use all of them to help the sick."

This would be his battle cry and the cry of those who have followed him! The Cross, the Red Cross like the Cross of Jesus which was meant to cause death and destruction, instead brought about victory and freedom, one from sin and the other from pain.

St. Camillus and the Angels

There are many recorded accounts of the Angels taking part in the Ministry of St. Camillus and his Ministers of the Infirm. One of them was witnessed by St. Philip Neri, and not by St. Camillus. The two Saints were praying over a man in Rome who was on the verge of death. St. Camillus was praying for a triumphant death for one of their benefactors, Signor Virgilio Crescenzi. St. Philip saw Angels surround St. Camillus as he prayed. They whispered in his ears and gave him the words to pray for the man's soul.

In another instance, a woman, who was in the throes of death, wanted St. Camillus to be by her side to help her through the passage from this life into the next. He wanted to be there also, or at least have one of his Camillians there to minister to her, but neither option was possible. So the Lord sent two Angels, dressed in the habit of the Camillians, to stay with the woman for three days until she died and bring her over the threshold into Paradise. This was witnessed by the parents of the woman, although they didn't know she was being ministered over by Angels. The parents went to the Church to thank the two Ministers of the Infirm who had stayed with their daughter for three days. When they looked through the book which held the names of all those who had been assisted, and the Ministers who had assisted them, they could find neither the name of their daughter who had died, nor any record of Ministers having stayed with her. It had been truly a gift from God.

St. Camillus de Lellis lives on

The Lord took St. Camillus into His bosom on the 14th of July 1614. As soon as he died, Camillus was invoked as the Saint of the poor and the sick. The Church officially canonized him in 1746, and with St. John of God, he was declared by Pope Leo XIII Patron of the Sick, and then later Patron of nurses and nursing associations by Pope Pius XI.

St. Camillus is by no means dead! What we have given you

here is but a thumbnail sketch of the life of this most powerful Saint in the Church. There are many miracles and Heavenly Visions given to St. Camillus, and yet his work would seem to many to have been basically social work, taking care of the sick. But as you can see from this short story of his life, and will see more if you delve into his life in more detail, none of what he did could have been accomplished without the grace of God, and none of it would have had any meaning if it had not been for the love of and glory of God.

His message is not dead, as long as love and charity is still alive. It lights up the darkness of our times, these times of death and destruction, man against man. As long as one man offers care or compassion to another, as long as one person cares for his brother or sister, St. Camillus is not dead. Wherever we see that Red Cross, the universal sign of hope that help is on its way, we will always remember St. Camillus de Lellis and his band of missionaries. We have said on other occasions: Whenever there is need in our Church and in our world, God sends us Saints and other powerful men and women in the Church. St. Camillus de Lellis is one of those men. Thank You Jesus, for St. Camillus.

St. Catherine de' Ricci
Bride of the Crucified Christ

An extraordinarily gifted Saint, St. Catherine de' Ricci received the Stigmata, was mystically married to Jesus, *literally* shared in His Passion, and experienced many Visions during her ecstasies.

April 23, 1522, a baby's cry cut through the quiet of the palace and onto the streets of Florence, Italy and Alexandrina, who would someday be known as Saint Catherine de' Ricci, was born. She came from a prominent family of the nobility. Her piety and spirituality was evident from an early age. Therefore, it was no surprise to her family and friends when, at age thirteen, she entered the convent of *San Vicenzo* in Prato, a small town outside of Florence.

She immediately embraced her Dominican Community. She took the name Catherine as her religious name, in honor of her mentor, St. Catherine of Siena, a powerful Dominican Saint of the Fourteenth Century. As with her predecessor and namesake, she suffered greatly all her life. Saint Catherine de' Ricci was a virtuous young girl, never complaining or trying to bring attention to herself through an illness which would be with her the rest of her life. She turned her afflictions into redemptive suffering. She was able to overcome the debilitating *consequences* of her illnesses by uniting her suffering with Her Lord's Passion, her eyes and heart constantly contemplating her Spouse Jesus as He agonized on the Cross.

This chapter is about a holy contradiction. Let us travel back in time to the Sixteenth Century. Summer has arrived and Alexandrina's (Catherine) family has left Florence to go on pilgrimage to Prato, as they have done every year. There is a convent in Prato with a miraculous statue of Mother Mary to whom her family and many of the inhabitants of Tuscany have always had a great devotion. Years before, Spain had invaded Italy, her forces barreling through Florence and on to Prato,

Below: ***Crucifix that spoke St.***
      Catherine de' Ricci

Above: ***Saint Catherine de' Ricci***
       Bride of the Crucified Christ

Right: ***On August 24,***
1542, Our Lord Jesus
came down off the Cross.
After St. Catherine had
received Communion and
had given thanks, she
returned to her cell and
was trying to arrange her
veil so that she could put
her   headdress   on
properly, when she heard
Jesus calling her from the
Crucifix.

He said to her: "My dear
spouse, I beg you that
together   with   my
daughters you desire to
intercede   for   the
conversion of sinners,
who offend me so much.
And I would like you to
make 3 processions."

killing and destroying homes and everything in their path. They came upon the Dominican Convent of *San Vicenzo*.[1] They entered the first level of the convent, planning to invade the cloister and harm the Nuns within. As they were about to attack the Nuns, the statue of our Most Blessed Mother Mary came to life, and said: *"Do not touch my sisters and I will promise you Paradise."* The soldiers went down on their knees, and although 5000 lives had already been taken, not one Nun was touched.[2]

Nuns from the convent would come begging for olives, oil, and wheat to make bread. Alexandrina's family was always generous to the Nuns, little knowing the gift they would exact from them. Now, Alexandrina could not help but be attracted to the simple piety and humility of these *Brides of Christ*. She grew to love them. At eleven years old, she decided she would become one of them. Her family said absolutely no and quickly returned with her to Florence. She had lost her mother when she was four years old and had no one to turn to when, at thirteen years old, a marriage was arranged. But her *Mother Mary* was watching over her. Alexandrina became seriously ill! Her family allowed her to enter the convent. The illness left her.

Jesus bends down from the Cross and embraces Catherine

Right from the beginning of her religious life, Alexandrina (who became Sister Catherine) had problems. The other sisters wanted to send her away. They did not understand her; she was an outsider; she was of the nobility; they did not trust her; they wanted her out, and they systematically went about executing their campaign. That is, until one day when, upon returning from Communion, they saw the Lord bend down from the Cross and embrace her.

The annals of the Community's history reveals that on August

---

[1]St. Vincent Ferrer

[2]This happened the 29th of August and the faithful of Prato celebrate this miracle each year at this time. The statue is processed through the streets, the Mother of God protecting this village and the monastery through many wars including the 1st and 2nd world wars.

24, 1542, Our Lord Jesus came down off the Cross. It goes on to tell us, it happened after Mass. After St. Catherine had received Communion and had given thanks, she returned to her cell and was trying to arrange her veil so that she could put her headdress on properly,[3] when she heard Jesus calling her from the Crucifix. She turned, immediately, to see Our Lord detaching Himself from the Cross and coming down towards her, with the nails still in His hands and in His feet. She ran to receive Him, and took Him in her arms. He said to her: *"My dear spouse, I beg you that together with my daughters you desire to intercede for the conversion of sinners, who offend me so much. And I would like you to make 3 processions."* Catherine held Jesus (from off the Cross), in her arms for almost one hour. He remained like that so that the other Nuns could come and venerate Him. They all filed by their Lord miraculously before them, kissing the Crucifix and the hand of the Saint.

The Nuns responded immediately to the Lord's request, and began to do the processions, two before the 24th of August, Feast of St. Bartholomew, and one on his Feast Day, and also the anniversary of the miraculous embrace of Jesus to St. Catherine. This tradition continues until today, after more than 400 years. The 24th of August, the Bishop and all the community march in procession with the Crucifix, inside the monastery, to implore God's Mercy for sinners.

Jesus gives Catherine a new heart.

Five years later, on Easter Sunday, she prayed to the Lord to give her a new heart, because she said, *"With this weak heart of mine, I cannot love you properly."* Then, on the Feast of Corpus Christi, she went into ecstasy, and Our Lord appeared to Catherine and gave her a new heart, made of flesh. She said that her heart felt as if it was on fire. She had asked to love Him with a heart that could love Him as He deserved. Whose heart could

---

[3]The author is trying to bring out a point that, St. Catherine had contact with Jesus on the Cross at times other than when she was in ecstasy. In this instance, she was doing everyday things, fixing her veil.

better love Him than that of Mother Mary! Who knew *how* to truly love her Son, if not His Mother? When she asked Our Lord for a new heart that could properly love Him, He gave her the heart of His Mother Mary. From that time on, she said her heart was no longer hers, but that of Jesus' Mother.

Catherine is mystically married to Jesus

The following year, the 15th of April, 1542,[4] *she was mystically married to Jesus.* Our Lord appeared to the young girl in a brilliance, reminiscent of the Transfiguration. He took her hand in His and kissed it; then He took a gleaming ring off His own finger and placed it on the ring finger on her left hand, saying,

"My daughter, receive this ring as pledge and proof that thou dost now, and ever shalt, belong to Me."

The ring actually manifested itself as a *physical* ring of gold and diamonds. That's how St. Catherine saw it all her life. It was seen and testified to by three of the Nuns in the community, all of whom were mature nuns. Only they saw a red mark around the finger, as if the ring had made a mark on her finger. There was a larger red mark, in the form of a stone, but not a stone, appearing where a stone would be on an actual ring.

The ring became an important area of contention not only in her lifetime, but later, in the process of her Beatification and Canonization. She was to learn that, as she was married to *Jesus Resurrected*, she was also married to *Christ Crucified.*

Catherine receives the Stigmata

A year after the mystical marriage, she went into a long ecstasy which lasted *twenty-eight hours!* She saw a beautiful Angel approach her with the arrows of the Passion, and felt the pains shoot into her hands, feet and side. She collapsed in complete ecstasy mingled with agony; now, she was truly the Bride of Christ.

---

[4]Many of the great gifts Catherine received came to her in 1542, when she was just twenty years old.

Her Stigmata[5] was somewhat different from any we have ever researched, in that it was manifested in different ways to different people. Some saw what is considered the *traditional* Stigmata, that is the hands, feet and side pierced and bleeding. Others saw a brilliant light coming from the wounds. Then there were those who saw healed wounds, with just the red puffiness and swelling of wounds that had healed, black spots appearing in the center (of the wounds). In these instances, the blood under the skin appeared to be flowing in a circular movement around the black center. Catherine actually experienced, in a mystical sense, the agonies suffered by Our Lord Jesus Christ during His Passion and His Crucifixion.

The following Monday, she saw a beautiful lady dressed in red, coming out of one of the cells in the convent. She walked down the corridor of the dormitory toward Catherine. *It was Saint Mary Magdalen![6]* She beckoned Catherine to follow her. Now, Catherine was bleeding and weak from the agony she had endured during the twenty-eight hours of the Passion. At first, she tried to beg off, but in the end she obeyed. She walked, her back bent, her shoulder aching and bruised from carrying the cross. But this all passed, for before her stood her Risen Lord, bathed in a shower of light and He was splendid to behold. She fell to her knees in adoration. All her aches and pains turned into joy!

Catherine shares Jesus' Agony

These visions began when she was in her early twenties, and continued until her mid-thirties. They took place every week. She actually went through Christ's agony, as if she were doing it in place of Jesus, or as if He was suffering in her body. This would begin Thursday evening, in memory of Holy Thursday and the Agony in the Garden, through to Friday in communion with

---

[5]The Stigmata refers to the wounds, scars, or skin abrasions that appear on the flesh of individuals. They correspond to the wounds suffered by Christ in the Crucifixion. (Catholic Encyclopedia - Broderick)

[6]the Mary Magdalene of Jesus' time

Our Lord's Crucifixion on Good Friday, ending on Saturday. She was lost in deep meditation, the entire time. The only time she came out of it, for a short period, was when she received the Eucharist each morning. She would regain consciousness, receive her Lord, and sink right back into the sorrowful mystery of the Passion.

This went on continuously for twelve years. When word got out, it became a real cross for the rest of the sisters in the convent. Prayers and penance were offered by all, *including Catherine*, for it to end. Finally, in 1554, it stopped. However, this did not mean, by any stretch of the imagination, that her ecstasies ended.

Catherine chooses the Crown of Thorns

Catherine was to be given an additional gift; she received the Crown of Thorns. One day, our Blessed Mother appeared to Catherine. She was holding crowns and offered them to Catherine: one of thorns and one of silver. She already had the Stigmata and was experiencing great pain; weak, she asked for the crown of silver. Our Lady said: *"Catherine which crown did your spouse wear?"* Catherine replied: *"Then Mother Mary, place on my head the one my Lord wore."* And with that she placed the crown of thorns on her head.

Catherine goes *Home!*

St. Catherine died when she was sixty-eight years old, on February 2, 1590. When her cause for Beatification was opened in 1614, most of the sisters who had been eyewitnesses were dead. The Devil's Advocate was a very renowned priest, who went on to become Pope Benedict XIV. He was disturbed about what appeared to be confusion and unrest over the mystical ring. However, the Lord worked through this diversion, and Catherine became a member of the Communion of Saints. She was canonized in 1747. Her body has never decomposed.

She suffered greatly all her life, but she accepted her role as a redemptive sufferer with celestial joy, and this was seen by everyone with whom she came in contact. She reacted to the great gifts the Lord gave her with humility, love and thanksgiving.

Catherine was a *living contradiction* to the *shallow values of her day*. In her life, we see the Lord fighting the evils of the Renaissance in a completely different, indirect way, through a *suffering servant*. While it's true that her mysticism, her ecstasies and her stigmata attracted the attention of many, she was basically *a cloistered Nun*. She didn't go out into the world and spread the Good News of Jesus. She *suffered* for the redemption of the world, as her Spouse before her. The power of God was manifested through this ailing daughter. Through Catherine, the Lord showed another way of life, another set of values, an option to the debasement being offered by the Renaissance. Was the Lord telling these people, and us, today, *"There is another way. You don't have to buy into this lifestyle. Come to Me. I have proven to you, through My people, that you can live a wholesome life, a life close to Me, and be happy. Where your treasure lies, there is your God. Make Me your God!"*[7]

---

[7]These are excerpts from Bob and Penny Lord's book, *Visions of Heaven, Hell and Purgatory.* For more on her fantastic life, please read about her or learn about her in their video on the Life of St. Catherine de' Ricci.

St. Catherine of Siena
Took the Crucifix as her Book

Catherine of Siena was a remarkable woman, one of only three women to be given the awesome title of Doctor of the Church in the Twentieth Century; St. Thèrése, the Little Flower and St. Teresa of Avila being the other two. She had an intensely personal relationship with the Lord from the time she was a child. She had a great many mystical experiences with Jesus. They included holding the Baby Jesus in her arms, being mystically married to Jesus, and receiving the wounds of the Crucified Lord in a powerful way.

The Crucifix was her book

We have written at length about this powerful woman,[1] but in this book we are only bringing you some of her mystical encounters with our Lord Jesus, especially the Crucified Jesus and His Passion.

As she had never learned how to read, and Catherine could not study the Gospel to learn more about her Lord, she spent long hours kneeling before the Crucifix. The Wounds of our Savior before her, she prayed she might share in His Suffering. She yearned to feel His Passion in her body.

At an early age, she made a commitment to turn her life over to Jesus. This was when she was a very small child. She knew exactly what she wanted to do with her life. She took a vow of Virginity, which did not endear her family towards her. She suffered a great deal in her effort to belong to Jesus alone. She wanted to serve the Lord as a religious, but she did not want to be in a cloister. In those days, women either married, or joined a cloistered religious community.

She wanted to become a Mantellate.[2] But even they didn't

---

[1]Bob and Penny Lord's book: *Saints and other Powerful Women in the Church*

[2]Mantellate - Third Order of St. Dominic, a lay or secular Order.

Left:
*One day Jesus appeared to St.
Catherine with two crowns, one of
thorns and one of gold, asking her
which she chose. Catherine
pointed to the crown of thorns.
Jesus replied,
"You have chosen well. That you
have chosen the crown of thorns
for your time on earth, you will
wear this crown of gold for all
eternity when you come to make
your new life with Me."*

Above:
*One day, while she was in Pisa, after having received Our Lord Jesus in
the Eucharist, St. Catherine meditated on the Crucifix (above) which was
on the altar. Flames shot out from the five Wounds of Jesus and penetrated
her body, hands, feet and side. She had received the Stigmata.*

want her. They only accepted widows - she was a virgin. She
was too young and too pretty. She prayed and the Lord worked
miraculously, so that the superiors saw her as a weak, ugly girl,
which she was not. But it did the trick. They were willing to
accept her. Then the enemy began to attack her: What was it, a
life of loneliness and hardship, in a dark, little room away from
all she loved? Catherine, with what little strength she could
summon, threw herself to the foot of the Crucifix, crying,

*"O my only, my dearest Bridegroom, You know that I have
never desired any but You! Come to my aid now, my Savior,
strengthen and support me in this time of trial!"*

Her eyes fixed on her Lord on the Cross, she heard the gentle
stirring of a silk gown. Before her was the Mother of God, Mary
Most Holy holding out to Catherine a silken dress, shimmering
from the golden thread, jewels and pearls adorning it. As Mary
clothed Catherine in the heavenly gown she had chosen, she said
gently, lovingly,

*"My daughter, I have drawn this garment from the Heart of
my Son. It lay hidden in the wound in His Side, as in a golden
casket, and I have made it myself with my own holy hands."*

Once more Catherine said *"yes"* to Jesus' call to an intimate
life with Him. She privately took the vows of Nuns who
belonged to Religious Orders, poverty, chastity and obedience,
although it was not required of her. She stayed in her room, a
recluse, except to attend Mass. For three years she lived this
solitary life, scourging herself three times a day, denying herself
sleep and adequate nourishment, not seeing or hearing anything
or anyone outside this little world of hers. Although she allowed
no one in her cell, she was never alone. Jesus, sometimes
accompanied by His Mother and other times by Saints and
Angels, would come and instruct her about God His Father, the
Truths of the Gospel, about salvation and sin.

Catherine does battle with the fallen angels

But, Jesus and His Heavenly Companions were not her only

spirited visitors. The fallen angels, with their lies and deceptions, never failed to take an opportunity to attack. They let her have it again and again. One night, drenched and drained from the battle that had been ruthlessly ensuing, she had a thought from the Holy Spirit. She remembered the day she had asked the Lord for the gift of Fortitude. The Lord's words came back to her, *"If you want to have the strength to overcome all the enemy's attacks, take the Cross as your refreshment."* Fortified by the Lord's words, she stood ground, to do battle with the little devils.

Finally, the demons dispersed. The Lord appeared for the first time since the attacks had begun. Catherine asked the Lord where He had been during the onslaught. He replied, *"I was in your heart."* Catherine told the Lord she could not understand how the enemy could be attacking her if He had been there. When He asked her if her temptations brought her enjoyment or sorrow, she shared her feelings of repulsion and her intense trial. He told her it was He who planted those feelings. If He had not been in the center of her heart, the thoughts and temptations of the enemy would have pleased her instead of displeasing her.

According to the Life of St. Catherine, written by Blessed Raymond of Capua, her confessor and confidant, in an Apparition which took place about the year 1372, she was given a special gift, one which would stay with her for the rest of her life. She was allowed to drink of the Blood of Jesus, from His Side. She shared with Blessed Raymond that after drinking the Blood of Jesus, she couldn't eat anymore. She was neither hungry, nor could she hold anything in her stomach, other than the Sacred Species, the Body and Blood of Jesus.[3] She became what is called a Eucharistic Faster. She lived on nothing but the Blessed Sacrament. This continued for eight years. Her fasting did not affect her life. She was full of energy during that period. As a matter of fact, some of her greatest work took place during that period. Nor did it have anything to do with her death. She

---

[3]excerpt from Bob and Penny Lord's book: *This is My Body, This is My Blood, Miracles of the Eucharist.*

was able to live a normal life on nothing but Our Lord Jesus in the Eucharist, and some sips of water.

Catherine chooses the Crown of Thorns

From her youngest years, Catherine was being called to a closer walk with Jesus. He always accompanied that call with a sign to strengthen her for the gift of that walk, and the days ahead with that gift. One day Jesus appeared to Catherine with two crowns, one of thorns and one of gold, asking Catherine which she chose. Catherine pointed to the crown of thorns. Jesus replied,

"You have chosen well. That you have chosen the crown of thorns for your time on earth, you will wear this crown of gold for all eternity when you come to make your new life with Me."

Jesus replaces Catherine's heart with His Own

Another time, Jesus took Catherine's heart and replaced it with His Own. During this exchange of hearts, Catherine later confessed to her Spiritual Director she was without a heart for days, as she waited for Jesus to replace her stony heart with His Unconditional, Loving, Compassionate, Merciful and Forgiving Heart, with which she was then able to love unconditionally, returning hate with love, envy with generosity, abuse with mercy and patience, forgiving all for their malice and gossip.

The Miracle of the Cross - Catherine receives the Stigmata

Whenever Catherine went anywhere, she drew people to herself. She radiated such a strong spirituality that people wanted to follow her example. She went to Pisa in response to an invitation she received. She spent a great deal of time at a little church called St. Christina. One day, after having received Our Lord Jesus in the Eucharist, she meditated on the crucifix on the altar. She was there for some time when she felt a strange sensation overcoming her. She felt herself coming closer and closer to the Crucified Christ. Then, in an instant, she saw flames shoot out from the five Wounds of Jesus and penetrate her body, in her hands, her feet and her side.

Blessed Raymond was in the chapel when it happened. In his words, she was transfigured into the Image of Jesus Christ. He had just finished celebrating Mass for Catherine and her companions when she went into ecstasy, *"her soul separating as much as it could from the body."* They saw her body, which had been prostrate on the floor, rise. Mid-air, she kneeled, her face aglow with the fire of Jesus' Love inside of her. Then with a tremor, her body fell in a heap onto the floor. Her companions waited for her words, as she came out of the rapture. It was her practice, always, to share what the Lord had told her or what had transpired during an ecstasy. This time, however, it was different. Catherine awoke after a few moments, and went directly to Raymond.

> *"Father, I must tell you, that by His Mercy, I now bear the Stigmata of the Lord Jesus in my body," "I saw our Lord fastened to the Cross, coming down upon me in a blaze of light. With that, as my spirit leaped to meet its Creator, this poor body was pulled upright. Then I saw, springing from the marks on His Most Sacred Wounds, five blood-red rays coming down upon me, directed towards my hands and feet and heart. Realizing the meaning of this mystery, I promptly cried out: `Ah, Lord, my God, I implore You not to let the marks show outwardly on my body.[4] Whilst these words were still on my lips, before the rays had reached me, their blood-red color changed to radiant brightness, and it was in the form of clearest light they fell upon the five parts of my body - hands, feet and heart."*

Although Raymond continued asking her if she did not mean the wound was in her side, she insistently repeated over and over again, no, it was in her heart. Raymond writes of the excruciating pain she suffered bearing the Precious Wounds of

---

[4] The members of her Company reported that the wounds of the stigmata, although invisible during her life, became *visible* upon Catherine's death.

our Lord Jesus. Although Catherine had known pain all her life, this so debilitated her, she was in a coma for a week. Fearing she was dying, all her friends, including Raymond, prayed night and day. Not able to stir from her bed, feeling all the torture of Christ's Wounds cruelly rubbing against the blunt hard nails, she, too, was sure she was dying. Nothing helped to alleviate the agony and exhaustion that were companions of the Stigmata. Catherine returned home from Pisa but this did not improve her condition. Her mornings were pure hell for her, as she tried to get up from bed, having had barely an hour's sleep the night before. Only the loving support of her friends in the Mantellate, and the eyes of her heart focused solely on the Eucharist, gave Catherine the strength to painfully rise from bed.

Feeling some relief from the pain, Catherine consoled Raymond, *"The Lord has heard your prayers, and it is now my soul which is afflicted with suffering; but as for my body, these wounds no longer cause it pain, but rather lend it force and vigor. I can feel strength flowing into me from those wounds which at first only added to my sufferings."*

Catherine gave her last ounce of blood for her Church. Near the end of her painful journey on earth, her friends heard her say,

"O Eternal God, accept the sacrifice of my life for the mystical body of Thy Holy Church. I have nothing to give save that which Thou hast given to me. Take my heart then and press it out over the face of Thy Spouse!"

She saw God take her heart from her body and squeeze it out over the Church. As long as Catherine had a breath of life in her to give, she prayed and sacrificed for her love on earth, Mother Church. She instructed her companions she would continue to fight for her Church even after death.

"Father, into Thy Hands I commend my spirit."

She had had a Vision in the early part of 1380, in which the ship of the Church crushed her to the earth. At that moment, she offered herself as a willing sacrifice. She was to be ill from this time until April 21 of that year, when she suffered a paralytic stroke from the waist down.   On April 29, she went to her reward.

Catherine, with her last faint breath of life, continued to gaze on her Spouse on the Cross, whispering over and over again, *"Blood, blood, blood."* She was joining Christ on the Cross, for the last time on earth; His Last Great Act of Love becoming her last great act. On Sunday, Catherine whispered for the last time, *"Father, into Thy Hands I commend my spirit,"* and she went *Home.*

On October 4th, 1970, a lay woman, a woman without formal education, considered by some almost illiterate, our sister Catherine, a Saint, only one of three women to be so honored, was chosen as a Doctor of the Church.

St. Clare of Montefalco
The Crucified Lord in her heart
"I am looking for someone I can trust with My Cross"

Throughout the History of our Church you read about Lovers of the Cross. This sounds like a paradox. How can you love the Cross which entails so much suffering? Once when we had a group of Nuns with us on Pilgrimage, Penny very honestly stated that she does not want anymore crosses. A Nun celebrating 40 years of faithfulness to her vocation, got up, came to the front of the bus, and spoke through the microphone to the entire group. *"I have prayed for crosses all my life. My days are not complete without crosses."* Penny replied, *"I know the kind of cross Jesus could hand me, and I want to be sure to let Him know I'm not asking for anymore."* Mother Cabrini used to say that if she did not go through crosses with any of her projects, they were not of the Lord. The Saints of old, Francis in particular, feared that if they did not suffer a cross on a particular day, the Lord was upset with them. Padre Pio would say on days like this, "What did I do that the Lord has taken these crosses away from me?" But he never had to fear. The crosses came back to him in short order.

St. Clare of Montefalco is one of those Saints, who begged for the privilege of helping Jesus carry His Cross. She is one of the most unique Saints we have ever met. She is so strong her community has stayed faithful to her and the rule she began, for over 750 years. She had such a commitment to the Lord! She loved Him and knew that He loved her. From an early age, she was totally committed to Our Lord in His Passion. Her sister began a community of sisters in Montefalco when Clare was just six years old. She became her first member. Clare used her own forms of penance and mortification, which became so severe that her mother superior, sister Joanna, had to stop her under obedience. She felt, as many Saints before and after her, that if she took on the sufferings of Jesus on the Cross, she would be taking them away from Him, and in this way, showing how much

191

Right:

St. Clare is looking up to Jesus, her hands outstretched touching the Cross, expressing all the years of longing to share Jesus' Cross. Our Lord's Face is no longer gaunt with exhaustion, but beaming with love and joy. His Journey is over. He says to her, "Yes Clare, here I have found a place for My Cross, at last, someone I could trust with My Cross," and He thrust it into her heart.

Below:

The incorrupt heart of St. Clare of Montefalco revealing a crucified Jesus At the moment of her death, St. Clare of Montefalco said to her Nuns, "... I have the crucified Jesus in my heart."

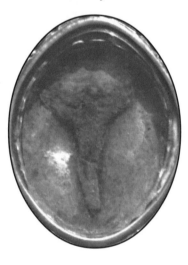

Above:

Chapel in the Convent of St. Clare of Montefalco in Montefalco, Italy

she loved Him in a real way.

How many of us have felt that way, that we could take a little of the pain and suffering away from Jesus if we would just take on a little of the agony, He endured for our sake? We follow Him through the Agony in the Garden, where He looked on to the Golden Gate where they had wanted to make Him King just days before. If we dare, we go with Him through that whole horrible night where He suffered so badly at the hands of the chief priests and elders of the synagogue. The Saints, like St. Clare, pleaded with Him to let them take away some of the pain He endured as He was whipped and scourged, His Precious Head pierced by the crown of thorns pressed down, penetrating His skull, His Back stooped, crushed under the weight of our sins, the agony He endured those hours on the Cross, the nails rubbing against His already Wounded Feet and Hands, and finally His Sacred Heart run through by a centurion's sword?

Our Bishop said the other day that all we do and feel is by and through the Grace of God. We all receive the Grace of God. The difference between Saints and sinners, is how we react to God's Grace.   Each of us respond differently to the Gifts bestowed on us by the Lord. Some of us cooperate with His Grace; offering our gifts back to Him of thanksgiving and praise, no matter the Gift He has handed us. Others complain, like the Israelites wandering in the desert. We each react to God's Grace differently. The making of Saints or sinners is no mystery - it is simply the reaction to God's generous gift of Grace. This Saint, as with others we are writing about, was filled with God's Grace to share in His Passion and she willingly embraced it.

"If you seek the Cross of Christ, take my heart;
there you will find the Suffering Lord."

These parting words, by St. Clare of Montefalco, were left not only as a clue from Heaven, which would lead the Church to investigate the Saint's heart after her death, these words were to be hope in, and understanding of the crosses we are all at one time or the other called to carry in our own lives. Clare adored and carried the Cross of Jesus, confident that she could trust in Him and His Promise to her.

From her earliest childhood, she had a burning love inside her for our dear Lord, especially in His Passion. This fire inside her was what gave her the energy and the zeal, her strength to live a life that would be demanding for most, but near impossible, when as a little girl, Clare would spend eight to ten hours a day, or more, in prayer, some nights falling down on her knees as many as one thousand times reciting the Lord's Prayer. As she walked with our Lord through His Passion, she pleaded to be allowed to help Him carry His Cross.

Clare was given a cross that all the crosses she was to carry in the future, could not equal that of the pain she was to suffer for eleven years. She was to know that loneliness that surpasses all others, the dreadful silence of God. God took this time with Clare in the desert, to toughen her, to prepare her for His Work, His Mission for her, which would continue even after her death.

Clare sees hell with all the suffering lost souls.

The year 1294 was to be a turning point for Clare. The Christmas of the past year had found her quite ill. Judging herself lacking in gratitude for all God had given her, Clare attributed the spiritual dryness she felt as God withholding His Divine Presence from her because of her sinfulness.

On the Feast of the Epiphany, after making a general confession before all the Nuns, she went into ecstasy, remaining in that state for several weeks. The Nuns kept her alive with a little sugar water they would give her to sip. During that journey away from the world, Clare had a Vision in which she saw herself in judgment before God; she "saw" hell with all the suffering lost souls without hope, and Heaven with the Saints enjoying perfect happiness in the Presence of God. She saw God in all His Majesty. He revealed to her how very uncompromisingly faithful to Him a soul must live in order to be in Him. When she came to, she resolved never to think anything, never to say anything, that would separate her from God. "And by the grace of God," she confided to a friend years later, "up to now I have been able to maintain this resolve."

"At last, someone I could trust with My Cross."

In the Chapel of the Holy Cross there is a fresco depicting Christ, dressed as a poor pilgrim, His Face weary from the weight of the Cross, His Body showing the outward signs of the long, hard journey carrying His Cross. In the foreground we see Clare kneeling, trying to keep Him from going any further, pleading, *"Lord, where are You going?"*

To which, Christ responds, *"I have searched the whole world for a strong place to plant firmly this Cross, and I have not found one."*

In the Nuns' Chapel, there is another small fresco. Clare is looking up to Jesus, her hands outstretched touching the Cross, expressing all the years of longing to share Jesus' Cross. Our Lord's Face is no longer gaunt with exhaustion, but beaming with love and joy. His Journey is over. He says to her, *"Yes, Clare, here I have found a place for My Cross, at last, someone I could trust with My Cross,"* and He thrust it into her heart.

The excruciating pain she felt in her entire body, upon receiving the Cross Jesus Himself planted in her heart, remained with her. From that first moment, she was always keenly aware of the Cross she could not only feel but sense with every fiber of her being. He was part of her; her Love; Jesus and she were one in His Cross.

"I have my Crucified Jesus in my heart"

"The life of a soul is the love of God," said Clare. She prayed that everyone she met would experience our Lord Jesus deep in their heart. She prayed, suffered and burned with passion, just as our Lord did; for, like Our Lord, she had completely given up her spirit to God.

On the evening of August the 15th, she called the Nuns together and left them her spiritual last will and testament,

"I offer my soul and all of you, the death of Lord Jesus Christ. Be blessed by God and by me. And I pray, my

daughters, that you behave well and that all the work God has had me do for you be blessed. Be humble, obedient; be such women that God may always be praised through you."

She asked for the Sacrament of Extreme Unction. When a Nun is dying, each of the Sisters blesses her with a Sign of the Cross. As they attempted to do so to Clare, she gently but firmly protested over and over again, *"Why do you sign me, Sisters? I have the crucified Jesus in my heart."*

The Nuns immediately got the body ready for all the friends of Clare to view. First they removed her heart and placed it in a flowered bowl made of wood. Had they remembered her words, *"I have the Crucified Jesus in my heart?"* That evening, the Nuns opened her heart preparing it to place in a Reliquary. To their amazement, Clare's words came alive; there before them were the marks of Jesus Passion! Cradled inside the softness of her grand heart, was the Perfect Form of Jesus Crucified, even to the Crown of Thorns clearly evidenced on his Head, and the lance Wound in His Precious Side. The Lord had not only planted His Crucified Body within the recesses of her heart, but the painful evidence of some of His Sufferings, the means of flagellation in a form of ligaments or tendons, the whip that was used to scourge our Beloved Lord, with the ends showing the metal balls and the jagged bones used to rip our Lord's Skin from His Bones.

The news of this miracle spread! The Bishop called together theologians, lawyers and doctors. The heart was carefully investigated and they all unanimously concluded that the "marks" were not of an explainable scientific nature or of human understanding, in other words, a phenomena, or as we are so happy to say, God leaving another Miracle of the Cross in our midst. There was not only a document drawn by the Church and affirmed by science, but the civil authorities did their own investigation and issued their findings. The heart of Clare did in fact contain this extraordinary sign and it was not the result of any false doings.

St. Clare's body exuded such a sweet fragrance, the Nuns never could bury her in the ground. Her body is still visible, nearly 700 years old, never having decomposed and is said to be supple (rigor mortis never set in).

More than 300 miracles (which occurred after her death), were attested to and accepted by Mother Church.[1]

This Shrine and Saint grasp the hearts of our pilgrims, more than almost any other; and they never forget her. Many come on pilgrimage with crosses: the death of a loved one, a painful separation after many years of marriage, a terminal illness, children on drugs or addicted to alcohol, family who have left Mother Church, an abusive spouse, and on and on. What is it about this Saint that touches them? Is it Jesus' Words, *"I have found a place for My Cross, at last, someone I could trust with My Cross."*

Someone I could trust with My Cross. Do we look upon our crosses as gifts from the Lord? Saints like St. Francis grieved when they had not received crosses. They would cry, *Did the Lord not find them worthy to share His Cross?*

The Saints who preceded us knew that the only way to know Jesus and follow Him was by Way of the Cross. Will you take up your cross and follow Him? The next time you go to church, will you look at Jesus on the Cross and tell Him, Lord You can trust me with Your cross.

After you receive the Eucharist, and the Mass is over, do you pause and pray? A prayer we would like to share with you is one we say after each Mass:

O Sacrament Most Holy,
O Sacrament Divine,
All praise and all thanksgiving
Be every moment Thine.

We adore the Wounds in Thy Sacred Head,

---

[1]For so much more on this powerful Saint, please read Bob and Penny Lord's book: *Saints and other Powerful Women in the Church.*

With sorrow deep and true.
May every thought of ours today
Be an act of love for You.

We adore the Wounds in Thy Sacred Hands,
With sorrow deep and true.
May every work of our hands today
Be an act of love for You.

We adore the Wounds in Thy Sacred Feet,
With sorrow deep and true.
May every step we take today
Be an act of love for You.

We adore the Wounds in Thy Sacred Heart,
With sorrow deep and true.
May every beat of our hearts today
Be an act of love for You.

O Sacrament Most Holy,
O Sacrament Divine,
All praise and all thanksgiving
Be every moment Thine.

The Miracles of the Cross
of St. Francis of Assisi

The Lord worked powerfully in the life of St. Francis of Assisi. The mandates He gave the little Saint, one at the beginning of his life, and the other towards the end of his life, came to him through Miracles of the Cross. Francis knew the power of the Cross. He spent his entire life with his eyes on the Cross, carrying his Cross, embracing his Cross, adoring his Cross. The Miracle which Our Lord gave him at the beginning of his life of ministry, put him on a path, in a direction, from which he never veered. The Miracle of the Cross he was given towards the end of his life was to make his body a beaten, broken crucified Christ. Francis always said *Yes* to the Lord, even though he might not have known what he was saying yes to, what he was getting into.

Francis was not aware he was born to be a Saint, a role model, a leader of thousands of men, at least not as a young man. He had been raised as a knight in training. He had the best suit of armor, the best horse. He had the best weapons. He learned how to play five instruments. He was the hit of all the parties of his social class.

St. Francis, a knight in training

St. Francis was truly a soldier, a knight in training. He was full of the chivalry of his time. He was of a higher station, and although he was not nobility, his father, a merchant, had always been able to give Francis the best of everything. In return, he expected the best of everything from Francis. That included going into battle for God and country. In the case of Francis' father, it was more for social status than for God. But Francis understood that. He was the son of a merchant; he would someday be a merchant. His father worked his way up from his bootstraps, becoming a success in business selling the fabric he bought from France; thus the name Francis for his son.

Above: *St. Francis of Assisi*
Cross of San Damiano

Below: *St. Francis of Assisi*   *Jesus spoke to St. Francis, "Go and*
receiving the Stigmata at the top of   *repair My Church, which as you*
Mount La Verna, Italy   *can see, is in ruins."*

Francis had only to follow the lead his father gave him and make use of all the talents he had mastered as part of his training. He was also trained in the art of gentlemanly warfare. This was all part of his father's plan for the role of his son as the proud offspring of a rich merchant, who yearned to achieve nobility through this boy, something he had not been able to claim. But Pietro de Bernadone had not considered one ingredient which was prevalent in the life of this boy, the power of God, the agenda of God.

Francis was always a good boy, but not deep, and not overly religious. As a natural course of events, he was embracing his father's plan for his life. He had a dream one night. He saw a huge palace filled with armor, and the coat-of-arms of Christ. He envisioned in his dream that he would have that palace to contain all the weapons necessary to fight for the glory of his town and his chivalry. He asked who this belonged to and was told it was for him and his knights. Not realizing what the Lord meant, he joined up with a military group to go to war against a neighboring town. It was a disaster for Francis.

Francis goes off to war.

He was captured early in the game, and sent to prison. There, he took ill and spent the bulk of the war in the hospital infirmary of the little town which could not have been more than five miles from Assisi. He had a dream one night. He saw the palace again. Our Lord appeared to Francis in the dream. The Lord asked Francis whom he would rather serve, the Lord or the servant. Francis replied "The Lord!" Then he asked, "What do you want me to do? The Lord told Francis he would be committed to fight all his life, but the battle would be for the Lord, and the weapon would be the Word of God, the Gospel. The Lord also told Francis to return to Assisi, where he would be told what to do.

Francis finally went back to Assisi, but not as the playboy who had left for the wars. Rather, he spent much of his time in meditation, searching for the meaning of his life. He went to churches quite a bit of the time. He thought the Lord would speak to him in a church. One such venture brought him into a broken-down roadside chapel, just outside Assisi, called the Chapel of San Damiano. The roof was off the church; it was in shambles. But Francis felt comfortable praying before the crucifix, which was still intact.

The First Miracle of the Cross

As he was praying, a blanket of silence covered the church. Even the sounds of the birds flying in an out, and the singing crickets and other insects stopped. It was as if the world had come to a complete halt. Francis looked up at the huge Cross in front of him. The eyes, huge brown, almond eyes, penetrated deep into his soul. Jesus came to life on the Cross. He locked His gaze on the frightened little man. Francis got up enough courage to ask him, ***"What do you want of me, Lord?"*** Jesus spoke to him. ***"Go and repair My Church, which as you can see, is in ruins."*** Francis stared at the Miracle which was taking place in front of his very eyes. The Lord may have spent more time with him than that. We're not told in the life of St. Francis just how much time the Lord spent with him, or what else he may have said to him. We do know that this was the absolute turning point of his life. This Miracle, which consisted in the Lord breathing life into a wooden image of Himself, and speaking some few words to this chosen apostle, would change the life of this young man forever, who would, in turn, save the Church of the Middle Ages.

Francis became totally committed to the Lord, but he didn't really know in what way or to what degree. He looked around at the little Church of San Damiano, which was truly in ruins, and did what he thought the Lord was asking him to do. He went about repairing it. His approach was simplistic; he used stone and mortar, but he was doing what the Lord told him. When the time came that the total plan of the Lord, or rather that part of it He wanted Francis to execute at that time, was laid out before Francis, he eagerly did what he did on that first key day in his life, he said *yes* and went to work.

The Second Miracle of the Cross

Francis on Mount La Verna

After the second Rule, the Rule of 1223 was imposed on Francis and his community, a great sadness overtook him. He lost all his zeal, that which had kept him going in good times and bad. He removed himself from the everyday workings of the Fraternity. It had gotten away from him. He didn't want to be part of decision-making, and yet, he couldn't keep his nose out of the everyday happenings.

He had to put distance between himself and his beloved Assisi. He spent a great deal of time in seclusion, with just Brother Leo, Brother Masseo and Brother Angelo[1]. It was important to Francis to surround himself with old friends, to be reminded of the way it had been in simpler times. He covered himself with a blanket of joy. Even in his sufferings, his illnesses which kept him in constant pain, he exuded joy. *This was a decision!* He instructed his Friars to go to the privacy of their rooms, if they wanted to bemoan their outcast state. But when they were in the presence of people, they must reflect the joy of Jesus. And so he practiced what he preached. He went off by himself. His companions stayed a safe distance, available to minister to Francis when he needed them, but always allowing him the space he needed, to let it all out with the Lord.

Francis and his faithful company of three, went to the mountain of Alverna (La Verna) to pray, from the Feast of the Assumption (August 15) to the Feast of St. Michael (September 29). He called this period the Lent of St. Michael. Francis had a special rapport with Mary and Michael from the early days of his conversion. He went to them often, for comfort and consolation, when things got rough. He was going there now to *give*, by

---

[1] These three brothers, Leo, Masseo and Angelo, are the three Friars, who compiled a book of narratives on the life of Francis, called The Three Companions.

fasting in honor of their feasts; but he knew he would be *receiving* from them as well.

He always had an exalted devotion to St. Michael. He felt that Michael should be honored because he had the office of presenting souls to God. He also said *"Everyone should offer to God, to honor so great a prince (Michael), some praise or some special gift."* He loved Mary reverently. As he loved Jesus, he could not do otherwise than love *"the womb that bore Him."* He sang to her, offered special prayers to her, shared his joys and sorrows with her. She was his very best friend, the Mother of his God. While he was honoring Michael during this time, he was also honoring Mary on the Feast of her Assumption into Heaven, August 15, and her birthday, September 8.

There was a crag on that mountain, a deep crevice which separated one part of that high place from the other. Tradition has it that at the very moment Our Dear Lord Jesus died, this mountain split in two, as the whole earth shook in protest over the demonic act of murdering our Savior. Francis loved to sit on that jagged rock, and meditate on the Passion of Jesus. The brothers brought him some bread and water from time to time, but for the most part, he was alone with his Lord and Savior.

According to the Divine Plan, another special Feast fell during the Lent of St. Michael. It took place on September 14, and was called The Exaltation of the Cross. Today, we celebrate it on the same day, but we call it the Triumph of the Cross. On that day, in 1224, the Lord gave Francis a distinctive gift, as reward for a lifetime of service. Might not our Lord also have been telling Francis that He affirmed all that Francis had done, that he had shepherded his flock the way Jesus wanted, but that all of it was dulled in comparison to what would happen this day? For on this day, Jesus gave His brother Francis, the gift of His wounds, His Stigmata.

Francis had been meditating deeply on the Passion of our Lord. He had asked his best Friend, Jesus, for two gifts. The first was that somehow, before he died, he might feel the wounds of Jesus in his own body and soul; and secondly, he might experience Jesus' love for those who inflicted the wounds on His Body, and killed Him. Francis went through *a dark night of the soul*. His mind kept interfering with his spirit. He thought of what he had given up, his Fraternity, his Rule. He tried desperately to put these things in the back of his consciousness, and just zero in on the pains of His Redeemer. His humanity fought him all through the night, but with the dawn, a stillness, a heavy blanket of peace came over the mountain. Everything was quiet; not a sound from any of the creatures. It was as if they knew what was to come, and were preparing themselves for the entrance of a Heavenly Being.

Light began to emerge from the darkness. Francis thought it was Brother Sun greeting him. But the light was too intense, much stronger than the sun. The curtain separating Heaven from earth split open. A figure came forth, slowly, and carried the brilliant light with it. Francis couldn't look at it; the light was too strong. Then the Lord allowed Francis' eyes to open. Before him, suspended in the air, was a huge Angel enveloped in a Cross, which appeared to be made of fire, he was so bright; but there were no flames coming from him. *He had six wings, two extended over his head, two extended as if for flight, and two covering his body.*[2] The angel was nailed to the Cross; the wounds of Jesus flared up, and shivered against the light. They were of a deep crimson, sprinkled with gold.

Francis receives the Stigmata

Francis stood up joyfully, to greet the Seraph.[3] At that moment, beams of heated illumination shot out from the Cross, and penetrated Francis' body, hands, feet and side. He fell from the force of the thrust; his body experienced devastating pain, mixed with inconceivable joy. His blood raced throughout his

---

[2]Celano First Life no. 94

[3]Seraph is the name of the Angels of the Angelic choir of Seraphim, which is one of the choirs who adore before God. The word comes from the Hebrew "fiery" (Is 6: 1-4).

body; he was sure he would die, but it was all right. Then the sensation calmed down to a constant throb of joy and pain. He looked up at the Heavenly creature. The eyes of the Angel were studying Francis. The stare was compelling. There was at once fear and bliss, mixed together. He didn't know what was happening to him. The eyes of the Angel were the most beautiful he had ever seen. He could not look away from them.

The Heavenly vision spoke gently to Francis' heart. He told him things he had to hear, which were for him alone; he would not in his lifetime, reveal them to anyone. He stayed with Francis for the better part of an hour. This is according to the testimony of the farmers, and mule keepers at the foot of the mountain. They mistook the brilliant light for the sun coming up, and began their day. Then, when it disappeared, and the natural sun came out, it was colorless by comparison. They became confused.

After a time, the Angel began to fade. The flames remained bright, outlining the Cross and then flickered like embers, after which they died. Francis kept looking at the image before him. The last thing he saw was the Cross.

Many insights were revealed to Francis on top of Mount Alverna on that September 14, Feast of the Triumph of the Cross. His whole life was put into perspective. He finally understood his journey, and while his humanity would tend to kick in over the next two years, he could always fall back on this time, and the revelations he received through this Miracle of the Cross, and a peace would come over him.

The story of Francis' *yes* to the Lord on that day, and his ongoing *yes*, fills history books. He began the largest religious order in the world. But as always, in times of crisis, Our Lord raises up Saints and Other Powerful Men in the Church, Our Lord raised up in the Thirteenth Century Saints Francis and Dominic for the salvation of the Church of the Middle Ages.[4]

---

[4]For more on St. Francis, read Bob and Penny Lord's book: *Saints and Other Powerful Men and Women in the Church.*

Saint Gemma Galgani
Her life - one great Miracle of the Cross!

The Lord sends down a Gem from Heaven to bless the world

In a small village not too far from the historic city of Lucca, the Lord blessed Aurelia and Enrico Galgani on March 12, 1878, with a tiny, precious little baby girl (as the priest who baptized her, exclaimed upon seeing her), *una Gemma* del Paradiso![1]

Gemma showed signs of sainthood from a very young age. She was her mother's life! They would pray together, the little girl joyfully keeping up with her mother. Her mother told her stories about Jesus and *His* Mother. But that was tragically to come to an end. When Gemma was only five years old, her mother became ill. For the few pain-filled years, she had left, her mother would hold her little girl close to her, cradle her in her arms and ask the Lord why He had sent this precious girl to her so late. Holding her close, she would tell Gemma, she wished she could take her up to Heaven with her.

Gemma, in later years, gave full credit to her mother for the great love, she had for God through the Cross. Her mother taught her the Faith, through the Lord Crucified, speaking of that loving God the Father Who sacrificed His only begotten Son for her, and of Jesus the Son Who willingly suffered and died for her. Knowing suffering first hand, her mother taught Gemma the value of the Cross. As death approached, her mother, completely bedridden, continued telling her stories about Jesus. But when she was nearing the end, she told her little Gemma that soon, she would learn from Jesus Himself Who would speak to her from the very depths of her heart.

As she could feel the debilitating ravages of consumption draining her of life, her mother requested Gemma be allowed to receive the Sacrament of Confirmation, before she died.

---

[1] a gem from Heaven

Above:
St. Gemma drank from the Wound
in the Side of Christ on this Cross.

Above:
Saint Gemma Galgani - Stigmatist

Above: *Saint Gemma Galgani receives the Stigmata*
Mother Mary appeared, accompanied by Gemma's Guardian Angel, and
told her that Jesus had forgiven her sins. Then Mother Mary opened
her mantle and placed it over her. Jesus appeared and showed her His
Wounds which were no longer bleeding. Instead flames of fire leapt
forth from them and pierced Gemma's hands, feet and heart.

Although she was only seven years old, her mother's instructions had fared her well, the Pastor agreed. The day of her Confirmation came; she felt so close to Jesus. After *that* Mass was over, she and her family stayed to give thanksgiving at the *next* Mass. As she was deep in prayer, praising the Lord for the gift of this Divine Sacrament that He had given her, Gemma heard a voice interiorly ask her: *"Will you give me your mother?"* She replied she would, but asked the Lord to take her, along with her mother. The Lord asked her to give her mother to Him, *unconditionally*. This was to be the first of many sacrifices that He would ask of her throughout her life, as she would join Him on the Cross.

Gemma carries her first cross.

It was September 17, 1886, and it was time for her mother to go Home to the Lord, whom she had so faithfully brought to her daughter, the future Saint. Her mother now with the God she had so often spoken of, Gemma knew there would no longer be anyone to tell her stories about her Jesus. Believing with all her heart that her mother would now help her from Heaven did not heal the emptiness she felt, losing her beloved mother and holy story teller.

Her first Christmas, after her mother's death, was a very quiet one. She looked like a little girl who had lost all her toys, as she tried to find the joy she had shared with her mother, when, in former Christmases, they had welcomed the Baby Jesus into their hearts. She sat at the window, looking off to the *Place* from where, she knew her mother was watching over her and tears began to flow. She cried, remembering how she had breathlessly helped her mother roll the dough to make ready all the baked goods, in anticipation of the precious Baby's birth.

When she pleaded to be allowed to receive her Lord in Holy Communion: *"Give Him to me; I long for Him, and I cannot live without Him,"* her confessor had no choice but to say Yes! It was then, she said, that she received her first embrace from Jesus *Crucified*. From then on, she would desire only to walk with

Him, sharing in His Passion. She later wrote,

"Do grant, oh my God, that when my lips approach Yours to kiss You, I may taste the gall that was given You; when my shoulders lean against Yours, make me feel Your scourging; when my flesh is united with Yours, in the Holy Eucharist, make me feel Your Passion; when my head comes near Yours, make me feel Your thorns; when my heart is close to Yours, make me feel Your spear..."

Gemma goes through The Dark Night of the Soul

Jesus had wooed little Gemma; she was ecstatic, sharing the sweetness of being loved by Him. But all good things come to an end. Gemma was to now know the Lord in His Passion, the Lord Who suffered in Gethsemane. She would share the abandonment that He felt, as she went through the *"Dark night of the Soul,"* experiencing *nothing* after receiving Holy Communion. Feeling spiritually alone, afflicted in body and soul, finding no consolation in prayers, nothing to affirm her faith, Gemma, like her Jesus before her, still *knew* and *continued to believe* she was not abandoned by God and tried even harder to please Him.

Gemma has to say good by to her brother Gino

It was 1894 and Gemma was sixteen years old. Once again, she had to say good-by to a loved one who would precede her to Heaven. Her brother Gino had always shared her love for Jesus. He was only eighteen years old. And so little Gemma's heart knew heartbreak once more, as her brother left her to join their mother and beloved Lord Jesus in Paradise.

Devastated by the death of her dear brother, Gemma became so ill, she was unable to rise from bed for over three months. Her father, seeing his precious child near death, pleaded with Jesus to take him and not her. The Lord answered his prayers and two years later, his spirit spent from the crosses he had borne, Gemma's father went *Home* to his wife and son.

The new year brings more crosses

At the end of a very difficult 1895, burdened down by heavy crosses, Gemma placed herself at the Lord's Feet on the Cross.

The new year did not promise to be any better:

"I do not know what will happen to me this year. I abandon myself to You, my God; all my hopes and affections shall be for You. I am weak, oh Jesus, but I trust in Your help and I resolve to live differently, namely, closer to You."

The new year came and with it, crosses. Her first cross was when, her leg became so infected, the doctor was going to amputate. Instead, he performed an extremely painful operation. Gemma, refusing all anesthetic, her eyes on Jesus on the Cross, cried out only once, for which she later begged forgiveness from the Lord.

That battle over, a worse attack was to ensue. Her father, a chemist, had given much credit to the poor and to those in *temporary* financial straits; except *temporary* became *forever*, and they never paid! The illnesses of his wife and son, and their subsequent deaths, had drained whatever resources he had; the authorities sold his farm and its machinery and his entire pharmacy. When Gemma's father was struck down by cancer of the throat and died November, 1897, his worries and pain were over; but those of Gemma and her brothers and sisters were only beginning.

Although they were left penniless, Gemma grieved more for the loss of her father than of all they had lost *materially*. The hurts were there though, and till her dying days, she recalled the creditors coming in, her father still laid out at home, taking what little they had left. But with all of this hitting her at one time, bitterness would have been an acceptable reaction. However, instead of vindictiveness, she prayed to that God Whom she never gave up on, the One Who never gave up on her. Gemma faced this at all of nineteen and a half years old!

Gemma has a vision of Jesus on the Cross

On Holy Thursday, 1899, Jesus came to Gemma for the first time in a vision and told her to sacrifice herself in atonement for the sins of the world. She had begun to meditate on her sins.

When she reflected on how deeply she had wounded Jesus by her sins, she began to cry as if her heart would break.

As she was grieving, Jesus appeared to her, Blood spilling from His Wounds, and said, *"Look at My Wounds and learn how to love. Look at this Cross, these Wounds, these nails, these bruises and lacerations, and this Blood. See to what extent I have loved you, Do you want to love Me? First, learn to suffer; suffering teaches how to love."*

Gemma receives the Stigmata

Because she had been healed through the intercession of St. Margaret Mary Alacoque, Gemma felt this was a sign she was called to be a Nun in the Convent of the Visitation. She was judged too fragile for convent life as a result of a debilitating illness. No amount of tears and begging would dissuade the Mother Superior or the Archbishop who had given the order she not be accepted.

Several days after she had been rejected, Jesus spoke to Gemma: *"I am waiting for you on Calvary."* On June 8th, two weeks after her rejection, she had an *inner thought*: She was about to receive some very special grace! She went to her confessor to shed herself of any sins she might have, so that the Lord would have a spotless soul, ready to receive whatever blessing, He willed to give her.

When Thursday came, Gemma began to think of all the sufferings, Jesus had endured for her. She became filled with such overwhelming remorse, she became rapt in *ecstasy*! The Blessed Mother appeared, accompanied by Gemma's Guardian Angel, and told her that Jesus had forgiven her sins. Then Mother Mary opened her mantle and placed it over her. Jesus appeared and showed her His Wounds which were no longer bleeding. Instead flames of fire leapt forth from them and pierced Gemma's hands, feet and heart. She was in such excruciating pain, she thought she would collapse and die, were it not for Mother Mary supporting her and covering her with her mantle. After she remained like this for hours, Mother Mary kissed her forehead and the vision vanished. *Gemma had received the Stigmata, and now bore the five Wounds of Jesus!* She was in such agony, she needed the aid of her Guardian Angel to help her into bed. The next day, she carefully bound and hid her bleeding hands and went to Mass.

From that time on, Gemma would receive the Stigmata, the five Wounds of Jesus, each week on Thursday evening, beginning at 8 P.M. They would continue bleeding until 3 P.M. Friday; then completely disappear that evening or early Saturday; by Sunday, freshly healed flesh would cover the wounds; the Stigmata was gone. The only visible signs left were white spots where the five open Wounds had been. The following Thursday the bleeding would begin again.

The last three years of her life, the ecstasies stopped. Her Spiritual Director forbid her to have them because of her weakened condition. Always working through the Saints' obedience to their Superiors, the Lord no longer shared His Five Wounds with Gemma.

Gemma levitates to embrace Jesus on the Cross

The Gianninis, a wealthy, very pious family in Lucca, having heard of Gemma's holiness, begged her brother and his wife to allow them to adopt Gemma. And so Gemma was adopted as a daughter of their family in September, 1900. There was an atmosphere of sanctity in this otherwise affluent home.

Setting the table in the dining room was one of her favorite tasks, as a huge Crucifix hung on the wall. Although venerated by the whole family, it was most especially adored by Gemma who would pause in front of it during the day and keep her Lord company with consoling words of love. Many times, she so desired to kiss the Wound on His Side, she would find herself rising into mid-air up to Christ on the Cross, embracing Him and kissing the Wound on His precious Side.

One day, as she was placing the tablecloth on the dining room table, her heart beating wildly, she cried out to the Lord, *"Let me get to You. I am thirsting for Your Blood."* The Image of Christ on the Cross came to life; Jesus held out one of His Arms from the Cross and beckoned Gemma to come to Him. She levitated up to Him; Jesus held her in His Arms and Gemma drank from the *Holy Spring* in His Side, staying aloft as if resting on a cloud. All this became known to the Church through a member of the Giannini household, Aunt Cecilia, her adopted mother. Gemma was under obedience to tell all her experiences to her; if not for that, all that came to pass would have remained a buried treasure inside Gemma's heart.

Jesus reveals God's imminent punishment on mankind

Father Germano saw in Gemma a holy soul who, like a child without guile, simply loved God and saw Him in all the circumstances surrounding her life, recognizing Him most in her suffering. Discerning her to be holy and pure, Father Germano believed her ecstasies were authentic and accepted her wounds as *the Stigmata*, a gift from the Lord of *His* five Wounds. Father spent the rest of his life being her Spiritual Director. But that did not mean Gemma's life would be without strife and dissension, the devil doing all he could do to cause problems. At times, Gemma even doubted Father Germano and all those who had been the first to believe in her.

Gemma's life was one of: *rejection* - God's gifts to her were often doubted and she, mistrusted; *hurts* - ill-will, spite and jealousy in the hearts of those around her; *abandonment* - feeling most sharply the absence of a family, she grieved because she judged she was a burden on those around her.

Gemma told a tender soul who was undergoing grave trials:
"...an interior voice seems to tell me we must remain at the foot of the Cross. If Jesus is nailed upon the Cross, we must not complain if we have to stay at its feet."

Gemma told this poor soul, we must all walk with Jesus on the way to Calvary, to the Cross and His death; or was she speaking with the *Heart of Jesus* asking *that* soul and us, *do we run away from Our Lord at the Pillar, not wanting to be wounded by and for the sins of others? Are we silent when we are mocked and humiliated, as Our Lord was when they put a Crown of Thorns on His precious Head? Do we deny Him when the going gets rough, like Peter? Do we choose the world's answers to our problems, as they did when Pilate asked "Which one do you want me to release to you, Barabbas or Jesus Who is called Messiah?" Are we willing to stand beside His Mother and die, as she did, with Him, for His beloved Church, this Church which flowed from His pierced Heart on the Cross?*

During Midnight Mass, at the time of the Offertory, as the priest was offering the gifts to the Father, Jesus appeared and offered *Gemma* as a victim to the Eternal Father. The Lord was radiant as He embraced Gemma and then presented her to her *Mama*, His Mother Mary, as *"the fruit of His Passion."*

The long painful journey *Home*

She was coming to the end of her journey to the Cross. Gemma's physical suffering was extremely painful. But the *physical* could not compare with the *spiritual* attacks to which this sweet soul was subjected, at the hands of the devil. He taunted her with: *She had led a useless life; all her suffering was for nothing; God had abandoned her because she had fooled people into thinking her pious; her gifts of the Stigmata and ecstasies were not of God and the devil used her to deceive everyone into believing they were divinely inspired; God was angry because she was a hypocrite, her humility and purity were false, and she was in truth a big sinner.*

The devil had her so convinced of her sinfulness that she wrote the story of her life, accusing herself of being sinful and deceitful. Seeking absolution for the dreadful sins the devil had deluded her into believing she had committed, she gave her story to her confessor, who read her story and assured her of her piety, charity and holiness. When she wrote, the devil smeared the pages with black hoof-prints of black ink and carbon from the fires of hell. These marks can still be seen on her writings.

Gemma communicates with her Guardian Angel

In a vision, her Guardian Angel had appeared to Gemma and

showed her two crowns, one of lilies and one of thorns. When the Angel offered them to her, inviting her to take *one* of them, Gemma responded, she wanted the crown that belonged to her Lord Jesus. The Angel handed her the crown of thorns! Gemma embraced the crown and kissed it. Then pressing it to her heart, she said, *"Be always praised my God! Long live Jesus! Long live Jesus' gifts! Long live Jesus' Cross!"*

Well, here it was, the end of Gemma's life, and she was wearing the crown of thorns she had chosen and would wear to the Cross. As with other Mystics who had the Stigmata, she had desired to share Jesus' Passion. Jesus allowed her to carry His Cross, bear His humiliation, loneliness, anguish, abandonment, yes, and even the taunts and temptations from the devil. Now, she would know the full meaning of her *Yes* to the Lord. Her final hours strongly paralleled those of her Savior. Gemma was walking the way of the Passion that her Lord before her had tread.

When the pain and the bombardment got heavy, the Lord came to her, accompanied by her Guardian Angel. He tried to reassure her and encourage her to persevere in fighting the temptations of the devil. But as soon as He left, the battles began to rage again; the enemy was back, more vicious than ever. As her Lord Jesus had cried out to the Father on the Cross, *"Why have You forsaken Me?"* now Gemma cried out, *"Jesus where are You? You know my heart; where are You?"*

Gemma could be heard crying out in ecstasy, *"Make haste, Jesus. Cut off the chain that binds me to earth, separating me from Heaven. Let me come to You."*

Gemma had asked Jesus to allow her to die on a Solemn Feast Day. Gemma had suffered the 40 days of Lent, and now it was Holy Week. Gemma would be given the final gift from Jesus: she would share fully in His Passion, agonizing with the suffering *Spotless Lamb*. On Holy (Spy) Wednesday, Gemma received Holy Viaticum with joy and thanksgiving. Prior to that, because of her constant vomiting, even the Lord in His Eucharist had been withheld from her. Since March 23rd, she felt as if she was alone in a desert, her lips and heart parched as she thirsted for the *Living* God. She had suffered the loss of her most precious consolation on earth, Holy Communion, and she was inconsolable.

When at last she received her Lord, Gemma fell into a deep ecstasy, and when she came out of it, she told the nurse, *"Oh, if only you could see the smallest part of that which Jesus has revealed to me, you would die of ecstasy."*

On *Holy Thursday*, she again requested Holy Communion. Soon after receiving, she fell into ecstasy and was overheard saying, she saw a crown of thorns, and she had more to suffer.

On *Good Friday*, the last one she would share with Jesus on earth, Gemma turned to her Aunt Cecilia and asked her not to leave her until she was nailed to the Cross. She said: *"I must be crucified with Jesus. Jesus told me, His children must be crucified with Him."* Everyone wept at Gemma's bedside as they witnessed that final dying on the Cross.

The morning of *Holy Saturday* the priest came to anoint her. Gemma, like her Savior before her, summoned her last ounce of breath, just enough to pray with the priest. She had asked to die without any comfort, as her Savior before her, and the Lord complied. When the devil launched his last attack, taunting her that she had been abandoned by the Lord she so loved, she replied, *"A Crucifix and a priest are all I need."*

At half past one, Holy Saturday, April 11, 1903, Gemma died, her Crucifix in her hand, exclaiming, *"Jesus, if it is Your Will, take me."* She kissed the Crucifix, placed it on her breast and closed her eyes.

On the triumphant anniversary of Christ's Ascension into Heaven, May 2, 1940, Gemma Galgani was hailed for the first time: *"Saint Gemma."* In the midst of war and hatred, of death and cruelty, of man's inhumanity to man, a light shone in the darkness and love was crowned.[2]

---

[2]You can read more about Saint Gemma in their books: *Visionaries,*

St. John of the Cross
Suffering Servant of the Cross

We have always admired the Pastoral Cross our dear Pope John Paul II carries. The image of Jesus crucified is so graphic, so inspirational, that we can't take our gaze away whenever His Holiness walks with this Crucifix. It has impressed us so that when we began taking Pilgrimages overseas in 1983, we had a manufacturer in Italy make these Crosses for us for our pilgrims to wear on Pilgrimage.

We have worn these Crosses all over the world, including the Holy Land, Jordan, Greece, Turkey, and all of Europe. The reactions we have received have been incredible. Everyone who has seen them have recognized these Crosses as the Cross of the Pope. In Italy, they would call them *"La Croce del Papa."* *(The Cross of the Pope)*. But in every language it has been the same. They connect the image of Jesus with the Pope. Over the years, people we have met in these foreign countries have asked us to give them a Cross like the one we were wearing. Very often, we have taken the Crosses off our necks and given them to these people. You cannot believe what a gift they felt they had received.

In 1991, the 500th anniversary of the death of St. John of the Cross, we went to Spain and made a documentary on his life. When we went to the Convent of the Incarnation in Avila, we saw an original drawing he made of a Vision he had of the Crucifix. The drawing was enclosed in an oval. In the opening of the documentary, we showed that beautiful drawing. So it has been an important part of our Ministry for at least twenty years. But it wasn't until we brought our most recent pilgrimage to the Incarnation Convent in September, 2001, that their in-house guide pointed out that the Papal Cross His Holiness uses all the time, was taken from the Vision of St. John of the Cross. We did a double take. We placed our pilgrim's crosses in the same position that John of the Cross would have seen his Vision of

Right:
St. John of the Cross, Doctor of the Church, had a vision of Jesus at a crucial time in his life which stayed with him all his life.
He is best known for his poems and commentaries, The Dark Night of the Soul; Ascent of Mount Carmel; Living Flame of Love and Spiritual Canticle.

Below:
A sketch of Jesus on the Cross hand drawn by St. John of the Cross

Above left:
St. John of the Cross - Dark Night of the Soul
The Dark Night of the Soul tells of a lover encountering the Lover, only to become one in Heavenly Communion.

Jesus Crucified, and sure enough, it was the same Cross as the Vision St. John of the Cross had experienced. Since 1983, we had been wearing a Pilgrim's cross, inspired, we thought, by Pope John Paul II, but in reality, inspired by St. John of the Cross, Spaniard, Poet, Visionary and Doctor of the Church.

Our story is about that Vision of Jesus, who came to St. John of the Cross at a crucial time in his life, and which inspired him to create that drawing which stayed with him all his life, and which inspired our Pope, John Paul II, to use in his pectoral Cross. But we can't just jump into that part of St. John's life without giving you a little background on him, which led up to his receiving this Vision of Jesus which he committed to paper and pen. He is a fascinating Saint, as well as Doctor of the Church.

As we turn the pages of St. John of the Cross' story, you will discover that he was born into a time of darkness and disgrace four hundred years ago. Martin Luther and his rebellion, under the pretext of Reformation, was spreading its venom all across Europe. But on the other hand, God always balancing the scales, there was an excitement that filled the air of Spain, as well. It was a time of pathos, not knowing when to cry and when to rejoice. It was the year 1542. After hundreds of years under the oppressive yoke of the Moors, a golden age was emerging for Spain.

Fifty years before the birth of St. John, Catholic Queen Isabella, believing in Columbus, had backed up that belief, financing him and his expedition. He set out to open a new route to India. His discovery of *America* for Spain, instead, opened an early gateway to the Americas, gaining a sizable advantage for Spain and her navigators. Her Treasury swelled as her ports buzzed with traffic from the sea.

And then, eleven years before the birth of St. John, almost as a reaction to the storm which was brewing in Germany, Our Lady went to Mexico, and as the Queen that she is, she appeared as Our Lady of Guadalupe, saved the newly founded continent for

God, and created 8,000,000 Catholics in seven short years. She averted holocaust, created family, and brought a new ethnic group under her mantle in the Catholic Church.

So to say St. John of the Cross was born into an exciting time in the history of the Church and the world is somewhat of an oversimplification. But it is surely a true statement. As the world of today, which seems like most everybody is going to hell in a hand basket, Our dear Lord tells us that we can be instruments in bringing about change. So it was with St. Francis of Assisi in the Thirteenth Century. And so it was with John of the Cross in the Sixteenth Century.

St. John of the Cross is best known for his poems and commentaries, *The Dark Night of the Soul; Ascent of Mount Carmel; Living Flame of Love* and *Spiritual Canticle*. Not poems of tragedy and storms, St. John and all his poems spoke of love and joy, that happiness that only the Father can provide! *The Dark Night of the Soul* tells of a lover encountering the Lover, only to become one in heavenly communion. His only true desire was to achieve that complete *union* when he and the Lord would be one. He wrote, *"There is no better or more necessary work than love" "We have been created for love" "As love is the union of the Father with the Son, so it is of the human soul with God."* While he is best known for his association with St. Teresa of Avila, and the Reform of the Carmelite Order of the Sixteenth Century, for which he sacrificed his life, he was proclaimed a Doctor of the Church for his deeply spiritual writings, which lifts one's soul to the heights of Heaven. While a great deal of who John of the Cross became had to do with St. Teresa, his soul burned with love for Jesus and Church from his earliest days.

He was born of little estate

He was born of peasants in a land where the earth and the weather can be an enemy for most. But to the poor, of which he was a part, it could be a *killer*. He was placed by God in a village called Fontiveros in the Castile section of Spain. Here, the villagers lived simple, hard lives. John, along with his two brothers and widowed mother, were colder and hungrier than most, his mother unsuccessfully trying to eke out a meager living doing some weaving. With not even her husband's relatives willing to help, the little family had to move to Medina del Campo or starve. *Here*, the little band would know some relief; they would be able to find some work and therefore, some food.

John, the youngest son, found work in a hospital serving men suffering from tumors. This brought some money into the house and still enabled him to go to school. All the deprivation, he had known, physical and emotional, had not affected his will or his mind. Right from the beginning, he showed himself to be enthusiastic *and* brilliant.

John was extremely spiritual all his life. Therefore, it was not surprising for a bright, gifted young man like Juan de Yepes (St. John's birth name) to enter a religious order. He sought and knew he would receive *support* from other members in the *religious* community. The strict rule, under which they lived, appealed to him. The tradition of those who had gone before him, strengthened him; it offered him the *security* he needed, to choose the path *God* wanted him to take. He looked for the strictest religious order he could find.

The Carmelite Order was one of contemplation and meditation. The object of the *Carmelite life* was to meditate night and day on God's Law and His Word. The rule came from St. Albert in 1209. The Carmelite history dates back to the hermits on Mount Carmel in the Holy Land. Their houses were purposely found in places far removed from the distractions of the world, very often in the desert, in hermitages. They would practice long and severe fasts. Their life was spent *communing* with their Lord in contemplation, meditating on this King of all Who loved them. In a word, they were to live austerely, centering on the World *beyond*, and their Creator.

St. Albert, Patriarch of Jerusalem, had written a simple rule for the Carmelites at the request of its prior, St. Brocard, in 1209.

The rule was straight and to the point. It called for complete obedience to an elected superior; a separate dwelling for each hermit, with a common oratory; manual work for all; long fasts and complete abstinence from meat; and daily silence from Vespers until after Terce.[1] It required that each hermit live in or near his cell, meditating day and night on the law of the Lord and persevering in prayer, unless engaged in some legitimate occupation, such as work. While each order desired to have their own rules, they all followed one rule handed down by St. Benedict, *"Ora e lavora,"* Pray and Work. If you consider the time frame of St. Albert's rule for the Carmelites,[2] 1209, he might very well be included with St. Francis of Assisi and St. Dominic, as defenders of the Faith of the Thirteenth Century. His rule was accepted about the same time as Francis' and Dominic's. While he was never himself a Carmelite, he was definitely inspired by the Holy Spirit, and would definitely fall into the category of a Saint and Powerful Man of the Church.

But that's the way the Carmelite Order was when it was founded, under the guidance of St. Albert. This is what St. John thought he was joining, and most likely what St. Teresa was trying to instill in the Incarnation Convent in Avila, but this was the Sixteenth Century. The Carmelites of St. Teresa and St. John's time were being invaded by the *world*. Literally thousands of lay people trafficked in and out of their houses, affecting and infecting those within, with the world and its standards. The convents less resembled houses of prayer and more reflected opulent houses of the *world*.

Everyone loved St. John; John loved everybody, in particular, his family. Leaving them to enter into religious life was possibly the most difficult thing he ever did. The night he made his decision to leave, to start his new life in the Lord, he waited till the house was dark and quiet. Fearing his family would try to dissuade him, not knowing if he could resist them and the love he

---

[1] The third of seven canonical hours
[2] He was an Augustinian canon

felt for them, he left the only way he could, not even saying good-by. What did the young man feel, as he ran through the night? Was he sad at all he was leaving? Was he excited at all that was ahead?

Months passed quickly for John, as a novice. He found his life full, each day bringing new excitement and joy. Many hours flew by in the worship of God and the reading of the Word. He loved it all - the reciting of the solemn offices of the Church, the long passages they read of the Bible, the chanting of the solemn office of the Eucharist where and when God once again came to him, Body, Blood, Soul and Divinity.

Unlike much of our vision of contemplative life, contemplation is often through *action*, caring for the household of a convent. There are rooms to be cleaned, meals to be cooked, tables to be served, dishes to be washed, provisions to be gotten; all in all, hard work making the hours fly. St. John not yet fully professed, like novices before and after him, was always being tested. It is so important that the religious die to the ego, or as we say in the ministry the "*I*" this and the "*I*" that part of our life.

It is imperative that the *religious* understand, as in any relationship, the courtship and the attraction period does not last forever. The life is lived in the everyday saying of "*yes!*" In every matter requiring obedience St. John excelled, joyfully proclaiming his *fiat*, his act of faith each day. This would be a stronghold for him in later years when that "yes" would be so painful. After six months of the *novitiate*, he professed his final vows, donned the scapular of the fully confirmed Carmelite. His professor, the one who would nourish his mind and spirit, drew *crowds*. Through him, students discovered learning could be stimulating. The professor's lectures were simply stated, clear, yet balanced with humor. He was everything the young man from the little town in Medina, needed.

Was his professor too popular? Was his teaching too innovative? Whatever the case, the Inquisition was to rear its ugly head and he was arrested! Accused and maligned, threatened and tortured, repeating over and over again his loyalty to Spain and the Church, *finally*, he was found innocent!

This professor and poet would influence St. John and his writings during his formative years in the University, but the greatest impact on him would later come from a cloistered Carmelite nun, St. Teresa.

Four years of studying with the greatest minds, at the University of Salamanca, no longer held the young friar. Medicine, astronomy, law, philosophy, even theology no longer fulfilled him. He longed for a more intense life, a closer encounter with his Lord. A romantic, St. John had a yearning to be silent and know his God. He was not finding it with the Carmelites. He had challenged his community to a more severe life, more like that of the original rule. Convents were in dire need of reform. Could it be this young friar, striving toward living the strict Rule of St. Albert, was a threat to others in the community, reminding them of what they could be and were not? In an effort to break him, they bore down hard on him. *They scourged him!* Three times a week, St. John bared his shoulders, so the friar in charge could discipline him, for his own good, of course.

Did he gather strength as he was being chastised? Was he being asked to accompany Christ, following the path He had walked, that of humility? It was during one of these times when St. John was being beaten, that Our Lord Jesus appeared to him. St. John saw his Savior before him, suffering terribly. John saw the apparition of Jesus from above, as if he were looking down on Our Lord, watching as His Head fell, the neck straining to lift itself up, the legs, so weak, they bowed out.

St. John could envision the legions of Angels, positioned all around Jesus on the Cross, begging Him to allow them to come to His aid, to kill those who were torturing their God. Jesus did not allow anyone to help him. John could visualize the suffering His Lord endured. As John took *his* blows, in his mind's eye, could he see his Lord Who did not defend Himself? Was this his way of sharing the Lord's Passion with Him? Rather than flee from the pain, St. John embraced suffering, refusing every comfort. His peace came, not through *personal* satisfaction, but was sown by each new flower of sacrifice he could place in the basket he, like the little boy at Capernaum, could offer His Crucified Lord. In the quiet of his cell, he drew the Vision of Jesus as he saw it. It gave him courage at a time when he hung on to his vocation by his fingernails. He carried that image with him for the rest of his life. During his turbulent career, that Vision of Jesus, imbedded in his heart, gave him comfort and courage. They still have that drawing today at the Carmelite Convent of the Incarnation in Avila, Spain.

St. John's life was one long dark night of the soul because of his loyalty to, and belief in, the necessity of the work of St. Teresa of Avila. He was not political; he tried to stay out of the politics, his mentor, St. Teresa endured in her battle to do the Lord's Will. But the more he tried to avoid politics, the more he became involved in the politics of religious orders and reform movements. It haunted him the rest of his life.

St. John went on to work for the Lord, side by side with St. Teresa of Avila. Together, they accomplished the work of reforming the Carmelite Order of Spain of the Sixteenth Century. He was not appreciated for it; he was berated, imprisoned, beaten; his body was virtually destroyed. But no one could ever destroy his spirit. His writings are proof of that. We believe that throughout the entire dark night of the soul of his life, he had that little piece of paper on which he had drawn the Vision he had seen early in his life of his Crucified Lord. We believe he kept it tucked away in a safe place, for when he would need it for comfort and consolation. And as he gazed at the Image, and remembered the Vision, he must have said to himself, "Can I do less?"

St. Joseph of Cupertino
Levitates to the Cross

St. Joseph of Cupertino had a great devotion to the Passion of Our Lord Jesus. He would spend hours before the Crucified Christ, meditating on His Passion and death. He practiced this devotion with him throughout his entire life. His greatest Miracles came as a result of meditating before the Cross, or Our Lord Jesus in the Eucharist, and our Mother Mary.

Joseph's life was not an easy one. He was born in Cupertino, a tiny farming village near Lecce, at the heel of the boot of Italy. His father Felix was a carpenter, a very good one. But he could not satisfy his debts, and the creditors seized his home as part payment and then threatened poor Felix with imprisonment, to satisfy the rest. Without the possibility of help forthcoming, Felix fled to a holy place and asked for asylum.

Frances, pregnant and also running from the authorities, was unable to reach a friend's home before Baby Joseph made known his urgency to be born, and so she found shelter in a stable. Here, as with Jesus before him, Joseph would be born June 17th, 1603, with only farm animals as witnesses.

Joseph's mother raised him. She often took him to church. When he was eight, he made a little Altar at home, where he would recite the Rosary and Litanies to Blessed Mother and the Saints, day and night. His ecstasies began at that time. His life *more and more* became God and His Church. He fasted sometimes two or three days in a row, abstaining from food of any kind. As he practiced *more and more* austere forms of penance and mortification, he desired *more and more* to leave the world and unite himself with things above.

Although Joseph never felt worthy, evidently God did, as He went about executing His plan to make Joseph a priest. On June 19th, 1625, Joseph entered the novitiate in the Monastery in Grotella. The brothers of his Order ultimately came to recognize

Right:
*St. Joseph of Cupertino levitates.
In the 17 years he spent at the
Monastery of Grotella, Father Joseph
levitated over 70 times.
On the Feast of St. Francis, our flying
priest, vested for Mass, levitated up to the
pulpit, close to 6 feet from the ground
and remained there suspended, in an
attitude of prayer, his knees bent, his
arms outstretched like his Savior before
him on the Cross.*

Above:
*Shrine of St. Joseph of Cupertino at Osimo, Italy
The most spectacular Miracle of the Cross occurred when the friars of
the Monastery were erecting a Calvary. The middle Cross was over 36
feet high, and by far the heaviest of the three. Ten men could not lift the
Cross. Upon seeing their plight, St. Joseph flew 70 yards, scooped up
the Cross, as if lifting a feather, and planted it in its appointed spot.*

Joseph as a true man of holiness in their midst. Because of his obvious virtue, although not having the required education, he took his solemn vows and made his profession as a Franciscan.

Joseph is visited by a heavenly messenger

Joseph returned to the Monastery at Grotella after his ordination. Father Joseph's life, through his own design, became more and more austere, as he deprived himself of all eating utensils and all but one poor garment. Throwing himself before the Crucifix, he cried, *"Look upon me, Lord; I am divested of all things; Thou art my only good; I regard all else as a danger and ruin to my soul."* The Lord's response was to take away all *His* consolation from Father Joseph, plunging him into the *Dark Night of the Soul.*[1] His agony became so unbearable one day, he cried out in anguish, the cry of his Savior before him, *"My Lord, why hast Thou forsaken me?"* A religious appeared to Joseph, someone he had never seen before. He handed him a new habit. Upon donning it, suddenly Joseph was no longer alone; he could feel the presence of his heavenly companions. Who was this stranger? Was he an Angel? Father Joseph believed so.

Saint Joseph of Cupertino is called before the Inquisition

His call to the Inquisition in Naples came as no surprise to Father Joseph. Three years before he had told a brother he would be called to Naples. Shortly before Joseph was to leave, Jesus came to him as a Child, His clothes shabby and ripped, His little Body weighed down by an enormous Cross, forewarning His little priest of the Way of the Cross he was about to walk. Was the Lord strengthening him for the forthcoming trials and attacks, he would suffer? Father Joseph had a choice! He could join his pain and rejection to the agony, His Savior encountered as *He* walked to His final act of love which would bring about the salvation of the world; or like the Disciples, he could run

---

[1]Read more about the Dark Night of the Soul in the chapter on St. John of the Cross in Bob and Penny Lord's book, *"Saints and Other Powerful Men in the Church"*

away from the persecution.

Armed with the two edged sword, *"the armor of God,"* a peace-filled joyous friar appeared before the Sacred Commission. The members of the Inquisition questioned him for weeks. But at the end of intense inquiries, they found him without any stain of self-interest or guile. Although Joseph did not agree, always judging himself a worthless sinner and scoundrel, the Inquisitors all concurred, he was leading a virtuous life of piety. As if their findings were not enough, the Lord manifested His Majesty once again through Father Joseph. He was asked to offer Mass in their church. Upon raising the Host in consecration, Father Joseph levitated, oblivious of everyone around him, completely enraptured in ecstasy.

Father Joseph goes to Rome and then on to Assisi

No pain would compare with the *Dark Night of the Soul*, he would once again suffer as Jesus withdrew *His Love and comfort* from Father Joseph. No more ecstasies; no more encounters with his heavenly family. When he read the Word of God, he felt nothing! Praying the Divine Office had always enriched him and instilled courage in him; now he experienced nothing! But most painful of all, during the celebration of the Holy Mass, he felt dead! He felt alone! Father Joseph cried out to the Lord, but it seemed God was deaf to his pleas and blind to his sorrow.

After two years of silence, the Lord spoke to him and told him he would return to Assisi. His heavenly gifts returned; he was once again experiencing heavenly ecstasies.

St. Joseph of Cupertino and the Miracles of the Cross

There are many Miracles attributed to the intercession of St. Joseph of Cupertino. We could spend pages and pages bringing them to you.[2] But we want to focus on Miracles of the Cross.

The most spectacular Miracle of the Cross occurred when the

---

[2]Read more about St. Joseph of Cupertino in Bob and Penny Lord's book, *Visionaries, Mystics and Stigmatists*

friars of the Monastery were erecting a Calvary. There were statues of Our Lord Jesus, Mother Mary, Mary Magdalene, St. John the Beloved, and the three Crosses of the Passion, including the middle Cross that was to hold the *Image of Jesus*. It was over 36 feet high, and by far the heaviest of the three. Try as they may, ten men could not lift the Cross. Upon seeing their plight, Joseph flew 70 yards, scooped up the cross, as if lifting a feather, and planted it in its appointed spot.

St. Joseph carried his Crucifix with him wherever he went. The lame and the crippled walked after they kissed the Crucifix Joseph held out to them. During the plague, which claimed many lives, he blessed a poor soul burning up with fever with the Cross. He made the Sign of the Cross on the sick man's forehead; the fever immediately dropped, and his temperature returned to normal. There are accounts of St. Joseph touching the bodies of dead people with the Cross, making the Sign of the Cross, and the dead were brought back to life.

An arrogant nobleman contemptuously challenged Fr. Joseph's ability to heal: *"Impious hypocrite, it is not you, but the religious habit you wear that I respect and because of it, I trust that if you make the Sign of the Cross on my wound, and touch me with your Holy Cross, it will heal."* Cheerfully, Joseph humbly agreed with the nobleman that what he said was absolutely true and wise. Then he did exactly what the nobleman said he would do, whereupon the wound was completely healed.

St. Joseph levitates

In the 17 years he spent at the Monastery of Grotella, Father Joseph levitated over 70 times. On the Feast of St. Francis, our flying priest, vested for Mass, levitated up to the pulpit, close to 6 feet from the ground and remained there suspended, in an attitude of prayer, his knees bent, his arms outstretched like his Savior before him on the Cross.

On Holy Thursday evening, Father Joseph was praying with the other friars of his Order before Our Lord Jesus, Who was reposing in the Tabernacle, His Holy Sepulcher, high above the main Altar. Overcome with the sad reality that His Lord would suffer the ongoing agony of Gethsemane that evening and that of His Passion on the Cross the next day, and feeling the terrible emptiness in the church without His Presence until Easter Sunday, Joseph could no longer contain his grief and levitated, soaring high up to the ciborium which contained His Lord.

Father Joseph foretells his death

His passion for his Savior grew, as the days moved closer and closer to the end of his life. He said,

"I desire to be dissolved and to be with Christ."

After he received his last Kiss from his Savior, Holy Communion, and then Extreme Unction,[3] he sighed: *"Oh what sweetness of paradise."* He asked that the Profession of Faith be recited; and then asked pardon of his brother friars. He implored them to bury his body in a secluded spot.

Before he drew his last breath, he cried out, *"Take this heart, burn and rend this heart, my Jesus."* Our Saint died at midnight, September 18, 1663, at the age of sixty.

Miracles kept happening through the intercession of Joseph of Cupertino, so much so that the Conventuals were joined by bishops and members of royalty entreating the Pope to open the Cause for Canonization.

The Pope accepted the Sacred Congregation's findings and approved the three Miracles credited to him, and Joseph of Cupertino went from the ranks of the Church Militant,[4] to the Church Suffering,[5] to the Church Triumphant,[6] as Saint Joseph of Cupertino was entered into the Company of Saints in Heaven, on July 16, 1767.

---

[3]Last Rites of the Church - Today it is called the Sacrament of the Blessing of the Sick.
[4]Church Militant - we, the Body of Christ on earth
[5]Church Suffering - the Souls in Purgatory
[6]Church Triumphant - The Communion of Saints

Julian of Norwich
Longed to feel the Passion of the Cross

"I saw two persons in bodily likeness, that is to say a lord and a servant; and with that God gave me spiritual understanding. The lord sits in state in rest and in peace. The servant stands before his lord, respectively, ready to do his lord's will. The lord looks on his servant very lovingly and sweetly and mildly. He sends him to a certain place to do his will. Not only does the servant go, but he dashes off and runs at great speed, loving to do his lord's will. And soon he falls into a well and is greatly injured; and then he groans and moans and tosses about and writhes, but he cannot rise or help himself in any way. And of all this, the greatest hurt, which I saw in him was lack of consolation; for he could not turn his face to look at his loving lord, who was very close to him, in whom is all consolation; but like a man who was for the first time extremely feeble and foolish, he paid heed to his feelings and his continuing distress.

"I looked carefully to know if I could detect any fault in him, or if the lord would impute to him any kind of blame, and truly none was seen, for the only cause of his falling was his good will and his great desire. And in spirit he was as prompt and as good as he was when he stood before his lord, ready to do his will. And all this time his loving lord looks on him most tenderly...with great compassion and pity."[1]

Lady Julian (as she was sometimes called) was a Visionary and Mystic born into the Fourteenth Century. Aside from her autobiography, there is little known about this extraordinary woman. Almost all our information comes from her writings, called *"Showings"* and her biography by Margery Kempe -

---

[1]from *"Showings"*, Long Text, chap. 51, in book by Joan M. Nuth, *God's Lovers in an Age of Anxiety*

*Lady Julian of Norwich
was a Visionary and Mystic born
in the Fourteenth Century.
She later revealed in her writings
that her
Visions shared the different kinds
of suffering Our Lord endured
during His Passion and
walk to the Cross.*

She had prayed to God for three gifts or graces: (1) that He would give her a deeper awareness of Christ's suffering, (2) that He would grant her an illness so critical it would bring her close to death, and (3) give her three wounds, of "contrition," of "compassion," and of "longing towards God."

another English Mystic. Further substantiation that she existed in that period comes from records of wills leaving money to a recluse called Julian of Norwich dating back to the Fifteenth Century, when she died. From her *Showings*, we learn that Julian was born in 1342, and lived to be at least seventy years old, spending most of her life as a hermit or recluse.

When she was thirty years old, she was struck down, completely debilitated by an illness that in fact threatened her life. By the fourth day, she was so far gone, they called in a Priest to administer the Last Rites. She held on, but the seventeenth day the doctors gave everyone the sad news that she was fading quickly. She couldn't move or speak; she just kept her eyes on Jesus Crucified on the cross in front of her. Then the morning of May 8th or 13th, all her pains left her and she had her first fifteen *Showings* which terminated in a sixteenth *showing* the following evening.

She later revealed in her writings that her Visions or *Showings* shared the different kinds of suffering Our Lord endured during His Passion and walk to the Cross. No sooner did she have her desire to share in His *pain-filled* Passion fulfilled, than she was filled with an awesome peace and joy, unlike anything she had ever experienced. But this was to be just a foretaste of the true reality. It would not be till much later that she would realize the *full price* Our Lord paid for our salvation.

It was at that point, she began her life as a recluse in a hermitage near the Rectory.

When Julian writes of her *"Showings'* she says that before she had received any mystical experiences, she had prayed to God for three gifts or graces: (1) that He would give her a deeper awareness of Christ's suffering, (2) that he would grant her an illness so critical it would bring her close to death; and in so doing, take away all desire for earthly things, and (3) give her three wounds, of *"contrition,"* of *"compassion,"* and of *"longing towards God."* Although zeal for her first two wishes were to eventually fade over a period of time, she never lost her *longing towards God,* till the day she died.

That He would give her a deeper awareness of Christ's sorrowful suffering, Julian writes:

"I wished that I had been at that time with Magdalene and with the others who were Christ's lovers, so that I might have seen with my own eyes the Passion which Our Lord suffered for me...Therefore I desired a bodily sight, in which I might have more knowledge of Our Savior's bodily pains, and of the compassion of Our Lady and of all His true lovers who were living at the time and saw His pains, for if I would have been one of them and suffered with them...I wished afterwards, because of that revelation, to have truer (mind) of Christ's Passion."

As she got older, Julian began to give less importance to her desire for illness and Visions. But as she lay helpless and in excruciating pain, she came to realize that the Lord had answered her prayers sending her this affliction. Upon meditating, she came to the realization that by praying for the grace of compassion, she perhaps would be able to unite her suffering with that of her Savior. She was so overjoyed! Then suddenly, to her amazement she had a vision of the Crucified Christ. The Priest had placed a Crucifix in her sickroom, and as Julian looked at it, she writes,

"Suddenly I saw the red blood trickling down from under the Crown, all hot, flowing freely and copiously, a living stream, just as it seemed to me that it was at the time when the Crown of Thorns was thrust down upon His Blessed Head. Just so did He, both God and Man, suffer for me...I was greatly astonished by this wonder and marvel, that He would so humbly be with a sinful creature living in this wretched flesh, I accepted it that at that time Our Lord Jesus wanted, out of His courteous love, to show me comfort before my temptations began; for it seemed to me that I might well be tempted by devils, by God's permission and with His protection, before I died."

Julian was relieved of her agonizing pain. She writes,
"And suddenly...all my pain was taken from me and I was sound...as ever I was before." Through this vision, she was made to realize how very much God loved her, that she was never alone and most importantly she had no need to fear eternal damnation. She writes:

"With this sight of His Blessed Passion, with the Divinity...I knew well that this was strength enough for me, yes, and for all living creatures who were to be saved, against all the devils of hell and against all their spiritual enemies."

It would not be until fifteen more years passed that she would hear in a locution:

"Would you learn the meaning of the vision revealed to you? Learn it well; love was His meaning. Who showed it to you? Love! What showed it to you? Love! Why did He show it to you? For love! Stay steadfast in your resolve to know more and you shall learn more of the same. But understand that you will never know the total suffering Our Lord."[2]

In another part of her autobiography she writes of having had inner locutions - Our Lord teaching her, for twenty years! Now something to remember, when she received her Visions and locutions, she was totally illiterate, reminiscent of Saint Catherine of Siena. Like the Saints before her and after, she became well-known and received visitors from every walk of life. As a contemplative, she did not venture out of her hermitage, so laity, religious, and even strangers hearing about her came to her.

Although her Visions began with the Crucified Lord, as all that is holy leads to the truth, it invariably ended in a deeper walk with the Holy Trinity: Father, Son and Holy Spirit. Through her Visions, she grows into the consciousness of *God in His Three Persons,* not only the God-Man Jesus but the other Two Persons of the Trinity suffering out of love for all humanity. She writes:

---

[2] cf. The Lord speaking to Julian in an inner locution

"..I saw this (bodily) sight (of the Head Bleeding). Our Lord showed me a spiritual sight of His familiar Love...He showed me something small, no bigger than a hazelnut, lying in the palm of my hand, and I perceived that it was as round as a ball. I looked at it and thought: What can this be? And I was given this general answer: It is everything which is made. I was amazed that it could last, for I thought that it was so little that it could suddenly fall into nothing. And I was answered in my understanding: It lasts and always will, because God loves it; and thus everything has being through the Love of God."

She goes on:

"In this little thing I saw three properties. The first is this, that God made it; the second is that He loves it; the third is that God preserves it. But what is that to me? It is that God is the Creator and the Lover and the Protector (the Holy Trinity)."

Her book has been called one of the most tender love stories of the Divine. Considering the love Our Lord has for us that He would become His own creation and be rejected, maligned, tortured and finally crucified by those He came to save, when she lapsed and committed a sin (as all the Saints confessed), she walked with confidence in the fact, He had allowed her to do so, and therefore would not hold it against her.

As even in her day, the world was a sorry place in need of hope, Julian shared the following message of hope and consolation given to her by the Lord, when she was at a low point in her life, a word which is as relevant today as it was then:

"I can make all things well. I will make all things well. I shall make all things well; and you shall see yourself that all manner of things shall be well."[3]

---

[3] ibid.

St. Louis Marie de Montfort
Bearer of the Cross

In the Marian Year 1987, in his Encyclical, *"Mother of the Redeemer"* Pope John Paul II recommended to the faithful, the writings of Louis Marie de Montfort.

Louis came from a very pious, very Catholic family. From the time he was a youth, he had a great devotion to Our Lady. All his life, she was his ideal. He prayed for her intercession before every major decision he made. When the determination was made to become a priest, a business acquaintance of his father's offered to pay his way to study at the Seminary of St. Sulpice in Paris.

Louis experiences many crosses in Paris

St. Sulpice was located on the Rive Gauche, the Left Bank, the Bohemian section, most likely even at that time. But he concentrated his time and efforts on the courses afforded him in these halls of learning. As he progressed in his studies, using Sacred Scripture as his basis, his mission manifested itself to him. He was to be an *itinerant preacher*, going from village to village proclaiming the Good News of Jesus. He wanted in effect to do as Jesus had done before him. Where he would carry on his ministry would be up to the Lord to decide.

Louis experienced many crosses during that time with the Sulpicians in Paris. But had he known in advance, he would have welcomed them anyway. He had learned to embrace the Cross passionately. And to accommodate him, God sent him *heavy* crosses, because He loved Louis so much.

After eight years in Paris, under extreme conditions, Louis Marie de Montfort was ordained on June 5, 1700, in the Church of St. Sulpice on the left bank of Paris. He celebrated his first Mass at the Chapel of Our Lady which had been such a special haven for him during his time at the Seminary. Although they ordained him, they did not give him his faculties as Preacher and Confessor. He accepted this as another cross from the Lord.

Above:
*Wax image of Saint Louis Marie de
Montfort in St. Laurent-sur-Sèvre
He died clutching his Crucifix, which
had been blessed by the Pope.*

Above:
*St. Louis Marie de Montfort
Bearer of the Cross*

Above:
*The Shrine of Calvary in Pontchateau, France
Here St. Louis Marie de Montfort built a replica of the Way of the Cross
and Golgotha the place of the Crucifixion.
This Shrine was torn down in 1710, rebuilt in 1747,
rebuilt in 1774, and again in 1854.*

Finally, he was given all his faculties, to hear confessions, as well as to preach.

Fr. Louis Marie *walks* to Rome!

Fr. Louis Marie knew what he wanted to do - preach missions. If he was not able to do that in Poitiers, he would ask the Pope where he should preach his missions, or what he should do. On St. Louis Marie de Montfort's way to Rome, he made a detour to the Holy House of Loreto. He spent time there with our Lady and the Angels, communicating with them. He may have gone to the Pope for his instructions, but we believe he got most of them right there in the Holy House of Loreto. Strengthened by the love of our Lady, his bloody feet bathed in the light of her love, Louis gathered enough strength to continue his journey to Rome. The Lord put a priest in his path, who just happened to be the *Pope's confessor,* and in June, 1706, Fr. Louis Marie de Montfort found himself in a special audience with Pope Clement XI. Louis talked about his ongoing wish to go to Canada to the missions of Ontario or Quebec and minister to the natives of North America. We believe the interview ended with a commitment to submit himself to whatever the Prince of the Apostles felt he should do.

The Pope answered immediately, without hesitation: *"Go back to France, and to work. It is a field big enough for your zeal. Work against Jansenism.*[1] *Teach the children their catechism. Teach all Christians to renew the promises they made, by themselves or through their godparents in Baptism."*

St. Louis went back to France a determined man. He was not going to let anyone stop him in his mission; after all it had been given to him especially by His Holiness, Pope Clement XI. The Pope had given St. Louis Marie the title *"Apostolic Missionary,"* and Louis Marie was taking it seriously. The Pope had blessed

---

[1] A heresy which taught that man was unable to resist temptation and denied the doctrine that Christ died for all men. It spawned an elitist society of "predestined saints." They also taught that only persons with perfect contrition could receive the Sacraments of Penance and the Eucharist.

Louis Marie's **Crucifix**, at which time he placed it on top of his staff to carry with him everywhere he went. He also gave Louis Marie the power to grant a Plenary Indulgence to anyone who would kiss the Blessed Crucifix on his or her deathbed. The only condition was that they repent of their sins, and call out in reverence - the names of Jesus and Mary.

The Shrine of Calvary in Pontchâteau

In 1709, St. Louis went to a little town called Pontchâteau, between Nantes and Redon. Louis Marie had always wanted to build a Calvary, in honor of Our Lord Jesus, Mother Mary and the other members of His Passion. After giving a mission in this town, he received an inspiration from the Holy Spirit. He shared his plan with the people at the mission who became very enthused. They chose a spot, a distance from the town and began to dig. In short order, it was determined this was not the right spot. So he brought everyone into the Chapel to pray for guidance from Our Lady.

When they went back outside, they saw two white doves come down out of the sky, and settle on the mound which had already been dug out. The doves took dirt into their mouths, and flew off. They did this quite a few times. Louis Marie prayed all the while this was happening. Eventually he realized that the doves were trying to bring them to a place. Louis Marie and the workers followed the doves to where they landed, some distance from where they had been. There they found a *"hive-shaped"* mound, on the highest point of the area. From this vantage point, a Calvary could be built and the crosses seen from miles around. They began to work.

Little by little, old-timers from the town came to the site. They shared a story which had happened some thirty six years before, whose meaning they had never been able to figure out. The people testified that they had seen **crosses** coming down from the sky, during the daytime with banners flying from them. The **crosses** hovered over this spot and stayed there for a time. Then there were very loud noises which frightened animals for miles around. This was followed by singing, Angelic singing, as if floating down from Heaven to earth. They said the date this happened was *January 31, 1673, the day St. Louis Marie Grignion de Montfort was born.*

At first, just the people of Pontchâteau took part in the project. But soon people from all over the district came with tools, ready to build Calvary. Statues of all the participants of the Passion, Our Lord Jesus, Our Lady of Sorrows, St. John the beloved, and St. Mary Magdalene were carved at the same time the mountain was being built. The statues were placed in the grotto which had been formed by the digging, for safekeeping. Every evening, after the workers were finished digging, they went down to the grotto and prayed to Our Lord Jesus and the other members of the Passion.

The main tree for Calvary was cut from a neighboring village. It took twenty-four oxen to bring it to the mountain. The trees of the two thieves were placed on either side of it, one on the right and one on the left. One hundred and fifty fir trees were planted for the Hail Marys, and fifteen cypresses for the Our Fathers. It was a most beautiful tribute to our Heavenly Family.

But as had plagued Louis all his life, the powers of evil were ready to destroy what had been built in honor of God. There was a war with England going on. Word got out that all this digging was going on. Those who hated the Church and especially St. Louis Marie de Montfort complained to the authorities: *Le Calvaire* (The Calvary) was in Brittany, which was right across the English Channel from England; if the English should attack, the Calvary would make a perfect fort to use against the French. The project had taken over a year. The solemn blessing was to take place on September 14, 1710, Feast of the Triumph of the Cross. A few days before the blessing, the Bishop was pressured by a small group of very vocal, special interests with an agenda, and orders were given to Fr. Louis Marie and the people of Pontchâteau to *tear down* the monument built to Our Lord Jesus.

The words of Pope Clement XI came rushing back into the

mind of this heartbroken priest, *"And always be obedient to the Bishop of the diocese."* The people of Pontchâteau and the surrounding villages tore down *Le Calvaire* (Calvary), the Shrine to the Crucifixion of Our Lord Jesus. Louis Marie was to learn again, *God Alone!* Strangely enough, however, that's not the end of the story. *Le Calvaire* was rebuilt *again* in 1747. Then the crosses had to be replaced *again* in 1774, after they had collapsed. And then *again* they were replaced in 1785. The Reign of Terror which spread throughout France tore down the crosses *once again.* But, the Church will never stay down, and after the French Revolution a *new* Calvary was built on the same site. Bronze crosses were erected in 1854, the same year that the Dogma of the Immaculate Conception was proclaimed. Pilgrimages began in 1873.

Le Calvaire cannot be wiped from this countryside, no more than His Death and Resurrection. The crosses loom high in the sky, a testimony of love and hope for the world.

Louis Marie de Montfort preaches his last mission

Fr. Louis' last mission was in St. Laurent-sur-Sèvre. It began on April 5, 1716. He took to his bed. One of his priests from the Company of Mary, later to be called the Montfort Fathers, gave him the Last Rites. Then Fr. Louis Marie made out his will.

Father Louis Marie focused his attention on his Crucifix, that great Crucifix which had been blessed by the Pope when he had been given the mandate and the title *Apostolic Missionary*, and a statue of Our Lady. These had been his weapons as he went forth to conquer evil and do good. He kept saying, *"Jesus and Mary."* He weakly began to sing the first verse of a hymn he had composed:

On, on, dear friends, to Paradise,
God's Paradise on high!
Whatever be our gain on earth,
'Tis surer gain to die!

His voice trailed off into a coma. After some time, he woke abruptly and cried out, *"Your attacks are quite useless; Jesus and Mary are with me; I have finished my course, I shall never sin again!"*

On September 7, 1838, one hundred and twenty two years after the death of Fr. Louis, Pope Gregory XVI declared him *Venerable*, the first step towards canonization.

His greatest crosses were given to him in the name of obedience. He embraced these crosses and carried them with joy.

We leave you St. Louis Marie de Montfort's prophetic words of the last days, all of which were taken from **True Devotion to Mary:**

"....towards the end of the world, ...Almighty God and His holy Mother are to raise up Saints who will surpass in holiness most other Saints as much as the cedars of Lebanon tower above little shrubs."

"These great souls filled with grace and zeal will be chosen to oppose the enemies of God who are raging on all sides. They will be exceptionally devoted to the Blessed Virgin. Illumined by her light, strengthened by her spirit, supported by her arms, sheltered under her protection, they will fight with one hand and build with the other. With one hand they will give battle, overthrowing and crushing heretics and their heresies, schismatics and their schisms, idolaters and their idolatries, sinners and their wickedness. With the other hand they will build the temple of the true Solomon and the mystical city of God, namely, the Blessed Virgin..."

"They will be like thunderclouds flying through the air at the slightest breath of the Holy Spirit. Attached to nothing, surprised at nothing, they will shower down the rain of God's Word and of eternal life. They will thunder against sin; they will storm against the world; they will strike down the devil and his followers and for life and for death, they will pierce through and through with the two-edged sword of God's Word all those against whom they are sent by

Almighty God."

"They will be true apostles of the latter times to whom the Lord of Hosts will give eloquence and strength to work wonders and carry off glorious spoils from His enemies. They will sleep without gold or silver and, more important still, without concern in the midst of other priests, ecclesiastics and clerics.   Yet they will have the silver wings of the dove enabling them to go wherever the Holy Spirit calls them, filled as they are, with the resolve to seek the glory of God and the salvation of souls. Wherever they preach, they will leave behind them nothing but the gold of love, which is the fulfillment of the whole law."

"They will have the two-edged sword of the Word of God in their mouths and the bloodstained standard of the Cross on their shoulders. They will carry the Crucifix in their right hand and the rosary in their left, and the holy Names of Jesus and Mary on their heart. [2]

---

[2]To read more on St. Louis Marie de Montfort, please read Bob and Penny Lord's book, Visionaries, Mystics and Stigmatists

Montagna Spaccata
The Mountain that Split

*"Now from the sixth hour there was darkness over all
the land until the ninth hour. And about the ninth hour
Jesus cried with a loud voice, `Eli, Eli, lema sabachthani,'
that is `My God, my God why hast Thou forsaken me?'
And some of the bystanders hearing it said, `This man is
calling Elijah.' And one of them at once ran and took a
sponge, filled it with vinegar, and put it on a reed, and
gave it to Him to drink. But the others said, `Wait, let us
see whether Elijah will come to save Him.' And Jesus cried
again with a loud voice and yielded up His Spirit.*

*"And behold the curtain of the temple was torn in two,
from top to bottom; and the earth shook, and the rocks
were split..."*[1]

The curtain of the temple was torn in two; the earth shook
and the rocks split! Bob has always said that the Angels, who
had to stand by, helplessly, because they were obedient to the
Father's Will, when their Lord and King suffered cruel
punishment and died on the Cross, they bellowed out such an
agonizing shout, it reached to the ends of the earth; the curtain of
the temple tore and the earth trembled and the mountains shook.
There were reports of earthquakes and mountains splitting all
over the world. In this book, we are going to tell you of two such
occurrences. One happened in Gaeta, Italy, where pilgrims flock
by the thousands to venerate our Lord on this Split Mountain, till
today. It is widely believed that the mountain split, the moment
Jesus died on the Cross in Calvary, thousands of miles off in the
Holy Land.

Does this boggle your mind? Is this too hard to accept?
Well hundreds of years ago, at the time the Saracens were
overrunning most of Europe, a Turkish pirate landed in Gaeta.

---

[1]Mt 27:45-51

Above Left: ***The Split Mountain where St. Philp Neri came and prayed and venerated the Crucifix*** (Above Right) ***in the Chapel located there***

Above:
A Turk came to visit the Montagna Spaccata or the Split Mountain and said he did not believe this mountain split at the time of the death of Jesus. He touched the rock wall of the mountain and his hand penetrated the solid rock, leaving his hand print.

When the locals warned him, sharing with him what had caused the mountain to split, and that since then the Lord has protected them and answered their prayers, he just scoffed, laughing disdainfully at their words. He placed his hands on the cave's stone and as if he were the devil himself, the stone melted under his touch and left an imprint of his hand, which is there till today. Now we have seen this with our own eyes, and you have the choice to believe or scoff at the idea of a man's hand making an imprint on a stone mountain, just as you can ridicule mountains all over the world splitting at the time of Jesus giving up His Spirit to the Father, although it is in Holy Scripture; but for me and mine we choose to believe.

Many Saints have prayed before the Crucifix at the *Montagna Spaccata.* One such Saint was Philip Neri on whom this place had a profound spiritual effect.

The Sixteenth Century was a time of no easy answers or quick fixes. Preachers were stemming from every hamlet, small and large, calling people to repent! And that was good, but they did it at the cost of unity and peace, supplanting the decadent past with a divided future. The Renaissance brought about a Luther and a Calvin, the pendulum swinging from the extreme left, to what was being touted as the extreme right. One of the big problems was that everyone became a lone ranger, teaching his own brand of religion.

What would stem the tide of promiscuity that threatened to flood Rome and then all of the papal states? Place a powerful apostle right smack into the womb of the Renaissance. So, in the year 1515, as a raging storm ushered in a loud tempest of dissent in the north,[2] in the haughty city of Florence a soft breeze, carrying the hope of the Church, introduced Philip Neri, future Saint and Apostle of Rome. God planted this true contradiction in his time, in the Province of Tuscany, a land of the proud, willful and insolent, to a family of the nobility, who although righteous and good, were far from spiritual; their god, as with the

---

[2]Germany

rest of the aristocracy, was the god of convenience and luxury. His father and Philip's mother were born into two of the wealthiest families in Tuscany.

From the time he was five years old, *"Pippo Buono"* ("good little Phil") was obedient, never willfully causing his parents any problems. His beloved mother died when Phil was very young, but the Lord sent him a very loving step-mother to care for him and his sisters. Phil's life of holiness, visiting the churches, praying the Psalms and etc. was to be interrupted when he reached eighteen years of age. It was decided that Phil would go to his uncle, where he would train him for the business he would one day inherit.

Phil left for his uncle and Germano (near Monte Cassino). After arriving, he soon realized his old life was over. He missed home and the time he had to meditate on the Lord and His Passion. There was little time and less opportunity for prayer. But Phil would finish his studies quickly and run off to a mountain near Monte Cassino called *"Split Mountain."* He would go there to pray and attend Mass. He would pray before the crucifix, as well as before a beautiful statue of the Blessed Mother. She appeared to him one day, told him he was to go to Rome, and his vocation was sealed!

He arrived in Rome. Once situated, he often spent hours praying outside locked churches, deep into the night, kneeling on the stone steps; or in the catacombs. In the Catacombs of St. Sebastian, the evening of the vigil of Pentecost, as Philip prayed for the Holy Spirit to descend upon him and fill him with His Spirit, he received the Holy Spirit in the form of huge ball of fire, soaring toward him. The ball of fire entered his mouth, traveled down to his heart, and finally rested there for the rest of his life. His heart was so on fire, he was filled with such passion, such ecstasy, he pleaded, *"Stop Lord! I cannot take anymore. Anymore and I will die!"* This fire would remain with him the rest of his days, from age twenty to eighty - sixty years! His heart became so enlarged, as a result his two ribs broke.

When he meditated on the Lord and His Sacrifice for us, his heart would beat so loudly, it sounded like the rumbling of an earthquake; for this reason, they dubbed him *Saint of the Earthquake*. They said that his heartbeat could be heard all the way to St. Peter's, about two miles away.

Those who knew him best, his first biographers, Cardinal Baronius and Galloni, said that the heart was so affected by *good Phil's* ecstasies, the third and fourth ribs on the left side broke to accommodate the size of the heart enlarging and decreasing with each ecstasy. Not only this but the ribs had to make room for the aftermath, resulting from the acute thumping, pounding, throbbing, palpitations of the heart and the effect it had on the other organs in his chest. [All this phenomenon was affirmed by doctors and members of the Church after Philip Neri died.]

St. Philip had a deep devotion to Jesus Crucified. As a young man he could not pray in front of Jesus hanging on the Crucifix before him, without grieving passionately, as if he were there at Golgotha and Jesus was breathing His last. At these times, especially before the Crucifix at Montagna Spaccata, he would get completely lost in the Passion of Our Lord Jesus.

When he became a Priest, he was never too sick to celebrate the ongoing *Sacrifice of the Cross every day.* He united himself so deeply with the Lord, and His last hours on the Cross, that at the moment of elevation, he would levitate, suspended over the altar for more than two hours. For this reason, toward the end of his life, in order to not attract attention to himself, he celebrated Mass privately in a little chapel adjacent to his room. His first biographer said he came upon St. Philip many times, six feet from the floor while saying the Mass.

Once, during the celebration of the Mass, he begged Jesus to give him the gift of patience; he heard an inner voice say, *"You'll have it; the road to Heaven is through the Cross."* Father Philip Neri was to know persecution; but as *The road to Heaven was through the Cross,* he bore it all with humility and patience.[3]

---

[3]excerpt from Bob and Penny Lord's book: *Defenders of the Faith*

Left:
***Statue of
Saint Nicholas of Tolentino***
Below:
***Jesus comes down off the
Cross and embraces a statue
of St. Nicholas of Tolentino.
Just as a procession came to
the front of a hospital, the
Crucifix approached the
statue of St. Nicholas. Our
Lord Jesus on the Cross
came to life. He moved His
Body towards the statue of St.
Nicholas and embraced him
with all His might.***

Jesus comes off the Cross to embrace St. Nicholas of Tolentino

St. Nicholas of Tolentino embraced the Poor Souls in Purgatory. His major ministry was to the Poor Souls. Because of him, every day Mass is celebrated for the Poor Souls in the Basilica of St. Nicholas.

Even his birth had miraculous overtones to it. His elderly parents had not been able to bear a child. Late in life, they made a pilgrimage to Bari, petitioning Saint Nicholas of Bari to intercede with the Lord that they might bring a child into the world, never suspecting the impact that child would have on the history of the Church. A boy was born and his parents named him after Saint Nicholas of Bari in thanksgiving. He was the gift of their golden years. They offered him back to the Lord, as his mother committed him to God at his baptism. Parents, having a problem conceiving, often turn to St. Nicholas of Tolentino, Patron Saint of difficult births because of his miraculous birth.

He entered the Augustinian community while still a child, and before he was eighteen, he joined the community as a brother. His first task was as *doorkeeper* at the monastery. The Lord had a plan for Nicholas, and that was to eventually bring his ministry to Tolentino. There, he would spend the rest of his days, evangelizing to everyone and anyone he could.

It was during this time, his early days in the Augustinian community, while being doorkeeper, that we hear of Nicholas' first miracle. A child came to the door with his parents. It was obvious he suffered a serious physical malady. Nicholas put his hand on the child's head and said, *"The good God will heal you."* The afflicted child was immediately healed.

There are many gifts for which St. Nicholas of Tolentino is best known. One is his great devotion to the Poor Souls in Purgatory. When his superiors encouraged him to enter the seminary in preparation for the priesthood, he hesitated. He wanted nothing to take away from his prayer time for the Poor

Souls. It wasn't until he was convinced that the greatest prayer he could pray for those suffering in Purgatory was the *Sacrifice of the Mass*, and that he could do best as a priest of God, that he finally consented to enter the seminary. He was ordained a priest in the order of St. Augustine.

He remained a man of prayer, praying day and night for the Poor Souls in Purgatory, sometimes as much as six to eight hours a night. But his devotion to those in Purgatory had to take a back seat to his vow of obedience.

One evening, while he was in prayer, a friar who had recently passed away, Pellegrino of Osimo, appeared to Nicholas. It was all too obvious from the expression on his face that Pellegrino was in agony. He mournfully shared with Nicholas that he was in the pits of Purgatory, suffering the most excruciating pain. He knew of Nicholas' devotion to the Poor Souls in Purgatory, and so he pleaded with his old friend to offer Mass, not only for himself, but for the many other souls who had asked him to implore the aid of Nicholas. Nicholas immediately consented. *Then* he remembered that he was under obedience to offer the conventual Mass of the Order for the next week.

Pellegrino brought Nicholas into the pits of Purgatory, so that he could see first-hand, the suffering of all those who had asked for his intercession. Before him were a multitude of souls of all ages and conditions, experiencing terrible torment. Pellegrino turned to Nicholas and said,

"Behold the state of those who sent me to you. Since you are agreeable in the sight of God, we have confidence that He will refuse nothing to the oblation of the Sacrifice offered by you,[1] and that His Divine Mercy will deliver us."

Nicholas could not hold back the tears. He went into prayer, after which he went to his superior and asked permission to pray *the Mass for the Dead*. When he shared his Vision, and the agonizing condition of the souls who had asked for his help, the superior, too, broke down into tears. He gave Nicholas a special

---

[1] when the priest consecrates the host during the Sacrifice of the Mass

dispensation from praying the conventual Mass for that next week, and granted him permission to dedicate his Masses as well as all his prayers, toward the deliverance of the Poor Souls from Purgatory. Nicholas celebrated those Masses *passionately* as (and with) the *Victim Priest*[2] before him, the One Who came that no one would have to suffer the pains of eternal damnation.

At the end of a week, Pellegrino of Osimo appeared to Nicholas again, only this time he was not in agonizing pain. He had been released from Purgatory, and was on his way to Heaven. The other souls were in the same way, clad in white garments and enveloped with a bright, heavenly light. They called him their liberator, and as they rose up to Heaven, they chanted the prayer,

"Thou has saved us from them that afflict us, and thou has put them to shame that hate us. "[3]

There were many instances of Nicholas' intercession for the Poor Souls in Purgatory. It became one of the greatest goals of his vocation, to help as many souls be released from Purgatory as he possibly could.

These are some of the things we know about St. Nicholas of Tolentino. But there are so many miracles, so many Marian apparitions our Saint experienced, so many cures and conversions which took place through his intercessions, it remains extraordinary that all these gifts would be given to one person. One extraordinary experience had to do with the Holy House of Loreto. It is believed that because of his sanctity, he was chosen by Heaven to be the representative of the area of Piceno, to be the first to welcome the Holy House of Loreto, and also the first to visit it.

This extremely exciting apparition or dream or Vision which our Saint had, took place in a little town in the Marches region of Italy, called Valdichienti. It was late at night on the tenth of

---

[2]Jesus Christ on the Cross offering Himself to the Father for the Redemption of the world

[3]Psalm 43

December, 1294, about 11 years before our Saint died. He was having difficulty trying to go to sleep. He had been awake for many hours in deep prayer. Now, he wanted to get some rest before it was time for him to get up. But there were no dreams for St. Nicholas that night. However, the Vision which he received actually seemed more like a dream than anything he had ever experienced. He reported that he felt as if he was dreaming, but he was wide awake! He spoke of having a great feeling of anticipation, of expectation, but of what, he did not know.

He heard the bells of all the chapels and churches in the little town ring in unison. He jumped up from his mat and ran to the window. There was a great light in the sky over the Adriatic Sea. He thought he could make out the Image of Angels surrounding the great light. But he didn't know what the Image meant. But one of the brothers in the house was given a locution. He told St. Nicholas, *"The meaning of the lights and all the bells are as follows: The House in which the Word was made Flesh has come in our midst and there will be a fountain of graces, miracles and blessings with it."* What St. Nicholas did not realize at that moment, but would soon become aware, was that the Holy House of Loreto was making Its voyage across the Adriatic Sea from Tersatto, Yugoslavia, to Italy, where it would rest, and with it would come many blessings, miracles and graces, as the brother had described to St. Nicholas as a result of his inner locution.

But there is another thing for which St. Nicholas of Tolentino is famous, and that is the bread of St. Nicholas. The tradition began when Nicholas was quite ill and beginning to show the ravages of old age; he was so sick and so debilitated, he was about to die. His superiors asked him to eat a little meat and some nourishing foods. After all, they pleaded, they needed him, they and the community *and his Souls in Purgatory*! He wanted to obey his superiors, but he also knew the power of fasting toward moving God's Heart. So he prayed to Our Lady. Now, we know how much she loves her priests, her favorite sons, especially ones like Nicholas of Tolentino. Mother Mary appeared with the Baby Jesus in her arms. She handed Nicholas a small bit of bread; the Infant Jesus was holding a chalice filled with water; Mother Mary enjoined Nicholas to dip the bread into the chalice and then to eat it. Upon obeying the Mother of God, *his* Mother, he immediately recovered from his illness, and had more strength than he had ever known before.

From that time on, St. Nicholas would bless little pieces of bread, which he would distribute among the people. Healings abounded. *Author's note: When we visited Tolentino for the first time in 1977, the Nun at the Shrine gave us some "St. Nicholas' bread." There were approximately six little crackers[4] enclosed in cellophane packages. Just having returned to the Church two years before, and not having had much real education in the Faith at the time, Penny asked how much we were to give someone who was suffering, to bring about a cure. The Nun made a very wise statement, a teaching which has stayed with us these many years. She said:*

"It takes a little bread and a lot of faith."

Eight days before his death, our Lady appeared to St. Nicholas and prophesied that he would die on September the 10th, the third day after the anniversary of Mary's birth.[5] St. Nicholas was on his death bed and suffering. The *enemy* was attacking him mercilessly, these his last days. His soul was in anguish, as the enemy persisted, taunting him, disrupting his praying to the point he could barely remember the prayers. St. Nicholas turned to his Mother Mary and pleaded with her, saying he had endured the torments of the devil all his life; could he, his last hours on earth be undisturbed so that he could prepare properly for his entrance before the Lord. Our Lady left without giving him an answer. St. Nicholas continued praying. An Angel appeared to him, told him his prayers had been heard, and he would have the peace he desired. St. Nicholas spent his last days

---

[4]little round crackers which look like small oysterette crackers that are sometimes put into soup

[5]September the 8th

in peace, without any attacks from the devil. Not only that but he spent his last days, as if he were already in Paradise, his face illuminated.

As Mother Mary had predicted, St. Nicholas of Tolentino died on September 10, 1305. At his death, his tomb became immediately a shrine of veneration. Forty years after his death, a tomb was erected where the faithful could come to venerate the Saint. One day, a disturbed fanatic, desiring to have part of the Saint to bring back to his country,[6] decided to cut off his arms. When he performed this sacrilegious operation on the Saint's body, the Saint's arms began to bleed profusely, *forty years after his death*. The rest of the body has decomposed, but from that time on, the miraculous arms have been incorrupt and are venerated in their own special chapel. They are still solemnly processed on the Saint's Feast Day.

In 1926, the body was investigated and the Church verified that it was the body of the Saint. At that time, the arms were reunited with the rest of the body, a silver mask was placed over the Saint's face and the remains of the Saint are exposed for veneration, at the base of the Altar of Sacrifice, fitting for a priest who had prayed for so many Souls as he celebrated Mass.

Because of the many Souls that were released from Purgatory through his prayers, and the Masses he celebrated for the Poor Souls, he became and is known as the *Saint of Purgatory*. Great pilgrimages began immediately to Tolentino. St. Nicholas was declared *Patron Saint* of many large cities in the rest of Italy, due to the miraculous deliverance from plagues and pestilences, through the intercession of St. Nicholas. Devotion to him came about in all of Europe, and then in the whole world. In Mexico, there are over 30 villages named after St. Nicholas, as well as a village in the Canary Islands. He is also venerated in South America.

He has among those who have been devoted: many Popes, Saints and Blesseds who spent much time in Tolentino, praying

---

[6]it is written that he was a foreigner

to our Saint. Now you may be saying to yourself, *"Well, that's all well and good, and we enjoyed learning about St. Nicholas of Tolentino. But where's this Miracle of the Cross?"* Actually, the Miracle of the Cross of Jesus coming to life and embracing St. Nicholas took place ***after his death!***

✝✝✝

Let us paint a picture of the devastation into which Our Lord Jesus placed Himself and St. Nicholas. The deadly plague had spread all over Europe. The death toll had become catastrophic. Devastation prevailed as the population of Europe were being annihilated by the deadly pestilence.   The people of a small village in northern Spain appealed desperately to St. Nicholas of Tolentino, through whose intercession the city of Genoa in Italy had been spared from the plague. They believed he was their last chance for survival.   To this end, the people of the town processed through the streets with a Crucifix and a statue of St. Nicholas.

The streets were littered with sick people, fearing they would be the next to go. Fathers and mothers, sisters and brothers, the rich and the poor, all were being assailed by this enemy. All were deep in prayer as the procession passed in front of the local hospital. There were so many infected people, they were outside on the lawn of the hospital. There was no room inside for any more and there was no effective medicine for any, inside or out. It was a catastrophic situation, beyond anything anyone had ever experienced. Tears poured down the faces of those in prayer; wailing could be heard from all quarters. It was like the end of the world.

Just as the procession came to the front of the hospital, the Crucifix approached the statue of St. Nicholas. Our Lord Jesus on the Cross came to life. His eyes traveled over the scene of destruction before Him. He looked at all His children with such deep compassion. He moved His Body towards the statue of St. Nicholas and embraced him with all His might. The people in the procession stopped walking. They looked with awe and wonder.

There was an expression of bewilderment, mixed with reverence. They knew the Lord had come to answer their prayers. Almost immediately, a great shout came from those in the hospital and those sprawled out on the lawn. They cried out that they were healed. The grey look of death on the faces of most of them was replaced with rosy cheeks. The blood pumped back into their bodies. They were healed; all the sick in the town were healed. None died from the plague. The town was saved from the deadly scourge.

To this day, the people of this town venerate St. Nicholas of Tolentino and Our Lord Jesus Crucified. They celebrate the Miracle which took place in their town every year. A procession still takes place down the center of the town to the hospital where the Miracle of the Cross of St. Nicholas of Tolentino took place.[7]

---

[7]Read more about St. Nicholas in Bob and Penny Lord's book: *Visions of Heaven, Hell and Purgatory* or view his life on video documentary taped overseas by Bob and Penny Lord

Padre Pio's Miracles of the Cross

One of the most powerful series of ongoing Miracles of the Cross that we have researched are those which were bestowed upon Padre Pio throughout his life. Jesus wrapped Padre Pio in the Cross and he accepted it as a gift. He spent his entire life as a Crucified Christ, desiring only the sufferings of Jesus on the Cross.

Padre Pio was gifted with the Cross of Jesus from his earliest days. His personal relationship with Jesus and Mary manifested itself to him from the time he was a child. His entire world centered around the little church of Our Lady of the Angels in his little home town of Pietrelcina. It might as well have been his home. He spent more time there than at his home. All the important events in his early life took place in that church. He was baptized there; he received his First Holy Communion and Confirmation there; he went into ecstasy for the first time in that church, and had an apparition of the Sacred Heart of Jesus at age five, there. *"Our Lord Jesus appeared to Francesco,*[1] *and beckoned him to come to the main altar."*[2] He placed His hand on Francesco's head. We don't know what transpired between Our Lord Jesus and the young boy, but we do know that after this, the course of his life, and his vocation were sealed. He offered himself as victim of the Cross at that early age, although he probably did not know it at that time. He just said yes.

There are literally thousands of stories of Padre Pio, with regard to the many spiritual gifts he received. Many of these have been documented, while others are legend, having been woven out of a sincere love people have had for him and a desire to make him bigger than life. But as Fr. Joseph Pio once said to us as we were writing the biography of Padre Pio,[3] *"The truth is*

---

[1] Padre Pio's baptismal name was Francesco Forgione
[2] Statement made by Padre Benedetto da San Marco in Lamis, Padre Pio's spiritual director
[3] *Saints and Other Powerful Men in the Church*

Above: *The Chapel at San Giovanni Rotondo where Blessed Padre Pio said Mass and heard confessions*

Above: *Blessed Padre Pio received his stigmata from this Crucifix in the choir loft of the Chapel at San Giovanni Rotondo, Italy*

actually more fascinating than fiction." And so the Miracles we will share with you in this chapter have been documented by the Capuchins in San Giovanni Rotondo.

The Miracle of the Crucified Christ

One of the Miracles of the Cross dealing with Padre Pio has to do with the experience the Lord gave him almost daily as he prepared for and experienced the Crucifixion of Our Lord Jesus in the Sacrifice of the Mass.[4] Eyewitnesses, such as Fr. Alessio Parente and Fr. Joseph Pio[5] have shared with us that when Padre Pio would begin preparations for the Sacrifice of the Mass, and this could have been more than an hour before he actually began the Mass, they could see his knees begin to buckle and his body become bent under a tremendous invisible weight as he got closer and closer to entering the church and the altar. He told them he was carrying the weight of the Cross on his shoulders, and as we know, the Cross held the weight of all the sins Jesus was dying for. To those closest to Padre Pio, and actually many of those who waited for hours in the bitter cold outside the Church in the middle of the night to take part in the 5:30 a.m. Mass with him, they could actually see him being transformed into the Crucified Christ before their eyes during those times.

The Miracle of the Cross in the body of Padre Pio

Shortly after he was ordained, Padre Pio began to notice what he termed *"red patches, about the size of a cent, accompanied by acute pain."* This is from a letter he sent Padre Benedetto on the Birthday of Mary, September 8, 1911. He went on to say, *"The pain was much more acute in the left hand and it still persists. I also feel some pain in the soles of my feet."* He told his superior that this had been happening, on and off, for almost a year. So from the time of his ordination, at twenty three years old, he began to feel in his body, the wounds of the Passion of Christ.

---

[4]The Council of Trent declared that the Sacrifice of the Mass is the ongoing Sacrifice of the Cross

[5]Both of whom have gone to the Father in the year 2000

He prayed that the wounds would not show. The Lord answered his prayers for nine years, and so while the physical signs disappeared, the pain continued.

The Transverberation of the Heart - A preview

As if in anticipation of the great miracle he was to be given very shortly, the Lord granted Padre Pio a very special gift, one that would give him joy mixed with pain all his life, agony and ecstasy. On August 5, 1918, he received the gift of Transverberation of the Heart. Padre Pio wrote of this experience,

"While I was hearing the confessions of our boys on the evening of the 5th (August), I was suddenly filled with extreme terror at the sight of a celestial being whom I saw with my mind's eye. He held a kind of weapon in his hand, similar to a steel sword with a sharp, flaming point. At the very instant I saw all this, I saw the person hurl the weapon into my soul with all his might. It was all done in a split second. I was hardly able to cry out and felt as if I were dying. I cannot tell you how much I suffered during this period of anguish. Even my insides were torn and ruptured by that weapon, everything lashed by fire and steel. From that day on, I was wounded to death. In the depths of my soul, I feel an open wound which causes me to suffer continual agony."

Another Saint we wrote about, who experienced the Transverberation of the heart, was St. Teresa of Avila. She described her experience as follows:

"She (St. Teresa of Avila) saw an Angel to the left of her. He was small and very beautiful. He was so illuminated he had to be one of the very highest of the Angels, the Cherubim. He had a long golden dart in his hand, with what appeared to be fire at the end of it. She said he thrust it into her heart several times, piercing her down to her innermost organs, leaving her burning with a great love for God."[6]

---

[6]*Saints and Other Powerful Women in the Church*, Bob and Penny Lord

As you can see from their writings, their reactions to the Transverberation of the heart differed drastically.   Teresa experienced such an overpowering feeling of love, which stayed with her all her life. Padre Pio, on the other hand, continued to record his suffering.   However, although Teresa stressed the ecstatic nature of her gift, she also mentioned the suffering, but even in expressing her agony, she lapsed back into *ecstasy*. She wrote,

"Even though it is a spiritual pain and not physical, the body participates in the pain, in fact a lot......In this state I was beside myself. I did not wish to see or speak to anyone, except to remain alone with my suffering, which seemed the greatest joy that could exist in creation."

In a letter to Padre Benedetto, on September 5, 1918, Padre Pio talked more about the suffering and anger he was enduring.

"I see myself submerged in an ocean of fire! The wound which has been reopened bleeds incessantly. This alone is enough to make me die a thousand times.

"The excessive pain of this open wound makes me angry against my will, drives me crazy and makes me delirious. I am powerless in face of it."

This letter was written 13 days **before** he received the visible Stigmata. He was referring to the Transverberation of the heart. The open wound of which he speaks, is a spiritual, supernatural wound.

We believe we have each been given gifts in accordance with our walk with the Lord. For Padre Pio, the Transverberation of the heart may well have been to prepare him for the Miracle of the Cross, the Stigmata, which he was to receive shortly after. It may also have been given to him as a source of strength and joy, that would offset the physical pain and agony which the Lord wanted to use for His glory. We say this because of a letter he wrote on January 12, 1919.

*"Because of the exultation of possessing Him in me, I cannot refrain from saying with the most holy Virgin, `**My spirit**"*

rejoices in God my Savior.' Possessing Him within me, I am impelled to say with the spouse of the Sacred Song, 'I found Him whom my soul loves; I held Him and would not let Him go.'"

Padre Pio experienced the bitter-sweet love of Jesus. The bitter pain of his physical wounds was mixed with, and overpowered by the sweet, spiritual ecstasy he tasted by containing his Lord within his heart. Jesus never gives us more than we can handle, and showers us with more grace than we can ever use. As Jesus was born to die for our sins, so we believe Padre Pio was born to share in the Passion of Our Lord for our salvation. There was a major reason the Lord wanted to give Padre Pio the Transverberation of the Heart. He was now ready to receive the greatest miracle that could be bestowed on him.

The Miracle of the Cross of the Stigmata

September 20, 1918 was a turning point in the life of Padre Pio. While he had gathered a small following, because of his intense spirituality, and great wisdom, he would truly be the *Crucified Christ* after this day. He described the events of the day himself.

"On the morning of the 20th of last month, in the choir, after I had celebrated Mass, I yielded to a drowsiness similar to a sweet sleep. All the internal and external senses and even the very faculties of my soul were immersed in indescribable stillness. Absolute silence surrounded and invaded me. I was suddenly filled with great peace and abandonment which effaced everything else and caused a lull in the turmoil. All of this happened in a flash.

"While this was taking place, I saw before me a mysterious person, similar to the one I had seen on the evening of 5 August. The only difference was that his hands and feet and side were dripping blood. The sight terrified me, and what I felt at that moment is indescribable. I thought I should die and really should have died if the Lord had not intervened and strengthened my heart, which was about to burst out of my

chest.

"The vision disappeared and I became aware that my hands, feet and side were dripping blood. Imagine the agony I experienced and continue to experience almost every day."[7]

This outstanding Miracle of the Cross occurred while Padre Pio was praying in thanksgiving before the image of the Crucified Christ hanging before him. This particular crucifix is very descriptive. It shows the wounds of Jesus, hands, feet and side in an extremely graphic way. To this day, each time we bring pilgrims to the choir loft, above the main altar of the old church, and kneel under this crucifix, before which Padre Pio was given the Miracle of the Stigmata, we can feel the Presence and Power of Jesus. It is an awesome sight. If there had ever been a doubt in our minds that Jesus, through this representation of His Passion and death, which hangs above the choir loft in the old church, could not be enough to bring the wounds of Christ to Padre Pio, all one has to do is kneel before the image and pray. He's there; there's no question about that.

This visible sign of the Lord's Passion, which had been with him invisibly for eight years, became an immediate cause of panic in the young Capuchin. He didn't know what to do. He couldn't let anyone know what had happened. He didn't quite know himself. Perhaps it would go away. If he could just be away from people for a while, but how? As he wrote in the same letter, in which he described his receiving the Stigmata, it was a source of embarrassment to him. Again, we come to the bitter-sweet, agony-ecstasy aspect of the Stigmata. As with the Transverberation of the heart, he wanted it and didn't want it. Physically, he couldn't stand the pain; yet spiritually, he felt himself lifted to the heights of ecstasy by the experience. It was truly a paradox.

Since the death of Padre Pio on September 23, 1968, the tribute to Our Lord Jesus through His suffering servant, has grown in great proportions. A Way of the Cross has been built

---

[7] Letters of Padre Pio, Vol. I - Voice of Padre Pio

on the side of the mountain next to the original church of Santa
Maria delle Grazie in San Giovanni Rotondo. We made a
documentary there some years ago. It is a place not to be missed
if you are ever given the gift of visiting the Shrine to Padre Pio in
Italy. On that Way of the Cross, we see Padre Pio carrying the
Cross with Jesus. At one point, we see him as Simon the
Cyrenian, helping Jesus with the Cross. At other stations, we see
him carrying the Cross for Jesus. Padre Pio is so identified with
the Cross, it's no wonder that Our Lord Jesus would give him the
gift of Miracles of the Cross. To paraphrase Pope Pius XII on
the occasion of the Proclamation of the Dogma of the
Assumption of Our Lady: ***"Jesus did it because it made sense to
do it, and He had the power to do it."***[8] We believe the same
applied to Padre Pio. It made sense to Jesus to imprint His
wounds on the body of this holy man, through the Miracle of the
Stigmata, and He had the power to do it. And if we may insert
our own thoughts on this Miracle, it may have been more for
mankind than for Padre Pio that this was done.

You must remember that there were those in the Church who
were heading at breakneck speed away from all the gifts the Lord
had given us in the Church. All our Treasures were being taken
away from us; all our beliefs being reduced into so much
superstition. The Supernatural was being eliminated in favor of
secular humanism, a heresy which had been condemned centuries
before. Sacrifice was being displaced by celebration. The God-
Man on the Cross was being replaced by decorative bands and
metal pipes. But then the Lord, *"...scattered the proud in the
deceit of their heart"* and *"...put down the mighty from their
thrones."* by setting aside the laws of nature and creating Miracle
in Padre Pio.

We wrote about Padre Pio in our book, *Saints and Other
Powerful Men in the Church:*
*"There were many people who didn't want Padre Pio to be
raised to the Communion of Saints. He did not fit the image*

---

[8]Munificentissimus Deus

they wanted to project of the Church of the Third Millennium.
To many of Padre Pio's adversaries, he was a throwback to the
Middle Ages. Everything that he represented was pulling us
back to where we came from, rather than bringing us into the
modern age of Science and Technology, this Twentieth and
Twenty first Century. Perhaps that's true. Padre Pio
represented back to basics, to those values which made our
Church and our world, grand.

"But the people loved Padre Pio. To the people of God, he
definitely was the kind of Saint they wanted to represent the
Church. They knew God was looking down from Heaven; they
wanted Him to see that this man was their man. And so the
people furthered the cause for the Beatification of Padre Pio.
One of those people shared about his personal experiences with
Padre Pio at the Beatification. That person was Pope John Paul
II, who had met Padre Pio when he was a young priest. And
that man, our Pope, saw Padre Pio as the image the Church
wanted to project to God the Father on this the year of the
Father."[9]

We once said that when Mother Church chooses to raise him
to the Communion of Saints, the qualities of sanctity in Padre Pio
will not be solely that he bore the Stigmata[10] for 50 years of his
life, that he had the gift of bi-location,[11] the fragrance of
Heaven,[12] or the many miracles attributed to him during his
lifetime. The proclamation of his sainthood will come from the
extraordinary spirituality he showed during his ministry, his

---

[9]*Saints and Other Powerful Men in the Church* - Page 458

[10]Stigmata - from the Greek, meaning "marks". This refers to the
wounds, scars or abrasions that appear on the skin of people, corresponding
to the five wounds of Jesus, in the hands, the feet and the side.

[11]Bilocation is the actual presence of one finite person in two places at
the same time. Padre Pio was known to have been seen in various parts of
the world, including St. Peter's Basilica, although he never left San Giovanni
Rotondo.

[12]A heavenly fragrance, unique and identifiable, which, in Padre Pio's
case, exuded from his open wounds.

enormous love for Our Lord Jesus in the Eucharist, his overpowering love for the Cross, his devotion to Mother Mary and the Rosary, his willingness to take on the sins of the world during his eighteen-hour days in the confessional, his inspired writings, his spiritual counseling, his obedience to his superiors, most especially His Holiness, the Pope, and possibly more than anything, his lifelong commitment to his Sacrament, his priesthood. In short, his loyalty to the *Body of Christ, the Mother of Christ, through the Vicar of Christ.*

St. Paul of the Cross
His Role Model, the Crucified Lord

Before we tell you of the Miracle of the Cross in St. Paul's life, we need to introduce you to a Saint who was Mystic, Missionary, Director of souls and Founder of the Passionists. He was a Saint whose book was the Crucifix and his Role Model, the Crucified Lord. We have researched and written about Passionists for the last ten years, including St. Gemma Galgani, St. Gabriel of the Sorrows, and Blessed Fr. Germano, who was the spiritual director for St. Gemma. But it never occurred to us that these holy people were following in the footsteps of a holy man, who had to be very charismatic. St. Paul of the Cross was all that and more.

St. Paul of the Cross was born Paul Francis Danei, on the 3rd of January, 1694, the second of sixteen children. One of his brothers, John Baptist would be very instrumental in the work Our Lord had chosen for St. Paul. His parents, although of nobility, were neither affluent nor privileged. Even though the town hall at Castellazzo had once been the family palace, St. Paul's father, a cloth merchant, was always in serious debt. Because of the financial situation, St. Paul had to discontinue his education at a boarding school. At one point, things became so dire, St. Paul pawned all his belongings, to help his father avoid disgrace. This was a great sacrifice for someone in Paul's position, but it prepared him for giving up far greater things in the future, and for receiving great gifts in return.

St. Paul was brilliant. Although deprived of a formal education, he studied on his own and completed his education through hard work and dedication. Industriously studying, he developed a profound knowledge of the New Testament, a command of the Italian language and a proficiency in Latin. Never compromising his love for the Faith, St. Paul attended daily Mass, received the Sacraments frequently and spent as much time as he could before the Blessed Sacrament.

Left:
**Symbol of the Passionist Order
This "Great Vision" was given to
St. Paul of the Cross by Our
Lady appearing to him wearing a
tunic with the emblem on it; she
told him this was the life he was
to lead, a life totally dedicated to
Jesus Crucified.**

Right:
**St. Paul of the Cross
founder of the
Passionist Order
Mystic of the Cross
"The Cross!
O Holy Cross, can I bear to
look opon You?"**

Left:
**While venerating the Cross,
St. Paul of the Cross levitated
to Jesus on the Cross and
Jesus took him in His arms,
and embraced him.**

This gentle, but strong-willed youth would become Paul of the Cross, founder of a religious Order, Barefooted Clerks of the Holy Cross and Passion, the abbreviated form of which was The Passionists. There was good reason for that title. It told the world who and what he was, *passionate* for the Cross of Jesus. There is a tradition that when he was a child, and became irritated or annoyed, and began to cry, his dear mother would show him a Crucifix, and speak softly about the Passion of Our Lord Jesus. Little Paul would stop crying, but the tears continued to run down his face, only now it was not because of the reason he began to cry in the first place. Now the tears were being shed for the suffering His Savior endured for Paul and all of us.

Paul was born at a critical time in the history of the world. There was crisis and chaos, wars being waged, elements finding their way closer and closer to the seat of his Church, Rome. The Turks were taking over more and more of Europe; and wherever they conquered, they persecuted Christians practicing the Faith. It became against the law, with a penalty of imprisonment or worse, execution, if caught practicing the Faith.

But when the Church is under attack, God raises powerful men and women to defend His Precious Jewel. Right from birth St. Paul of the Cross was destined, no, chosen to serve and save the Church. As we were saved by Jesus on the Cross, so by his devotion to Christ Crucified and His Passion, St. Paul of the Cross would be an instrument to save the children of God. You might ask, How did he save the Church? Did he do battle? Yes, on his knees: he took part in the Passion, sharing with His Lord His Pain; he scourged himself in imitation of the Wounds inflicted on Our Lord. But we are getting ahead of ourselves.

Although St. Paul began his devotion to Jesus Crucified from the time he was a baby, it would be a homily he would hear at age eleven that would seal his vocation. As he listened to the Priest, he began to grieve, because he thought he was not cooperating with God's Bountiful Grace. He made a general confession and began his walk of suffering and sacrifice. He started to sleep on the ground; rising at midnight, he prayed hours on end; then in imitation of the Savior's Passion, he scourged himself. His younger brother John Baptist soon joined him, practicing the same forms of penitence. In very short order, more young men joined them, some of whom would later enter Religious Orders.

In the year 1774, Pope Clement XI called upon young men to volunteer in the Venetian Army and fight against the Turks, who were threatening Europe. Desiring to die for the Faith, St. Paul fashioning himself a crusader, joined the Army, prepared to do battle. But after serving one year, while praying before the Blessed Sacrament, he had an inner *thought, or was it an inner locution* - this was not his vocation. Did the Lord tell him he would be fighting a different battle, not using the weapons he thought, but the Cross and the Gospel? He resigned his commission and received his discharge from the Army whereupon he spent some time in Venice, before returning home to Castellazzo. After long hours meditating, he discerned that a life in the world was not where he could best serve the Lord. He relinquished a large inheritance and future married life, to spend years praying endlessly to discern God's Will.

St. Paul has "the Great Vision," which will determine his life.

The summer of 1720, St. Paul was to get his answer. He had what he called *"the Great Vision."* A black habit appeared, with a coat of arms on it, embossed with a heart bearing the Name of Jesus spelled out in white letters, and a white cross appearing over it. Then in the third Vision, Our Lady appeared wearing the same tunic; she told him this was the life he was to lead, a life totally dedicated to Jesus Crucified. Further, he was to form a congregation with members who would wear this tunic and mourn without ceasing the Passion and Death of Her Beloved Son.

Always obedient to Mother Church, St. Paul submitted a scrupulous detail of what had transpired during the Visions to his Bishop. After much consultation with several spiritual directors, including St. Paul's former director, and in view of the pious life he had led since childhood, the Visions were determined to be from God. St. Paul received authorization to follow his vocation, and the Bishop of Alessandria vested him, for the first time with the black habit of his Visions, but not without the caution, he was not to wear the emblem before receiving approval from the Pope.

It was time to start drafting up a Rule for his company. Under the direction of the Bishop of Alessandria, St. Paul went on a forty day retreat, in a tiny cell in the sacristy of the church in Castellazzo, living only on bread and water and sleeping on straw. On that retreat, he wrote his *Spiritual Diary* and drafted the Rule that is without change, that of the Passionists till today. The drafting of the Rule took a mere five days, but it would take years of suffering and rejection, before it would be accepted - He knew hope one day only to have that hope dashed into hopelessness the next. It would take *twenty-one years* before, in 1741, St. Benedict XIV would approve the Rule!

On that forty day retreat, St. Paul had a persisting thought: *Pray for England's conversion.* He prayed for the conversion of England for fifty years, and passed on that devotion to those who have followed. He would share, *"That country is always before my eyes. If England again becomes Catholic, immeasurable will be the benefits to Holy Church."*

[This is the second Saint we have written about who felt strongly about England and her place in the Church. St. Dominic Savio's dying words for the Pope were: *"...he must not stop taking care of England. God is preparing a great triumph for the Catholic Church here."*][1]

St. Paul and his saintly brother John Baptist returned to Castellazzo. They remained there a while, helping local clergy in the small village by teaching the children their Catechism and giving Missions. Then one day, he knew he had to take his next step to Rome, to seek approval of his Rule by the Pope! He set out alone, bareheaded, barefoot and penniless. He wouldn't even

---

[1]Excerpt from Bob and Penny Lord's book: *Holy Innocence*

allow his faithful companion, his brother John Baptist, to accompany him. As soon as he arrived at the Vatican, he presented himself at the Quirinale Palace (the Pope's residence at that time); but as he had no credentials or letters of introduction, he was turned away. They thought he was a beggar! He accepted the rejection as a sign from God that it was not His Will he do it at this time. Thanking God for the privilege of sharing in the Humiliation His Son suffered on the Way of the Cross, he went to the *Basilica of Santa Maria Maggiore*,[2] and, kneeling before the statue of Our Lady, *"Salus Populi Romani,"* he and his brother John Baptist (who had now joined him) took their first vows - to consecrate themselves to the memory of the Passion of Jesus Christ. That done, he left, and retired to a hermitage in the mountains, with his brother.

Three years pass, and the two brothers return to Rome to be ordained. Not only were they ordained by Pope Benedict XIII in the Basilica of St. Peter, they returned to the hermitage with permission in hand to accept novices. It sounds so simple, so wonderful; but when you set out to serve the Lord, especially through the Cross, you can count on attacks upon attacks. New recruits found the life too difficult and left. Then there was a threat of war in the air, benefactors stopped sending aid. To compound the problems facing the brothers, an epidemic broke out in nearby villages. The two brothers worked tirelessly ministering to the dying, nursing the suffering, and bringing sinners back to Jesus and the Church.

New recruits joined the brothers, and in 1737 the first Passionist Retreat was completed. The work continued successfully, but not without disappointments and hardships. But through it all, the Passionists became well-known throughout Italy and their missions were in demand. St. Paul evangelized every one of the Papal states, personally,[3] his ongoing theme - *the Sacred Passion of Jesus.* Cross in hand, arms outstretched in

---

[2]Basilica of St. Mary Major
[3]which at time constituted much of the Italian states of the North

love, like his Savior, he preached about Jesus' sorrowful Passion; his body and face taking on the suffering of his Lord. Each word became a flaming sword piercing the stony hearts of all who were present and if that did not melt their hearts, seeing the little Passionist scourging himself in atonement for their sins and unrepentant hearts moved even hardhearted soldiers and thieves to tears; and then to confession.

St. Paul was gifted by God with many supernatural gifts. He prophesied future events. Everywhere he went, he brought about healings of the sick. He bilocated, appearing to people in faraway places. During his lifetime, he became known as a living Saint. People strained to touch him; they tore off pieces of his tunic to use as a relic.

He and his company earned the title: *Missionaries of the Eighteenth Century!* From his first mission at Grazi's Ferry till his last, at seventy-five years old, in the Basilica of Santa Maria in Trastevere, Rome, he worked and preached tirelessly on the place of the Cross in the every-day life of the Christian. During his missions, he involved the laity, invoking them to participate in Processions, preaching in the streets, making vigils before the Blessed Sacrament, practicing penitential works in honor of the Crucified Lord. He was so successful the Order grew and grew.

But of all he did, our Saint is best known as *Mystic of the Cross.* His main reason for living was to keep alive in the hearts of the Faithful, the Price paid for our freedom from the bondage of sin, on the Cross! He wanted to perpetuate the Cross and the Sacrifice Jesus paid on the Cross not as something of the past, Ancient History, but of the ever-living, ongoing present.

His life, like that of any true Ministry, was a dizzying series of ups and downs. Against his protests, St. Paul was unanimously elected first Superior General, which office he held until his death. Before his death he had founded twelve foundations, opened two provinces, presided over six general chapters, and founded a second Order - that of Cloistered Passionist Nuns. In addition, always in love with the souls of

God's children, he took on the sometimes very painful task of directing souls. He wrote over ten thousand letters of spiritual direction and many small treatises on mystical theology. But with the gifts always comes the Cross.

The Cross! O Holy Cross, can I bear to look upon you?

After all did St. Paul not embrace the Cross? Did he not desire the Cross? But this, Lord? He was to lose his dear brother John Baptist to the Angel of Death. St. Paul was inconsolable. They had been more than brothers; they had been linked by their mutual dream of serving the Lord; they were inseparably tied to each other and their mission. He was two years younger than St. Paul; it wasn't fair John Baptist should die first; but die he did; and live St. Paul must do. Now he was to know not only the Passion through Jesus' Eyes, but through Mother Mary's grieving heart.

The Miracle of the Cross

St. Paul focused completely on Jesus Crucified. He spent more and more of his time venerating the Cross, and the price Our Lord Jesus paid for our salvation. He meditated on how much Jesus loved us and loved him, in particular. He found himself in tears often, weeping before His Lord in agony. On one of these occasions, Our Lord Jesus came to life on the Cross. Paul levitated to where He was. Jesus took him in His arms, and embraced him. That feeling stayed with our Saint for the rest of his days. While he wrote of it, he could never quite put in words the bond, the brotherhood, the love between the Savior and the saved.[4]

In memory of the work the two brothers did for Mother Church, Pope Clement XIV imparted on St. Paul of the Cross *The Basilica of Sts. John and Paul,* named after two martyrs of the early Church, in honor of St. Paul of the Cross and his

---

[4]After his canonization, the image of St. Paul being embraced by the Crucified Christ was placed on the back of the main altar in the new Basilica of Sts. John and Paul.

brother, John Baptist. The new Passionist Order received final approval, placing them on the same footing as other Religious communities. They have headquartered out of the Basilica of Sts. John and Paul from that day to this.

It was time to retire! St. Paul was tired; he was not well; he longed to spend his final days among his brother missionaries, in contemplative peace; after all his work was done, wasn't it!

St. Paul of the Cross was given the house adjoining the Basilica of Sts. Giovanni e Paolo,[5] on the Celian hill, near the Coliseum. St. Paul spent his final days here. He was visited by two Popes, Clement XIV in 1774 and by Pius VI in 1775. Shortly after Pope Pius VI's visit, our Lover of Jesus Crucified went *Home* to the Lord He had adored on earth, no veil separating them.

There were many miracles credited to St. Paul's intervention, in addition to those used for his beatification and canonization; the most noteworthy were the many conversions that came about of sinners who had appeared hopelessly lost in sin, their hearts hardened and distant.

May 1, 1853, St. Paul was beatified by Pope Pius IX and then canonized by him on June 29, 1867. April 25, 1880, the relics of St. Paul of the Cross were transferred to a chapel that had been recently completed. Our Saint can be venerated there till today.[6] His Feast Day is April 28th.

What Cross do you carry? Is it heavy? Is it unbearable? Turn to St. Paul and ask him to help you, not to just carry it; but to embrace it. ***Crave the Cross!***

---

[5]Sts. John and Paul
[6]Ss Giovanni e Paolo

Jesus Comes off the Cross to Heal St. Peregrine of Cancer

The Lord healed his leg of cancer.

Thirteenth Century Italy

Peregrine was born in Forli, Italy in 1260, into a time of unrest and rebellion. His family was well-to-do and actively involved in affairs of state.

By 1283, Peregrine was a full-grown product of the narrow, self-centered world of the upper class he grew up in. Italy was a hotbed of unrest and rebellion. Pope Martin IV imposed an *interdict*[1] on Forli, because of the city's open *anarchy*. Priests were not allowed to administer the Sacraments.[2] *All* divine services, including the Holy Mass, were forbidden.

The people of Forli countered the Pope's actions with attacks on the clerical. Things got so out of hand, the Pope sent a mediator, future Saint Philip Benizi[3] to try to *move the hearts* of the warring citizens of Forli. A group of young rowdies infiltrated the group he was addressing. They criticized; they jeered; they mocked his every word. When they could not provoke him into answering them, they pulled him down from the pulpit, as he was preaching. They resorted to *manhandling* him mercilessly, until they finally ran him out of town.

One of these rowdies was *Peregrine*! Along with the villagers of Forli, his parents were anti-papal and so naturally, Peregrine was anti-papal! All of eighteen years old, he outdid the rest of his friends. *He struck St. Philip on the face.* Now, St. Philip Benizi, known to have an Italian trigger temper, just stood there and offered Peregrine his other cheek.

---

[1]Interdict - A censure that deprives the faithful of certain spiritual benefits.

[2]except administration of the Sacrament to the dying if regulations are observed.

[3]called by Jesus and Mary, in two different visions to propagate the Servite Order

Below:
Fresco of the Crucifixion in the Chapter room of the priory where St. Peregrine was healed by Jesus on the Cross.

Below:
Shrine of St. Peregrine the Cancer Saint in Forli, Italy

Above:
Jesus heals St. Peregrine of Cancer

No sooner had he struck St. Philip, than he felt pangs of guilt and remorse. He ran after St. Philip. He begged his and the Lord's forgiveness. St. Philip opened his arms and forgave him, absolving him not only of this sin, but others he had committed.

Turning completely away from his old life and old *friends*, Peregrine began to spend more and more time praying in the Cathedral, his eyes riveted on the beautiful statue of our Lady in her chapel. While praying in the Church of the Holy Cross, our Lady appeared and told him to seek out the Servites. Mary sent an Angel to accompany him to Siena. Arriving in Siena, he rang the bell of the house of the *Servants of Mary* or Servites. There, he was brought before the *Prior General*.

The *Prior General was* the very man he had slapped.[4] Peregrine entered the Order around 1290, as a *choir-brother*. With the same conviction and determination, he had defied the Lord and His Church, he now defended and obeyed Them! Once he received his habit, he truly, untiringly lived his philosophy, *"one must never rest in the way of virtue."*[5] It is said, he never sat down for thirty years. But he did take whatever free time available to observe silence and solitude, his *wonderful* time alone with his Lord and his Lady.

Peregrine returns to Forli

After approximately five years, his superiors sent Peregrine back to Forli, to open a house, there. He was available to everyone who called on him, never too tired to counsel whoever came to him. Because of this, he earned the name, *"Angel of Good Counsel."* His life was salvation of souls, and consolation to the suffering and impoverished.

---

[4]St. Philip Benizi was not only a priest-maker, he was a Saint-maker. Notably good men he called to the Lady's service were: St. Peregrine, Bl. John of Frankfort, Bl. Joachim Piccolominin and on and on, over seven powerful men who have been beatified, and in addition the well-known *Saint* Juliana Falconieri from which sprang up the third order regular of the Servants of Mary.

[5]Butler's Lives of the Saints

He ministered tirelessly to the sick. A plague broke out in Italy and spread to Forli. No one was safe from the spreading ravages of the disease. Peregrine would not even take time out to be sick. Now, a very tired and sick *sixty years* old, he could barely stand. A cancerous growth, on his right leg, had spread dangerously, and there was no way out. He had to be operated on! He had worked among the sick, ignoring his own pain and the seriousness of *his* illness, for years. Now, it seemed, the Lord was saying, through the doctors, there was nothing that could be done; the leg had to be amputated!

The night before he was scheduled to be operated on, he went into the *chapter room* of the Priory. He was all alone. He prayed before a fresco of Jesus Crucified. He fell into a deep sleep. He had a vision of the Lord. Our Lord came down from His Cross and reaching out to his cancerous leg, He touched it, ever so gently, with His Healing Hand.

The next morning, Peregrine awakened, resigned to the operation, only to discover his leg didn't hurt. He could stand, he could walk, without pain! He was completely healed!

The operation never took place. When the surgeons investigated the leg, they reported there was not a trace of the illness. News of the miracle spread. People, who knew and loved him, had been following anxiously the progressive deterioration of Peregrine's health. Imagine when they heard, he had been completely cured! And overnight!

Peregrine lived for another *twenty* years. People continued to come to him, for help. Before, it had been for spiritual direction and healing of the soul; now they came seeking miracles of the *body*. Like with his Lord, he didn't care why they came, he said *yes!* There were miracles, even before his death. Many were healed of the cancer that attacked their bodies, but we are sure as many, if not more, left cured of the cancer that spreads and kills the *soul*.

Peregrine was eighty years old, but when he looked upon his Lady, it was like the first time; he was young! The young cavalier in the old body was ready to ride gallantly forth with his Lady. On May 1st, 1345, consumed now by fever, with his last spark of life, Peregrine's spirit soared, like a *rocket of fire*, to his Lord and to the Lady he so loved. She had called him from the world, to life as a *religious*. Now, Mary was calling him out of the world, to live eternally with her and her Son, Jesus.

All his life as a *religious*, had been a preparation for this, his entrance into eternal life. We know, as Peregrine called out, *"Jesus! Mary!"* They lifted him and carried him *Home*.

Their Saint was dead

The faithful filed by, for days. Their Saint was dead! So many continued to come, they left the gates of the city unlocked at night. They came, those he had loved and helped, those he had visited and served! First, the poor! Then the sick! They testified how he had been an *instrument* by his example, as well as, by his words. Testimony after testimony came forth, from the faithful, who had come to witness to St. Peregrine's *sanctity*! A delightful aroma of flowers, from the body of St. Peregrine, filled the church. People said they could smell a fragrance of flowers unknown to them, strong but not sickening, *delightful*!

Days passed. They had to say good-by to their old friend. The Servants of Mary placed the body of St. Peregrine in a coffin or sepulcher. But they could not place it in the cemetery. The fragrance continued, and the body showed no signs of decomposition. Instead, they kept it above ground in the Chapel of *Our Lady of Sorrows,* next to the Lady he had loved for over sixty years of his life. *It remained there until 1639.*

They wanted to canonize him immediately! The faithful brought evidence of the multitudes of miracles, through Peregrine's intercession. News spread rapidly of the *Saint of Forli*. Devotion to the Saint began, long before he was canonized. As early as from 1350 to 1375, a fresco was painted by the school of Lorenzetti in far-off *Siena*. In Italy and to the four corners of Europe, devotion to this holy Saint began. Miracles, through the intercession of St. Peregrine, were being proclaimed, from almost every corner of the earth.

So many miracles were reported after his death, they stopped recording them, after awhile. Over 300 miracles occurred before he was canonized. Pope Pio V, in the 16th Century, approved the cult of praying to Peregrine for his intercession, and declared him a *Blessed.*

His cause was brought to Rome. All historical testimony of his life as a *religious*, and miracles attributed to his intercession, were examined by the Sacred Congregation of Rites. These affidavits were carefully scrutinized, under the supervision of such as St. Robert Bellarmine, who was then a Cardinal and Jesuit.

In response to the investigation of the Sacred Congregation, in 1609, Pope Paul V issued a Papal Bull *officially* approving the cult (devotion) of venerating Peregrine, allowing the use of *Beato* or Blessed before his name. The Pope added his name to the Roman Martyrology[6] with permission to celebrate Holy Mass in his honor, May 1st of every year. A beautiful chapel was added to the church in honor of the new *Blessed*. On the 15th of June in 1626, the first stone was laid.

On May 16, 1639, the body of Blessed Peregrine was solemnly processed from the Cathedral to the church where he is till today. The Process of Canonization of Peregrine, began in the 17th Century. On the 27th of December, 1726, Mother Church *officially* added Blessed Peregrine to the Communion of *Saints*. Pope Benedict XIII, on the High Altar of St. Peter's Basilica, declared, the Church had a new Saint, for all ages, *Saint Peregrine!*

Three hundred years after his death, when they investigated his remains, they discovered his body had never decomposed. At that time, they placed him in a glass urn, so the faithful could

---

[6]Roman Martyrology, a liturgical book, is the listing with readings of the Saints honored in the Church, and the names of newly canonized Saints are added to it. It first was published in 1584, and now numbers more than five thousand entries.(Catholic Encyclopedia-Broderick)

view his body when they venerated him. He was then placed above the altar in that side chapel that had been constructed when he was Beatified. This has been a place of Pilgrimage, for most of Europe, since that time; but until now, not for Americans who were unaware it was there.

The first time we visited the Shrine of St. Peregrine, the priest told us, although most of his body, now over 500 years old, was little more than a skeleton, the leg our Lord miraculously cured, was still completely intact with *flesh* on it.

We knelt and prayed in front of that same fresco of our Lord Crucified, before which St. Peregrine had prayed. The Spirit of the Lord is here. He never left. He touched our Saint *here*. These walls remember it well; and they echo what happened, over and over again, when the helpless come crying, Science having failed them, without hope, their hearts breaking.

St. Rita of Cascia
Pierced by the Cross

St. Rita of Cascia is a role model for women of our generation. There is nothing that any woman has experienced that Rita did not experience during her lifetime. She was an obedient daughter, a faithful wife, a battered wife, wife of an alcoholic and woman-chaser, a widow, a single parent who lost her children when they were young. She was a Nun who was unwanted by her Community. She was given a Miracle of the Cross, during which time she received the gift of the Stigmata,[1] a thorn in her head. Her body is incorrupt, never having decomposed after 600 years. In Italy, she is considered the *Saint of the Impossible*.[2]

One night, Rita had a Vision. She saw a tall ladder leading Heavenward with Jesus at the top. He was beckoning her forward. He was calling her to that perfect mystical union with Him, that could only be achieved by her, through her daily obedience to the life He had chosen for her, her life in Him, as an obedient Nun. He would be her Teacher, her Strength in her weakness, her Companion, her Love in her otherwise loveless life. He would be her very Life! With Jesus to sustain her, St. Rita chose the most mended and worn clothing for herself, barely eating enough to maintain her strength. Word of her holiness reached the world outside of the Monastery and people began to speak of the Saint in their midst.

With the threat of heretics on one side and barbarians on the other, all the Christian world was experiencing a return to devotion to **the Cross**. The Saracens were invading, conquering

---

[1]Stigmata - Wounds that appear on the flesh of individuals, corresponding to the wounds suffered by Jesus in the Passion. Usually very painful.

[2]To read more about St. Rita of Cascia, get Bob and Penny Lord's best-selling book, *Saints and Other Powerful Women in the Church.*

Above:
Saint Rita of Cascia
A thorn fell from the Crucifix and
pierced her forehead.

Above:
The Crucifix which gave St. Rita
the wound on her forehead with
one of the thorns from His crown.

Above:
Saint Rita of Cascia implores her community to go on Pilgrimage.

and desecrating all that Christians held dear, not excluding the Shrines in the Holy Land sanctified by the Lord Himself by His Incarnation, His Crucifixion and His Resurrection. The wars fought to protect the Holy Places were called the Crusades.

St. Rita was to stage her own kind of crusade, the shedding of her own blood to stop the atrocities and abuses against our Loving and Suffering Lord. St. Rita grieved that she had not been able to share in the Passion of our Lord Jesus Christ. She spent many hours meditating on all the insults, the rejections, the ingratitude, the apathy our Beloved Lord suffered as He walked to His Agony on the Cross. She built a small Calvary of stones on the floor of her cell (bedroom), and kneeling there, she would relive the beatings, the scourging, the thorns in the head, the horror of our Lord's Passion, and the sorrow of His mother as she watched her Son. In the process for her canonization, witnesses (fellow Religious) testified they would visit her in her cell at times, only to find her on the floor, fainted after having shared the pain of the Savior's Passion.

The Miracle of the Cross

During Lent of the year 1443, St. James of Marches, a great preacher of his day, came to the convent in Cascia, and gave a very personal, fervent sermon on the Passion of our Lord to the Nuns. Rita was so taken by the sermon that she returned to the Monastery and began to pray, with all her heart and soul, before a fresco of Jesus Crucified. As she humbly asked for a part of His suffering on the Cross, admitting that she was unworthy to share His full Passion on Calvary, a thorn fell from the Beloved Head of our Savior and pierced the forehead of St. Rita. She could feel the pain down to the depths of her heart. She immediately began to bleed profusely, and the wound that kept bleeding has been accepted by all as the gift of the Stigmata of our Lord.

In the case of most holy people who have been graced with the Stigmata, like St. Francis of Assisi, and the saintly Padre Pio, the fragrance exuded from the holy wounds smells like a beautiful perfume from Heaven, more pleasing even than that of flowers. With the wound of St. Rita, came humiliation, estrangement and isolation. The wound had such a pungent, putrid odor emanating from it that she had to suffer the ostracism and rejection of her fellow Nuns who, at best, feared it might be infectious and, at worst, could not bear the smell. She spent the next fifteen years alone, suffering more and more excruciating physical pain. But although she was isolated from her Community in a small cell far away from any of the consoling companionship of other Nuns, she had *the Consoler*! Instead of looking toward herself and her pain, she focused on Jesus and His bleeding Crown of Thorns and all the thorns in her life were turned into roses of love by her Lord as she offered them to Him.

In 1450, Pope Nicholas V declared the first Holy Year, proclaiming Rome, once and for all, the center of the Christian world, and of our Faith. The Popes had been away from Rome for sixty seven years. Our Lord wanted to unite His Church, to end the scandal of division and dissension caused by self-interest and resultant schism,[3] so He inspired the Pope to institute this Holy Year. And unite He did! All the Religious of Italy, as well as pilgrims from all over the world converged on Rome.

The Nuns of Cascia were also planning to go to Rome on pilgrimage, which was not to include St. Rita. Knowing and understanding the reasoning behind her exclusion (her wound which continued to bleed, fester and emit unbearable odors), she nevertheless did not take it lying down. She went to the Big Boss! She prayed that her wound be temporarily healed, that there be no external signs, only the internal pain of the wound to remain. Her petition was almost immediately granted; the wound disappeared and St. Rita was on her way to Rome with the other Nuns.

---

[3]Schism - from the Greek, which means crack or tear or flaw. It meant breaking away from the Church. In this instance, it was the Great Schism, in which the Popes of Avignon and the Popes of Rome each claimed to be the true pope. It lasted until 1417.

The pilgrimage to and from Rome was a walking pilgrimage. And if you have ever climbed the mountain to Cascia, even by bus or car, you know that it is extremely arduous. Their journey was one of hardship, deprivation, suffering and sacrifice; the walking and living on the road, at times, more than the little band of pilgrims from the Monastery of Cascia could bear. But the always patient, never complaining joy of the eldest Nun, St. Rita, now in her late sixties, encouraged and sustained them.

The wound did not bleed or reveal any evidence it had ever existed during the entire pilgrimage, but upon their return to the Monastery, not five minutes passed when the wound opened, with all the accompanying signs. Rita was again quarantined into seclusion with her Beloved Lord.

Three days before St. Rita died, she had a Vision of our Lord Jesus and our Lady. The room, so often Calvary for Rita, was now flooded with a beautiful, bright light. *"You will be with Me in Paradise, in three days,"* our Lord told her, and three days later, on May 22nd, 1457, Rita was to join the annals of those who have lived for God; she was with Him.

The ugly wound she had borne uncomplainingly over the years, healed as she breathed her last, only to be replaced by a ruby spot, like a kiss. A strong fragrance, sweet and heavenly, poured forth from where the wound had been, replacing the stench she had lived with those many years. This fragrance has continued for many centuries, because St. Rita was never buried! Till today when you visit the shrine of St. Rita in Cascia, there is a feeling of family; she's one of us. Here, in a glass urn, honored by God and her brothers and sisters in Christ, the mystical body of Christ, lies a daughter, an obedient daughter whose parents did not make the wisest of decisions by man's standards, but possibly by God's; a wife of an alcoholic, an abuser, a carouser, a man easily provoked whose deadly silence could erupt into rage; a widow who loved her husband before and after his conversion only to lose him by an act of violence; a mother who watched her children grow up taking on the violent, non-Christian personality of their father, afraid they might commit murder, only to lose them to death through illness; a Nun who was rejected, judged, ostracized, laughed at, tested and glorified. Here lies our sister, Rita, a Saint, a woman for our time. And we love her and thank God for the gift of her to remind us what we can be.

St. Teresa of Avila
Faithful Daughter of the Crucified Lord
"I believe our love is the measure of the Cross we can bear."

Teresa of Avila, lovingly referred to as *Teresa la Grande*, is a powerful woman who truly rose to the battle cry to become a strong part of the Counter-Reformation in her native land. She sought solitude all her life in the bosom of Jesus, but said yes to the mandate He gave her to bring about a major reform in the Carmelite order.

She had an overwhelming devotion to Our Lord Jesus in His Passion, and Jesus crucified. The Cross was her strength in good times and bad. We have seen, through our research for this book, how all our Saints have had an extraordinarily great respect and love for, and understanding of the *power of the Cross*. And these are super role models. Before we begin sharing St. Teresa and the Cross with you, allow us give you just a little background on this most Powerful Doctor of the Church. She has earned our love and enormous respect, not only for who she was, and for what she accomplished, but for her relentless quest for unity with Our Lord Jesus in His Passion. But let's get on with our story.

God balances the books

Teresa was born into a time of upheaval in the world and in the Church, with protesters calling rebellion "Reformation." In 1514, the year before Teresa was born, Pope Leo X granted an indulgence to members of the Church who donated money toward the building of the new Basilica in Rome, St. Peter's. Let us just give you the official Church teaching on Indulgences:

"An Indulgence is obtained through the Church who, by virtue of the power of binding and loosing[1] granted her by Jesus Christ, intervenes in favor of individual Christians and opens for them the treasury of merits of Christ and the Saints to obtain from the Father of

---

[1]Mt: 18:18

Left:
Saint Teresa of Avila
Faithful daughter of the
Crucified Lord
Below:
Convent of the Incarnation
Avila, Spain

Above:
St. Teresa of Avila receives the Transverberation of the Heart.
An Angel of the Lord pierces her heart.

mercies the remission of the temporal punishments due for their sins. Thus the Church does not want to simply come to the aid of these Christians, but also to spur them to works of devotion, penance, and charity."[2]

Although the indulgence called for the usual conditions of prayers, penance and contrition, devious enemies of the Church were to use this most normal practice as a means to fracture the Church and eventually separate innocent believers from their Faith.

The year Teresa was born, 1515, was the same year Martin Luther was to attack the very Foundations of the Catholic Church using the selling of these indulgences as a tool. Actually, Martin Luther was a pawn in the hands of various princes of Germany who did not want to pay the royalties to the Vatican due them for the lands which had been given over as gifts to the Church. They wanted to take the lands away from the Church and use them for themselves. They also wanted to be able to have in effect, their own religions, with rules which they made up for their own particular desires. Many actually did start their own religions, in effect, using Martin Luther's attack against what he called a corrupt church, as an excuse. But nothing is by accident with the Lord. We would be foolish to believe it was merely a coincidence that Teresa was born the very year Martin Luther came out with his dogma of salvation through grace alone. In retrospect, we can see that the Lord was raising up powerful people in the Church, such as St. Teresa of Avila, St. John of the Cross, St. Francis de Sales, St. Vincent de Paul, St. Charles Borromeo, just to name a few, placing them in key places, so that He could defend His Church against this devastating attack.

We would be doing you and St. Teresa a disservice if we didn't spend just a little time sharing about her passionate love for the Church and her determination to make the Carmelite Order more focused on Our Lord Jesus and the Gospel life as projected by the primitive rule of St. Albert of 1209, upon which the

---

[2]Catechism of the Catholic Church # 1478

original Carmelite order was founded. Her entire life was dedicated to Our Lord Jesus through His Passion and suffering, and to projecting that love in a very fervent but forceful way on the women in her community.

Hers was a herculean task, which could never have been accomplished without Heavenly intervention. She encountered formidable enemies, mostly from within the Church, who made it next to impossible for her to complete her mission as the Lord manifested it to her. A great deal of the resistance she had to deal with came from her own community of sisters at the Incarnation Convent in Avila, Spain.

There is so much that can be written about St. Teresa,[3] but in this book we are concentrating on her love for the Cross and the miraculous ways the Lord made the Crucifix come alive. The Incarnation was a Convent of holy Nuns, but problems arose because of the never-ending stream of visitors coming and going. The Rule of St. Albert was the strictest of all the rules in the Church. The Rule encompassed, in addition to the vows of poverty, chastity and obedience, *the Nuns were to maintain complete silence at certain hours; to remain in their cells meditating on their God when not busy with other tasks; to fast from September 14, Feast of the Exaltation of the Cross, to Easter, unless physically unable; to eat no meat (unless it was required for health reasons); be engaged in doing all sorts of physical work for the community.*

But this was not what the Nuns of the Incarnation Convent wanted. This was not what the town wanted. As a matter of fact, she found herself being attacked from the pulpit at Mass. A priest from Avila delivered a homily accusing her of plotting against the Church. And she was sitting there in the pew!

If that was not bad enough, even her friends began to doubt her, not her sincerity, nor her spirituality, but the wisdom of fighting the establishment. For most people this would be

---

[3]for more on St. Teresa, read Bob and Penny Lord's book: *Saints and other Powerful Women in the Church.*

enough to make them quit, or at least bemoan their outcast state. But not Teresa. She held strong. And to be honest, this was when the Lord would come to her, to comfort her, to fortify her, to give her strength. And He did not come alone. He brought with Him some of her strongest advocates, Our Blessed Mother, St. Clare of Assisi, her role model, and always, her mentor, St. Joseph, to whom she had absolute faith, and who never let her down. So you can see how the Lord always balanced the books. He never let her suffer more than she could handle, and whenever she did go through serious times, He gave her what we would call today "Perks," extra benefits which made all her adversity seem like nothing.

Teresa and the Dark Night of the Soul

A perfect example of this would be the twenty years, from age twenty four to forty four, Teresa was to know Purgatory on Earth. Her physical pains were to be joined by spiritual and mental ones, in the *conversion* from sinner (as she often called herself) into Saint. Teresa speaks of how necessary it was for her, and is for anyone in their walk towards Jesus, to go through the *"dark night of the soul."* She described it as *"turning your back on all the pleasures of this world, if you would know that oneness with our Lord."* Being put to the test often, Teresa was to fail over and over again.

To exemplify the seriousness of the problem of the laxity of the Incarnation Convent before the Reform, an elderly Nun once strongly cautioned Teresa to stop seeing one of her friends, that her talk, more like gossip, was a threat to Teresa's soul. But the *younger* Teresa chose to ignore, conveniently judging the Nun too old and too worried about too little. Teresa was slowly, but surely, sacrificing her prayer life and eventually her Lord, by unwittingly giving in to temptations by her friends, their world and its vanities. And so, Jesus appeared to her as the Gardener one day, pruning shears in Hand, while she was entertaining the friend and visitor, whom the Nun had warned her against. Teresa became aware of the Lord's Presence. *"I saw Him with the eyes*

*of my soul more clearly than I could see Him with those (eyes)
of the body."* It made such an impression, that even twenty-six
years later, she felt That Presence before her, just as she had that
day. That was enough for her. She never saw that person again.

Our Crucified Lord appears bleeding and broken

Around 1555, someone brought to the Convent, a painting of
Our Lord and Savior in His Passion, bleeding, bruised and
broken. She was so touched by the anguish, the suffering of Our
Lord Jesus on the Cross, she fell to her knees. She kept looking
up at His visage there on the Cross, so real, so filled with pain. It
was not just a painting; it was Jesus on the Cross! She prostrated
herself before Him, begging Him to release her from the bondage
of the liar and his lies, with his false gifts of the world and the
flesh. All her many sins and transgressions appeared before her.
It was like her entire life was on a big picture screen. She asked
His forgiveness for the many times she had foolishly been
tempted and tricked by people and things of the world, *"My Lord
and my God, I will not get up from here until you grant me this
favor."* This was to be the turning point in Teresa's life. Her
breathing became labored. Her heart pounded, as she waited for
the Lord to speak to her, to forgive her. She would not back
down. She could not possibly continue her life without having
her soul cleansed.

*She could see Jesus, broken and bleeding, on the Cross
before her. She had passionately prayed with her heart and
soul. The Savior lifted up His face, blood dripping from His
beard, perspiration burning His eyes, His breathing strained
and laborious. He looked at her intensely, but with so much
love. He lifted His Body up, exerting all the strength and energy
He could summon, and spoke to her;* **"Your faith has saved
you. Your sins are forgiven. Pick up your mat and walk."**
*She was free at last of the lure of the devil and his kingdom, the
world. It would never control her again. God had conquered.
Jesus disappeared, but she never forgot the Vision.*

Teresa had a small statue of Jesus at the Pillar, Our Lord,

blood dripping from the more than five thousand blows He received at the hands of the centurions, His Head hanging helplessly, His Hair matted with His Precious Blood, His back filled with mound-shaped welts from the brutal scourging, His Eyes piercing your very soul, speaking volumes, as He peers out at you and asks, *"My child, what did I do to you? All I wanted was to love you."* He appears no older than a teen-ager, His Eyes innocent and loving.

This statue reminded Teresa of the Vision she had had of Jesus Crucified when He gave her the Miracle of Conversion. She brought this small statue of Jesus to every house she founded. In the Church of Saint Teresa in Avila,[4] there is a life-size statue of Jesus at the Pillar, where we have seen grown men cry, when they look up at Our Lord suffering.

St. Teresa's words are at times easy to write and read, but hard to live: *"All who wish to follow Christ must walk the way He went, the Way of the Cross."*[5] They are not unlike those of Jesus, *"If any man will come after Me, let him deny himself, and take up his Cross daily, and follow Me."*[6] What is my Cross, my Savior, the one You ask me to carry *today*? And will I betray and deny You because I seek the Resurrection without the Cross? Can we truly experience the Joy of Easter Sunday without the pain of Good Friday? Not any more than we can celebrate the Eucharist without going through the Sacrifice of the Mass.

Teresa warns that in the beginning of our Spiritual Walk, we will experience our own Dark Night of the Soul, loneliness, "dryness,"[7] and disgust, judging that everything we are doing is of no avail, worthless. We can expect to be barraged by

---

[4]This church was built over the house where Teresa was born and she and her family lived.

[5]St. Teresa

[6]Mk 8:34

[7]dryness - refers to that time when a soul doesn't feel or sense the Presence of the Lord...an emptiness...to be dry spiritually.

temptations; but in the end, the Lover who has been testing us, before granting us greater treasures, will give us the understanding that we have been helping Him to carry the Cross, drinking from the chalice from which He drank.[8]

We want to take a moment and share a revelation given us by a Franciscan priest at Osimo, Italy, when we were making the program on St. Joseph of Cupertino. We talked about the Dark Night of the Soul which St. Joseph experienced. This priest, filled with the Holy Spirit, said very quietly, *"Every Saint has to experience the Dark Night of the Soul."* We looked at him. He just smiled.

The Angel of the Lord pierces her heart

She received, what she called, *a terrifying caress, a Transverberation of her heart.* She was deep in prayer before the same Crucifix which had played such an important part in her conversion. With her eyes closed, she could feel the strong presence of someone in the chapel. She looked up to see an Angel appear to the left of her, small and very beautiful. He was so radiant! He had to be one of the very highest choirs of the Angels, the Cherubim. The Angel had a long golden dart in his hand. She could see a glow at the tip of the arrow, as if there were a flame at the end of it. It pulsated, then sparkled. Teresa said he thrust the dart into her heart several times, piercing her down to her innermost organs, leaving her burning with a great love for God. Her body weakened; her legs crumbled; she fell to the floor. It was virtually impossible for her to explain the feeling she received throughout her body and soul. The closest she could come in the way of explanation was agony and ecstasy, both at the same time, both as intense. This feeling stayed with her the rest of her life.

After the Transverberation, Teresa's raptures became more and more frequent, lasting longer, and deeper. She would see

---

[8]from chapter on St. Teresa of Avila in Bob and Penny Lord's book: *Saints and other Powerful Women in the Church*

Christ in the Eucharist during Mass, especially after receiving Communion. She would go into ecstasy! No longer able to feel her body, it levitated with a weightlessness that lifted her whole body into the air.[9] Some of her Nuns testified that one day they saw her body rise high above the window from which she had received the Host from the Bishop of Avila. Teresa was thoroughly saddened when this occurred in front of others, not wanting to be judged holy. In response to her requests of anonymity, Our Lord would gift her with such outward signs of radiant beauty, it was impossible for her to conceal these gifts of sanctity. Like Moses after he came down from the mountain after having been with the Lord, Teresa had such an aura about her, she glowed.

After St. Teresa's death, when they investigated her heart, it appeared to be pierced through the center as if by a dart. In 1872, at the request of the Prioress at Alba de Tormes, three physicians, professors of medicine and surgery at the University of Salamanca, examined Teresa's heart. They found the heart still incorrupt and untouched by the ravages of death, after almost three hundred years. The heart was punctured on both sides, leaving a perforation above the left and right auricles, verifying what Teresa had said, *even to the angle of the thrust of the Angel's arrow.*

Our Lord takes Teresa's crucifix

Teresa suffered greatly at the hands of her confessors. She felt required to share about her Visions of Jesus and her mystical experiences. They didn't believe she was having Visions of Jesus, but judged, if anything they were something demonic. They told her to denounce the Visions, to rebuke them, throw holy water on the apparitions. She was fearful to do the things they wanted of her. But Jesus told her to obey her superiors, and her confessors. He said He would work through it, and triumph over these attacks, as long as she remained obedient.

---

[9]it is called Levitation

One day, after suffering one of her worst trials at the hands of her confessor, she was exhausted. She didn't think she could last any longer; then she felt the Presence of Jesus. Fighting back the tears, but too weak to do anything but obey her Confessor, she held up her Crucifix defensively, so that if, in truth, it was not her Lord Jesus, but the evil one, as her confessor insisted, he would disappear. Of course He didn't disappear; *it was Jesus.* Instead, a beautiful Vision of our Lord came toward her, extending His Hand. He took the Crucifix from her; He held it for a short period of time, then He returned it to her. *"When He gave it back to me, it was of four large stones, much more precious, beyond compare, than diamonds. It had the five wounds very exquisitely wrought."*[10] He told Teresa that was how she would see the Crucifix from that time on, but she alone would see it.

Teresa never really doubted the authenticity of her Visions. However, her many spiritual directors and confessors confused her. She finally came to know that her Visions were of the Lord by the way of the heart. After going through many confessors and spiritual directors (over 100), who could not fathom the spiritual level on which St. Teresa lived, the Lord sent a very holy Priest into her life, *Fray Pedro de Alcántara.* Father Peter could see, kneeling before him, a holy and courageous lover of the Lord, and cautioned her confessor to not interfere with her spirituality.

The holy friar wrote a brilliant plea to the Bishop to grant Teresa permission to open the Convent. Not only did the Bishop refuse, but rejected the Friar's request for a meeting, hastily leaving for his country home some thirty-two miles away. Fray Pedro de Alcántara, more dead than alive, barely able to stand, journeyed to the Bishop's home and extracted from him a promise to talk with Teresa when he returned to Avila. The Bishop's heart of stone melted when he met Teresa, as did most hearts. He pledged his protection of her and her Monastery. He remained her true and loyal friend till the day he died, requesting

---

[10]St. Teresa

he be buried beside her.

As for the Franciscan friar who the Lord used to aid St. Teresa, he went on to form a reform Franciscan community in which St. Paschal Baylon became a member. He is now St. Peter of Alcántara.

Alba de Tormes: Teresa's Final Journey

Mother Teresa was tired. She had walked with the Crucified Lord, right up to Calvary and it was time, as with her Savior before her to go *Home!* She had dreamed of this Spouse she so adored, now it was time. She had founded her last house. Everyone present on that occasion, agreed that this was to be the most difficult act of obedience Teresa would ever be asked to make, as she was now showing clear signs of weakness. This last battle was one Teresa would not have the physical strength to win.

At long last, they arrived in Alba de Tormes. The Nuns seeing how gravely ill she was, died to their desire to talk with her and carried her to her bedroom. On September the 29th, she went to bed never to rise again. As she lay dying, between bouts of total collapse and speech loss, her pulse rising and dropping rapidly, Teresa dictated her last Testament.

According to her nurse, *"She asked for the Blessed Sacrament. . . When they were taking It away she sat up in bed with a great surge of spirit and said joyfully: `My Lord, it is time to be going. Very well, Your Will be done.'"*

It was the 4th of October, 1582. Teresa was 67 years old. She had lived a hard life. She closed her eyes thanking the Lord she had lived and was now dying a daughter of the Church.

Teresa was one of three women to be declared Doctor of the Church in the Twentieth Century; St. Thèrése, the Little Flower and St. Catherine of Siena being the other two. We thank You, Lord for the gift of St. Teresa and all that You allowed her to do in her lifetime.

Saint Veronica Giuliani
Lover of the Cross

Pope Pius IX said, after reading Veronica Giuliani's Diary that she was not merely a Saint, but a *great* Saint!

Ursula Giuliani (who will later become Sister Veronica) was born on December 20, 1660. Her father was a well-respected member of society and her mother was a deeply religious woman. She would die before she reached her 40th birthday, leaving Ursula and her four surviving siblings (two having died) to their father's care. *But before she died*, her mother would consecrate each of her five children to the precious Five Wounds of Our Lord Jesus. To the Wound in Our Lord's Side, she entrusted Ursula, who was all of seven years old. Without her understanding the full implication of her mother's bequest, nevertheless this was the beginning of Ursula's betrothal to Jesus' Heart, the very Heart Which bled on the Cross.

She began doing penances from an early age in silence, striking her body with rope, all in a desire to imitate the Saints before her. She began walking on her knees, her little arms outstretched in the form of Jesus Crucified. Ursula desired to carry the Cross as her Jesus had done. She fashioned a Cross, putting two pieces of wood together. She later wrote that it was so heavy, she could not carry it; she found herself falling with every step she took. Our Lord, too, fell under the weight of the Cross made heavy by our sins and the sins of the world.

She asked the Blessed Mother to teach her how to suffer. And the Baby Jesus, speaking from His Mother's precious arms said, *"I have suffered so much."* To which Ursula replied, *"I want to do everything You did."* Jesus then said, *"The Cross awaits you."* But little Ursula was so filled with her Lord, so overflowing and abounding was His love, she wanted to offer herself completely to Him. So, at only ten years old, she offered the Lord her total abandonment, in the quiet of night pleading:

"My God, don't delay, any more. My Lord, I do not want

Above: *St. Veronica Giuliani*

Above: *Crucifix that spoke to St. Veronica Giuliani. Jesus asked her to be a mediatress between Himself and sinners.*

Above: *St. Veronica Giuliani receives the Stigmata. An arrow is sent deep into her heart.*

to separate from You, until You give me the grace to be Crucified with You. Crucify me with You! Give me Your thorns, Your nails, Your Cross, and all of You; here I am, hands, feet and heart. Wound me, O my Lord!"[1]

Ursula begins the Way of the Cross as Sister Veronica

On the day she received her heavy coarse maroon-colored habit, Ursula was given the name of the Saint who had the courage to wipe Our Lord's Face on His Way to the Cross - no longer Ursula but now *Veronica of Jesus and Mary*. This was to be the sign of her life with the Lord, that of His Passion. When did it begin? Was it at age seven when she saw Our Lord covered in wounds? At that time He told her to be devoted to His Passion and then disappeared. When He again appeared, He looked so wounded, His Wounds forged a stamp onto her heart, carving themselves so deeply into its cavity, she was unable to think of anything or anyone else.

When she was vested in her habit, *Sister Veronica* asked three things of the Lord: *One,* that she would have the strength to live up to the life she had pledged to follow; *Two,* that she never wander far from His Will; And *Three* that He keep her on the Cross with Him. He promised Veronica she would do all she desired, but cautioned her that the price would be much suffering. She would drink from the cup of bitterness, as she shared the Lord's Way of the Cross.

The Lord was calling her to *"make up in her flesh what was lacking in the sufferings of Christ"* for the good of the whole Church.

In the first year of her religious life, her novitiate, Veronica was to suffer the slings and arrows of the devil through her sister novices. They constantly strived to show her in a very bad light in front of her Novice Mistress who took up the persecution of Veronica with gusto, causing the little novice to struggle against the temptation to fight back! She later wrote, *"What a struggle*

---

[1]from Bob and Penny Lord's book: *Visionaries, Mystics and Stigmatists*

went on inside of me, to overcome myself!"

Where are You, Lord?

It has been called the **Dark Night of the Soul** by the Mystics, like Saint Teresa of Avila and Saint John of the Cross. Saint Veronica was to write:

"One occasion, when I was dry and desolate and longing for the Lord, but unable to find Him, I would come out of myself and run from one place to another. I called for Him out loud, using all kinds of magnificent names, repeating them several times. At times, I seemed to hear Him, but in a way I cannot explain....I felt as though I were on fire, especially around the heart."

Pain was the road she would travel to complete union with Jesus. Through this pain, she would know the Spouse Whom she had chosen and Who had chosen her. Her walk was to be to the Cross, to *literally* hang there with her Spouse Jesus *alone*, deserted, mocked and rejected. She would cry out, as He had before her: *"My God! My God, why have You forsaken me?"* in her Dark Night of the Soul.

She would hang almost every evening (and during the forty days of Lent *every* evening), after her work was done, for anywhere from an hour to an hour and a half. She would tell the nun who helped her climb onto the cross, to return and help her off the cross when her time was up. One evening, the nun overslept and did not come for Veronica until the following morning (around three hours later, possibly more). When they found Veronica, she was close to death. Her confessor forbid her to hang on the cross from that time on, and she obeyed.

Veronica began suffering from aridity. She went to confession sometimes four or five times a day! She desired a complete union with her Spouse; He was not responding. Even as He withheld Himself from her, she had an unexplainable urgency to prepare herself for that moment when He and she would be one.

As Veronica shared His thirst for souls, He allowed her to

experience the pains of Purgatory and Hell. Our Lady who had prepared her told her that *"Many do not believe that Hell exists, and I tell you that you yourself, who have been there, have understood nothing of what hell is."*

Veronica receives the Stigmata

One day, while praying in her cell, Sister Veronica had a Vision of Jesus. He was carrying His Cross on His Shoulder. He asked her, *"What do you wish?"* She replied, *"That Cross and I wish it for You, for Your Love."* He took the Cross from His Shoulder and placed it on her shoulder. It was too heavy! She fell under the weight of it, and her Lord lifted her.

Still another time, Our Lord appeared to Veronica, covered with open sores, a Crown of Thorns on His Head. Blood spilled from His precious Body, as He said, *"See what sinners have done to Me."* Veronica wrote in her Diary:

"Seeing the great agony that my Lord was in, I begged Him to give Me His Crown. He placed it on my head; I suffered so much, I thought I was dying."

Another time, Jesus came and showed Veronica a Chalice filled with liquid. She wrote that it seemed as if the liquid was on fire. The Lord told her, *"If you want to be Mine, you must taste this liquid for My Love."* She later wrote that when He placed just a few drops of the liquid on her tongue, she was filled with such indescribable bitterness and sadness, she thought she would die. Her tongue became dry and from that day on, she could not taste anything.

On Christmas Day, the Infant Jesus appeared to Veronica. He sent an arrow deep into her heart. When she awakened, she found her heart bleeding. The burning flame roaring inside her heart was so painful, she could not rest day or night. He told her He wanted her heart to bear the marks of His Wounds; He said, her heart had to feel the lance and her feet and hands, the nails He felt on the Cross.

Our Lord chose to make Veronica as much Himself as is possible, and what better way than to share His Passion with her.

He had asked her many times what she wished, and she had replied, His Cross. Well on April 5, 1697, Veronica had a Vision of Jesus Crucified, accompanied by His Mother *Our Lady of Sorrows* as she appeared at the foot of the Cross on Golgotha. Veronica's heart, as with her Savior before her, was pierced. She experienced the crowning of thorns, the scourging, the crucifixion, *her* own death and that of Our Lord Jesus Christ.

The other Nuns could see the impressions of the crown of thorns on her head through her veil, the blood at times dripping from her eyes because of the deep wounds inflicted by the long sharp thorns. Sealed with this Stigmata, Veronica's body became an indelible sign of the Lord's total communion with her, one of everlasting unity and love. She wrote:

"In an instant, I saw five shining rays shooting out from His Wounds, coming towards me. I watched as they turned into little flames. Four of them (the flames) contained the nails, and the fifth one contained the lance, golden and all aflame, and it pierced my heart. The nails pierced my hands and feet."

Veronica took the crucifix off the wall in her cell and embraced it saying:

"My Lord, pains with pains, thorns with thorns, sores with sores, here I am all Yours, crucified with You, crowned with thorns with You, wounded with You."

Veronica takes up the Cross

Veronica received the Stigmata. Now it was time for her to take up the Cross! She could not help Jesus carry His Cross, that dark and infamous day He walked to Calvary. He had told her, she would be the bride of the Crucified Savior. Now to be completely *one* with Him as His bride, in imitation of her Spouse, she would carry *her* cross each evening. At those times she would wear a robe, lined with sharp long thorns which pierced her body, especially doing damage to the shoulder upon which she carried the cross.

Laden down by the weight of the cross, she staggered as she

tried to maintain her balance. She would walk through the monastery's orchard or within the monastery itself until she was at the point of collapse. When she completed her Way of the Cross, she would then climb up many steps to a painting, in the convent chapel, of St. Francis receiving the Stigmata, where she would flagellate herself.

At times Veronica would take a very heavy log and carry it across her shoulders as a cross beam to reenact more authentically Our Lord carrying the cross to Calvary. There are crosses there till today, which the Nuns carry on Good Friday.

Sister Veronica's internal suffering was so intense, that after she died they found the traces of her life as a victim. Her heart had Divine incisions on it of the instruments of Our Lord's Passion: the *Cross* He had carried, the *Lance* which pierced Our Lord's Heart, the *Pliers* used to rip the nails from our Lord's Hands and Feet so He could be taken down from the Cross, the *Nails* that mercilessly ripped away at the Flesh on His Hands and Feet as His Body collapsed, completely exhausted, after trying to summon enough breath to speak, begging forgiveness for us all.

As you cannot separate the Son from the Mother, Veronica's heart also bore the seven swords that pierced the heart of Mother Mary. It was further engraved with letters representing the vows she had taken, a sign of her faithfulness to her vocation: **P** for Passion, **O** for Obedience, **V** for *Volunta*,[2] **F** for Faith and **C** for Caritas.[3] She described each sign to Blessed Florida (one of her Nuns), as it was being imprinted on her heart by the Lord, and Blessed Florida would sketch the heart with the sign, until finally, she sketched the heart containing all the signs the Lord had inscribed. When Veronica died, the bishop, doctors, and Nuns, including Blessed Florida, were present at the autopsy. They saw the signs Veronica had spoken of, clearly imprinted on her heart when it was dissected in half.

---

[2]Volunta - the Will of God
[3]Charity - love, compassion

Attacks from within the Monastery, from within the Church

After she received the Stigmata, Veronica was ordered by her confessor to remain locked away in a room in the infirmary for 50 days, to leave only to go to Mass, and then accompanied by two other Nuns. The devil kept attacking her, throwing her against the walls and door in an attempt to scare her into disobeying her confessor. Veronica obeyed her confessor! At other times, the *Holy Office* ordered she be placed under round-the-clock scrutiny for days on end. She never refused or complained, as they examined and probed her mind and her body. She submitted without complaint.

Veronica became so spiritually attuned to Christ's suffering and passion she asked to not die, but to be allowed to remain on earth so that she could suffer *more!* At times, when Veronica was going about performing her duties among them, she would pass by the Crucifix in the Infirmary, and Jesus would take His arm off the cross and scoop her up to Him, holding her close to Him. She spent very little time sleeping. She walked the Way of the Cross, prayed and wrote down all that Blessed Mother and Jesus dictated to her in the *evening hours*, after her chores were completed.

Veronica drank mystically from the *Chalice of the Blood of Christ* and that of the *Tears of Mary*; she shared in what really happened at the foot of the Cross.

The Lord reveals the graces He bestowed upon Veronica

The Lord told her He had renewed the sorrow in her heart *500 times* to bring her closer to Him. He told her, He had renewed His marriage to her *sixty times*, and He would allow her to experience His Passion *thirty-three times*, for every year He had spent on the earth that she might know the price, He had paid for His children on earth. He said, He revealed this only to His specially chosen ones.

The Lord Jesus Comes to Life on the Cross

The Lord showed Himself to Veronica wounded and bleeding, His precious Blood spilling from His open Heart and other Wounds. He once again asked that she do His Holy Will. How loving Our Lord is to those who carry the Cross with Him. Veronica wrote in her Diary that on *three* different occasions, Jesus pulled His Arm away from the Cross, and lifting her, brought her close to Him and held her beside Him on the Cross. *Five* times Our Lord allowed her to drink the Blood and Water from His Side. *Fifteen* times He washed her heart in His precious Blood which shot forth from His Side like a ray and struck her heart. *Twelve* times He searched her heart, purifying it, emptying it of all imperfections and remnants of past sins.

Was this to strengthen her so that she could, with her sacrifices make retribution for the Church that flowed from that Holy Side? She wrote, *"He gave my soul delightful embraces in a special way, not counting the others which He gave constantly."* He pierced her heart with *one hundred* loving Wounds, to be known to the world only after her death when all would see the signs Our Lord had imprinted on her heart.

Veronica goes *Home*

Veronica's last years were spent in total communion with God, enjoying the special Graces of being one with God, a new perfected creation, as are all the Saints in Heaven. When it was revealed to her that she had received the gift of sanctifying Grace, she exclaimed, over and over again, *"Forever and forever...Love has conquered and love itself has been overcome."*

The time for her to enter the Kingdom was at hand. Veronica suffered a stroke on June the 6th, right after having received Holy Communion. Now paralyzed, the Nuns carried her to a bed in the infirmary, she had so faithfully served. But, the Lord would not take her Home to Him, until she suffered *thirty-three* days of Purgatory on earth. For those *thirty-three* days, she was attacked mercilessly: *physically,* as she knew the most excruciating pain; *spiritually,* as she had all the temptations of such Saints as St. Thérèse, the Little Flower, the devil taunting her with her sinfulness and unworthiness to enter Heaven, how she had been a poor nun and led many to sin; on and on, *diabolically* torturing her, pulling out all stops, in a last ditch effort to have her for himself.

She suffered all the pains and sufferings of Our Lord, the complete Passion of Christ, a day for each of His *thirty-three* years on earth. As you meditate on the last days of Jesus' life, you get a glimpse of what pain, rejection, abandonment, complete vulnerability Veronica shared with Him.

At dawn, July 9th, Veronica asked permission from her confessor to go to her Spouse in Heaven. Having received it, she closed her eyes! Then she uttered final words to her sisters at her bedside: *"Love has let Himself be found!"* No more pain, no more Passion on earth, job well done, her soul soared up to Heaven where she would experience the Beatific Vision for all eternity.

Mother Church declared Veronica **Blessed** in 1804. Then in 1839 she entered the Company of Saints and became known to the world as **Saint Veronica Giuliani**. Please continue to read about Saint Veronica Giuliani.[4] Her road to perfection is a loving, spirit-filled journey to the Lord for all those reaching for eternal life with the Father.

---

[4]For more on St. Veronica, read chapter on St. Veronica in Bob and Penny Lord's book: *Visionaries, Mystics and Stigmatists*

No Cross! No Pain! No Sacrifice!

"The shrill, piercing cry of the aging Archbishop Fulton J. Sheen ricocheted off the walls of the Church of St. Agnes, in New York City, on Good Friday, April 8, 1977.

"'If you're the Son of God, come down from that Cross.   Come down and we'll believe.'[1]   Sure they'll believe; they'll believe anything, just no Cross.   No mortification, no self-denial!' He continued, *'Many say `I'll believe anything!   I'll believe He's Divine!   I'll believe in His Church; I'll believe in His pontiff, only no Cross! no sacrifice!'   George Bernard Shaw said of the Cross; `It's that that bars the way.'   Sure it bars the way. It bars the way to hell.'"*[2]

Lord, I want to cry out, *What pain did You feel* when You stood before Pilate, and looked at Your children, Your loved ones, the ones You had come to earth to save, and they were chiming in with a small band of self-serving dissidents, choosing a murderer in place of You?

How did you begin the Way of the Cross, when more dead than alive, the centurions having made sport of You, You were flung into a pit. As minutes ticked slowly into hours, the walls of the cave, marked with blood and sweat, bore silent witness to those who had suffered before You, Dear Lord.   The centurions, products of years and ancestry worshipping false, empty gods, dared to disdainfully peer down on You, jeering, taunting, jabbing at Your brutally bruised Body.   But Your spiritual pain was greater than any they could physically inflict on You.

Did Your thoughts wander back to another time, a time lost in the all too short, wonderful yesterdays of life with two devoted parents?   Did you remember the look on their faces, when, at twelve years of age, after furtively searching for You for three

---

[1]*cf*Mk 15:32
[2]excerpt from *Scandal of the Cross and Its Triumph, Heresies throughout the History of the Church* by Bob and Penny Lord

days, they found You preaching in the Temple? I am sure they thought nothing could ever equal the stark fear and torturous anguish of that moment. Was Your greatest Cross, thinking back to that time in the Temple, or to the present moment on the Cross, and the impending pain looming before Your dear Mother, the sorrow She was at that very moment enduring, and the fear that was piercing her Heart, once again not knowing what terror had befallen You?

In the Garden of Gethsemane, Lord, had You seen all the sins that had been committed and those that were yet to be committed, down through the centuries, some even in Your Name? Did You see one holocaust after another, one more horrible than the one before? How You must have wept, when You foresaw Your chosen people being herded into cattle cars, leading them to their horrible deaths in the concentration camps! If man had not done enough to wound You, a new holocaust would follow, a greater holocaust, killing more of your people, only one of innocent babies, trustfully awaiting birth in their mothers' wombs! Is that why You sweat Blood and Tears in the Garden of Gethsemane?

Lord! Lord! Lord, I cry out in the silence of my heart, ***How did You walk to the Cross*** and the most horrible, degrading death, knowing how unfaithful and selfish some of the best of Your children would become, how quickly and easily they would succumb to the wiles and lies of the enemy of God?

Dawn began to slowly, mournfully rise, a sword of light cut through the darkness of night, exposing that which had been done and that which was to follow. The Angels had been standing guard, during the long night. Now they stood as heralds of man's conscience wanting the world to know the part man had played. Then it was time! You stood before them, bleeding, Your Skin hanging pitifully, barely hiding the trauma to Your Precious Body. Your Hair no longer gleamed as it had when You walked among them, teaching, healing, bringing new hope. Now all they could see was a cruel crown, scornfully formed with thorns more than four inches long, piercing Your Skull, Your Precious Blood matting Your disheveled hair, already caked by mud from the earth You had created.

They handed You a Cross meant for another, Lord. Though more dead than alive, you opened Your Arms to warmly embrace it. You began the Walk to the Cross. Lord, we have followed Your footsteps along the Via Dolorosa in Jerusalem during Holy Weeks past and would You believe, they still stand outside their stores hawking their wares, business as usual? We stop, pray and pause at each station. As humanity presses in, closer and closer to us, at times almost crushing us, the reality of what happened here is vividly coming to light. I can still hear Archbishop Fulton J. Sheen: It was not those who had rejected Him, denied Him, abandoned Him, spit on Him, mocked Him, nailed Him to the Cross that hurt Him the most; if was those who just stood by and did nothing. *They didn't care! My God, they didn't care!* I want to cry! How could they have not cared?

But then Lord, it is 2000 years later. We should know Who You are, by now! Why do we not run beside You, take the Cross from Your precious Shoulders and carry it part of the way? *Do we know You?* Better yet, do You have a place in our lives today, in this world of haves and want mores? Lord, if you were to ask any one of those who call themselves Christians, if they believe in You, they would say yes, and they would mean it! But ask them if they have any time for You. Oh, Lord, I'm sorry, I have poured salt into Your Wounds. It is not for You we have written this book. You and we know how we feel about You. It is for that one child of Yours who loves You and does not know he can do more to show his love for You; and in so doing save the world.

We adore Thee O Lord and we bless you
Because by Your Holy Cross, You have redeemed the world.

Bibliography

Sermons of St. Anthony
    Edizioni Messaggero Padova 1998

Butler, Thurston Atwater - *Lives of the Saints*
    Christian Classics, Westminster, MD 1980

Bellato, Franco - *The Cathedral of San Martino in Lucca*
    Edizioni Cattedrale di San Martino - Lucca 1998

Wonders of the Miraculous Crucifix of Limpias, Spain
Benedictine Convent of Perpetual Adoration - Clyde MO 1928

Montfort, St. Louis - *God Alone* -
    Montfort Publications, Bayshore, NY 1987

Joáo S. Clá Dias - *The Mother of Good Counsel of Genazzano*
    Western Hemisphere Cultural Society - Sunbury, PA 1992

New Catholic Encyclopedia - 18 Volumes
    Catholic University of America - Washington, D.C. 1967

Catechism of the Catholic Church -
    Libreria Editrice Vaticana - 1994

Aquinas, St. Thomas - *Summa Theologiae*
    Image Books - 1964

Brizzi, Mario - *Sant' Agnese da Montepulciano*
    Edizione BiEmme - Proceno (VT) Italy - 1995

Testa, Cristoforo OP - *La Rosa sul Piatto*
    Firenze, 1977

De Sanctis G.A.-*L'avventura carismatica di S. Paolo della Croce*
P.P. Passionisti - SS Giovanni & Paolo - Rome, Italy 1975

Rondinara, P. Francesco - *Piccola Vita di S. Camillo de Lellis*
    Ministri degl' Infermi - Rome, Italy 1988

Frati, Antonio - *Caterina de' Ricci, La Santa di Prato*
    A.C. Grafiche - Citta di Castello, Italy 1990

Smith, Jody Briant - *The Image of Guadalupe, Myth or Miracle?*
    Doubleday Image Books - New York 1979

The Holy Bible - Revised Standard Version - Catholic Edition
    Ignatius Press - San Francisco - 1994

Lord, Bob and Penny - Journeys of Faith - Morrilton, AR
    This Is My Body, This Is My Blood Book I - 1986
    This Is My Body, This Is My Blood Book II- 1994
    The Many Faces of Mary - 1987
    Saints and Other Powerful Women in the Church - 1989
    Saints and Other Powerful Men in the Church - 1990
    Scandal of the Cross and Its Triumph - 1992
    Visionaries, Mystics and Stigmatists - 1995
    Visions of Heaven, Hell and Purgatory - 1996
    Treasures of the Church - 1997
    Defenders of the Faith - 1998

Bob &Penny Lord with Pope John Paul II and Mother Angelica, foundress of EWTN

In Recognition of their Media Apostolate
Authors Bob and Penny Lord
Recipients of
2001 Poverello Medal

Franciscan University of Steubenville's highest award
in recognition of their media apostolate that
preaches the Good News of Jesus Christ in
virtually every corner of the world
through Print, Television, Radio
and the Internet

*Fr. Terence Henry, TOR, President of Franciscan University of Steubenville,
presents Bob and Penny Lord the 2001 Poverello Medal*

318

Holy Family Mission
P. O. Box 845 - 65 Holy Family Mission Drive
Morrilton, AR 72110
1-800-633-2484 - 501-354-6100 FAX 1-501-354-1783

Email - info@bobandpennylord.com Website - www.bobandpennylord.com

Holy House under construction

Bob and Penny Lord are lay Catholic Evangelists, who are authors of 21 books and producers of over 200 television programs shown on **Eternal Word Television Network (EWTN)** and heard on **WEWN.**

They have brought their Apostolate to Morrilton, Arkansas. Here they founded the Holy Family Mission, which houses all their facilities. In addition to the work Bob and Penny continue to do, the goal of the Mission

Senior citizens day

is to strengthen the family unit and the faith of Catholic Christians around the world and to call back those who have left the Church.

The Mission contains a conference center, kitchen and dining rooms, chapel, Holy House of Prayer, and an audio-visual production and distribution center.

Celebration of St. Joseph's Altar

Confirmandi retreat

Services include:
Seminars/Workshops
Family Retreats
Youth and Adult Conferences
Missionary Training Sessions
Good Newsletter
Books, Videos, and Audio Tapes
Pilgrimages

Call or write us for more information or specific requests.

Save the family; if you destroy the family,
you destroy the Church, you destroy the world.